A GUIDE TO THE BEST  RESTAURANTS IN AMERICA

WHERE THE LOCALS EAT™

LOUISVILLE

1

Editors/Writers: Pat Embry, Charles Harris, Catherine Johnson, Rachel Lawson, Elizabeth Ramsey and Jeff Walter

Researchers/Writers: Brandi Fleck, Connally Penley, Jessica Tower and Kathryn Tower

Book Design: Brian Relleva

Website: Byron McClain, Tom Mason and Kelsey Weaver

Contributors: Bethany Arthur, Leigh Belanger, Katie Dodd, Amanda Hardesty, India John, Jacklyn Johnston, Melanie Klink, Andria Lisle, Lee Lueck, Catherine Metts, Eleanor Morgan, Nicki Pendleton, Tracy Pulley, Mike Ricceti, Virginia Roberson, Heather Spencer, Emily Voorhees, Kyle Wagner and Marie Yarbrough

MAGELLAN PRESS, INC.
Nashville, Tennessee

WWW.WHERETHELOCALSEAT.COM

Where the Locals Eat: Louisville

First Edition

Published by Magellan Press, Inc., P.O. Box 1167, Brentwood, Tennessee 37027.
Printed in the United States of America.

Printed by Fidlar Doubleday, Inc., Davenport, Iowa

Library of Congress Control Number: 2008924668

ISBN: 978-1-928622-27-7

24-1-1-042408

Welcome to Where The Locals Eat: Louisville

At Louisville's Churchill Downs racetrack, the annual Kentucky Derby has made the Kentucky bourbon-fortified mint julep famous — or is it the other way around? The concoction typifies the city's thriving restaurant scene, a mix of Old South gentility and New South sophistication.

Here at Where The Locals Eat, we think it's every bit as important to honor the greatest hot dog and finest meat loaf as it is to recognize the white-tablecloth restaurants where you might celebrate your anniversary or dazzle your date. Our hope is that *Where The Locals Eat: Louisville* will reconnect you with some old favorites and lead you to some new, out-of-the-way and totally unexpected dining discoveries.

Tell them a local sent you.

Pat Embry
Editorial Director
Magellan Press

*At **Where The Locals Eat**, we've assembled a hardy band of certified foodies — passionate gourmands to near-omnivores — who eat out a lot and know the difference between a restaurant special and a special restaurant. They're adventuresome in their grazing and don't mind trekking across town in search of the new and the different. We supplement that foodie group with our own team of finicky writers and researchers, who have a fine eye for the unusual and a keen sense for what makes a great kitchen, a creative menu and a memorable dining experience. Add to that surveys taken by more than 50,000 diners across the country, and the result is our list of the top 100 very best restaurants in each of the top 50 cities in the United States.*

LOUISVILLE KENTUCKY

TABLE OF CONTENTS

LOUISVILLE KENTUCKY

***The newer additions to Louisville's thriving culinary scene** fit in nicely with the history of this river city, with Southern comfort food such as biscuits and gravy for breakfast making way for Latin ceviche and rack of Australian lamb for dinner.*

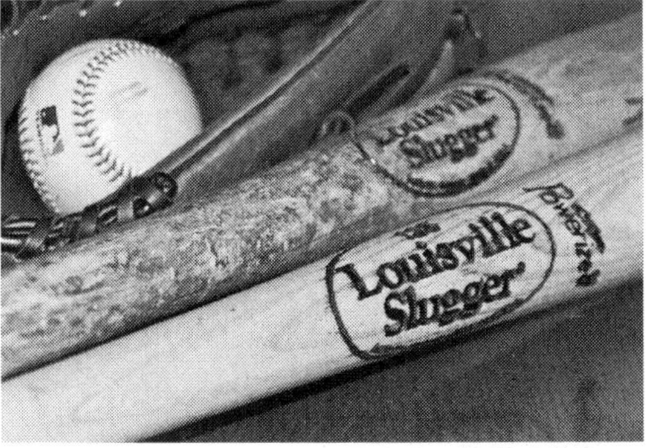

The locally produced Louisville Slugger®

211 Clover Lane

Owner Andrew Smith's elegant fine-dining destination, hidden in the rear of a St. Matthews shopping center, conjures up images of the French countryside. White picket fencing and a garden highlight the exterior. Inside, hardwood floors, fine antiques, soft lighting and tranquil music create a relaxing mood that prepares you for the gloriously simple French- and Italian-inspired cookery. Local ingredients are featured prominently on the menu, which changes daily and strives to please all. Potential starters are almonds with marinated olives or veal sweetbreads with wild mushrooms and creamy veal jus. The salads are masterful, with such ingredients as Indiana goat cheese, golden beet carpaccio and roasted shallot dressing. Among the main courses, you might enjoy potato gnocchi with vegetables, prime rib eye with Roquefort cheese, or rabbit braised with Dijon and cream. The wine list is stellar, and desserts are amazing, with choices including chocolate mousse flavored with Woodford Reserve bourbon. Alfresco dining on the patio is a desirable warm-weather option. 211 also offers an excellent Sunday brunch (10:30 am–2:30 pm). Reservations suggested. Full bar. Serving lunch and dinner Tue–Sat. Closed Mon. 211 Clover Ln, Louisville, KY 40207. (502) 896-9570. www.211cloverlane.com. Go to: www.wtle.com/118. ***Brunch, Contemporary. $$$.***

60 West Bistro & Martini Bar

Bistro, Contemporary; $$
3939 Shelbyville Rd, Louisville, KY 40207
(502) 719-9717, www.60westbistro.com
Go to: www.wtle.com/187

610 Magnolia

When Edward Lee took the reins as 610 Magnolia's owner/chef in 2003, he inherited a restaurant that for 25 years had been regarded as one of the nation's finest (under founder Ed Garber). Lee takes a holistic approach, emphasizing the importance of everything from food, wines and lighting to crystal, napkins and bathroom soap. His six-course, prix fixe menu, which changes weekly and includes a vegetarian option, is served three nights a week. Hot and cold amuse-bouche courses offer miniature delicacies such as the 610 BLT or the smoked salmon crêpe with caviar. Past entrées have included pistachio-encrusted lamb chops and skate stuffed with lobster. Reservations required. Full bar. Serving dinner Thu–Sat. Closed Sun–Wed. 610 Magnolia Ave, Louisville, KY 40208. (502) 636-0783. www.610magnolia.com. Go to: www.wtle.com/5. ***Contemporary. $$$.***

Artemisia

With its own art gallery and live jazz on Thursday, Friday and Saturday nights, Artemisia is a hip gathering spot for those who like their "contemporary Continental cuisine" (as the restaurant describes its fare) served with artistic flair. The eclectically flavorful dishes are complemented by the bold-colored and contemporary artworks that highlight the dining room walls. Lunch selections include an array of soups, salads and sandwiches, along with entrées such as a quiche of the day and a pan-fried fish tostada with onions, peppers, garlic and sweet chili sauce. Dinner entrées may include marinated sirloin steak, pan-roasted salmon or Cajun smoked rabbit. An extensive martini list adds to the restaurant's sophisticated appeal. Full bar. Serving lunch Tue–Fri, dinner Tue–Sat. Closed Sun–Mon. 620 E Market St, Louisville, KY 40202. (502) 583-4177. www.artemisiarestaurant.com. Go to: www.wtle.com/266. ***Contemporary. $$.***

Annie Café

Vietnamese; $
308 W Woodlawn Ave, Louisville, KY 40214
(502) 363-4847, www.anniecafe.com
Go to: www.wtle.com/382

Asiatique ~ *Best Asian Fusion*

Asiatique, opened by chef Peng Looi in 1994, moved to its current Highlands location in 2002. Several small dining rooms compose the multilevel restaurant, which features a minimalist black-and-white décor with wood and glass accents that allow the artful food presentation to shine. Highlights of the dinner menu, which is dominated by seafood, may include peppercorn ahi, and scallops and freshwater tiger prawns sautéed with garden vegetables in a spicy Thai basil sauce. There are ample non-seafood options as well, such as chargrilled, lemongrass-scented Angus medallions and a five-spice pork chop. Full bar. Serving dinner nightly. 1767 Bardstown Rd, Louisville, KY 40205. (502) 451-2749. www.asiatiquerestaurant.com. Go to: www.wtle.com/21837. ***Asian Fusion, Seafood. $$.***

August Moon Chinese Bistro ~ *Best Chinese*

Well-regarded chef Peng S. Looi, who does double duty at his other restaurant, Asiatique, has gloriously expanded the scope of Chinese cuisine at August Moon Chinese Bistro. The simply breathtaking digs feature both indoor and alfresco dining (in season) with a gorgeous view of the wooded area behind the restaurant. The four-star menu retains Looi's impeccable modern interpretations of classic dishes, as influenced by his native Malaysia and the Pacific Rim. Even when the name of a dish is familiar, there's nothing standard about it, from soups to appetizers (including the excellent goat cheese-crabmeat won tons) through salads, entrées and desserts. In addition to about 14 signature dishes — try the spicy calamari with Indonesian sambal sauce and julienne of snow pea or the spicy lamb with scallion, carrot and ginger-black bean sauce — there are seafood options as well as chicken, beef, pork and veggie entrées. Along with a fine wine list, there's also an impressive selection of hot teas. A separate brunch menu is offered from noon–4 pm Sundays. Full bar. Serving lunch and dinner daily. 2269 Lexington Rd, Louisville, KY 40206. (502) 456-6569. www.augustmoonbistro.com. Go to: www.wtle.com/37. ***Brunch, Chinese. $$.***

Avalon

According to Celtic legend, Avalon is the isle of the dead, the afterlife home for heroes like King Arthur. In Louisville, however, Avalon is more widely known as a trendy Bardstown Road eatery serving "fresh American cuisine." After owner Steve Clements opened his establishment in 2002, it quickly made a name for itself with the warm, art-filled, romantic ambiance of its multiple interior dining levels, its lush and inviting patio, and its creative, seasonally changing cuisine.

The menu has remained essentially the same: American with notable Southern accents as well as Asian and Middle Eastern influences. A dozen or so starters include a soup of the day and salads as well as the intriguing truffle and lobster macaroni and cheese. Entrées such as beer- and chili-braised boneless short ribs, pan-seared scallops with fried cheddar grits, and grilled beef tenderloin highlight the menu. There are also sandwiches and pastas. Desserts include vanilla crème brûlée and the marvelous fried apple cheesecake. Full bar. Serving lunch and dinner Tue–Sat. Closed Sun–Mon. 1314 Bardstown Rd, Louisville, KY 40204. (502) 454-5336. www.avalonfresh.com. Go to: www.wtle.com/114. ***Contemporary. $$.***

Baxter Station Bar and Grill

American Traditional; $$
1201 Payne St, Louisville, KY 40204
(502) 584-1635, www.baxterstation.com
Go to: www.wtle.com/270

Blue Dog Bakery & Café ~ *Best Bakery*

Baker Bob Hancock has been called a "human bread machine" because of the passion and single-mindedness with which he pursues his craft. Well, that and the fact that the result of his passionate pursuit, conducted with the aid of a $55,000 wood-burning oven imported from Spain, is some of the best bread you'll find anywhere. Hancock's Blue Dog Bakery & Café produces croissants and pastries as well as artisan *levain* (naturally leavened) breads that are sold in fine groceries and other retail outlets throughout Louisville. And the attached café serves food that is worthy of the breads. Sandwiches, which come with a side of wheat berry salad, include a marvelous goat cheese, pear and walnut pesto panini as well as a cold tuna and tapenade sandwich. Egg dishes are a specialty at breakfast and during Saturday brunch (8 am–2:30 pm). The fine desserts include what many consider Louisville's best chocolate chip cookie. Blue Dog also offers a well-chosen wine list, craft beers and fine European-style (read: strong) coffee. Serving during breakfast and lunch Tue–Sat. Closed Sun–Mon. 2868 Frankfort Ave, Louisville, KY 40206. (502) 899-9800. Go to: www.wtle.com/21. ***Bakery, Brunch, Café, Dessert. $.***

Bourbons Bistro

Bistro, Contemporary, Home-style; $$
2255 Frankfort Ave, Louisville, KY 40206
(502) 894-8838, www.bourbonsbistro.com
Go to: www.wtle.com/116

Bristol Bar & Grille ~ *Best American Traditional*

With five Louisville-area locations (plus one location, called Café Bristol, in the Speed Art Museum), Bristol Bar & Grille is known by some for its green chili won tons appetizer (deep-fried, golden won tons filled with creamy jack cheese, chilis and jalapeños, served with cooling guacamole), but you'll find plenty to enjoy for the rest of your meal. The original Bristol location opened in 1977 on Bardstown Road, helping launch the road (now widely known as Restaurant Row) as a prime restaurant location. Menus at the locations vary, as each chef offers his or her own signature dishes, but a handful of "Bristol Classics" are available at all sites. Those include the Bristol Burger on a toasted English muffin, the Filet Mandarin (marinated in soy, honey, garlic, ginger and Mandarin liqueur) and the steak au poivre, encrusted with peppercorns and pan-seared in a cognac sauce. Selected appetizers, soups, salads and pastas, plus the individual chefs' specialties, round out the menus. A very popular Sunday brunch buffet (10 am–3 pm) includes breakfast standards, waffles, fried chicken and beef carving stations. A Saturday brunch menu is also available at the Bardstown Road location. Brunch items vary by location. Full bar. Serving lunch, dinner and late-night daily. Hours vary by location. 1321 Bardstown Rd, Louisville, KY 40204. (502) 456-1702. Multiple locations. www.bristolbarandgrille.com. Go to: www.wtle.com/392. ***American Traditional, Brunch. $$.***

Browning's Restaurant & Brewery ~ *Best Brewpub*

Few things go together as well as beer and baseball, which makes Slugger Field, home of the Louisville Bats, a terrific location for a brewpub. Browning's Restaurant & Brewery is named for Louis Rogers "Pete" Browning, a Louisville native and legendary 19th-century major league baseball star. (Appropriately enough, Browning was purportedly a heavy drinker.) History credits Browning, aka The Gladiator, as the inspiration behind the Louisville Slugger bat. The brewmasters at Browning's keep about five regular beers on tap — a light, German-style lager, an India Pale Ale, an English-style bitter, an English brown and a porter, for example — along with seasonal brews. Despite the sports bar atmosphere, the cuisine is certainly not neglected. Choices include prime beef tenderloin chili, salads, sandwiches and more substantial entrées such as the Louisville Hot Brown, beer-battered grouper and meat loaf. Full bar. Serving lunch Mon–Fri, dinner Mon–Sat. Closed Sun. 401 E Main St, Louisville, KY 40202. (502) 515-0174. www.diningonmain.com. Go to: www.wtle.com/32. ***American Traditional, Brewpub, Sports Bar/Pub Food. $$.***

Buck's Restaurant and Bar

If F. Scott and Zelda Fitzgerald were to visit Louisville today, there's a good chance you'd find them dining at Buck's Restaurant and Bar. Housed in Old Louisville's venerable 1920s-era Mayflower Hotel, Buck's has been going strong since the early '90s. The ambiance, a combination of Old World luxury and contemporary style, manages to be simultaneously classy, down-to-earth and even a bit whimsical. With dark woods, white linen tablecloths, candlelight, white flowers, a jazzy pianist and mismatched fine china setting the tone, Buck's is a favored spot for an intimate Valentine's Day dinner or other special occasion. The gourmet fare is a blend of American, Continental and Asian influences. The crispy fish with a hot, sweet chili sauce nicely illustrates the Asian influence. There are several options for seafood lovers, including a mixed Caribbean grill. Beef tenderloin, grilled pork chops and rack of lamb are also available. The reasonably priced lunch menu features a selection of appetizers, salads and sandwiches, as well as some less expensive versions of dinner entrées. Full bar. Serving lunch Mon–Fri, dinner Mon–Sat. Closed Sun. 425 W Ormsby Ave, Louisville, KY 40203. (502) 637-5284. www.bucksrestaurantandbar.com. Go to: www.wtle.com/267. ***Contemporary. $$.***

Café Lou Lou

Café, Pizza; $$
106 Sears Ave, Louisville, KY 40206
(502) 893-7776, www.cafeloulou.com
Go to: www.wtle.com/272

Café Metro

Since 1981, Café Metro has been setting the standard for culinary excellence along Louisville's so-called Restaurant Row, also known as Bardstown Road. Convivial owner Nancy Shepherd regularly makes the rounds among the three German-art-deco-accented dining rooms, greeting diners and making sure experiences exceed expectations. Start your evening with the escargots with garlic butter, Parmesan cheese and puff pastry, or try the seared beef carpaccio. Continue with one of the fine salads, such as the tomato, fresh mozzarella and asparagus salad. Entrées include exquisite seafood dishes (the jerk-seasoned red snapper and the sea scallops wrapped in phyllo are just a couple of choices) as well as veal, beef and pork. And Café Metro, which has two pastry chefs, is renowned for its desserts; some consider the decadent Concorde — alternating layers of chocolate mousse and chocolate meringue topped with curls of chocolate meringue — the best dessert in Louisville. Full bar. Serving dinner Mon–Sat.

Closed Sun. 1700 Bardstown Rd, Louisville, KY 40205. (502) 458-4830. www.cafemetrolouisville.com. Go to: www.wtle.com/268. ***Contemporary, Dessert, French. $$$.***

Chick Inn

Like the mythical phoenix, this longtime favorite haunt for down-home eats has risen from the ashes and is going stronger than ever. The bird of choice here, however, is the chicken, in a rendition that has achieved something close to mythical status in Louisville. After fire destroyed the original Chick Inn in 2002, many locals were distraught. But the casual riverside restaurant was rebuilt and reopened in 2004, when it once again started packing them in. In addition to the delicious, crispy-on-the-outside, tender-and-juicy-on-the-inside fried chicken, you can also get authentic Buffalo wings, excellent fried catfish, frog legs, shrimp, country ham steak, burgers and other sandwiches — all served in generous portions with a wide selection of side dishes. Build-your-own-basket options allow you to select pieces of chicken and combine them with as many side dishes as you like, à la carte. Try the golden ripple-cut fried potatoes known as Chick's chips and the thick and creamy Boston-style clam chowder. Full bar. Serving lunch and dinner Tue–Sun. Closed Mon. 6325 Upper River Rd, Harrods Creek, KY 40027. (502) 228-3646. Go to: www.wtle.com/192. ***Fried Chicken, Home-style. $.***

City Café

Café, Deli; $
505 W Broadway, Louisville, KY 40202 *(Multiple Locations)*
(502) 589-1797, www.citycafelunch.com
Go to: www.wtle.com/423

Claudia Sanders Dinner House

This Southern Colonial manor in rural Shelbyville, 30 minutes from Louisville, is named for the wife of "Colonel" Harland Sanders, founder and icon of Kentucky Fried Chicken. They moved to Shelbyville in 1959 from Corbin, Ky., where he had developed his famed chicken recipe. It was from Shelbyville that he built his empire. The couple lived in Blackwood Hall, the circa-1860s home next to the Dinner House, adding a building for office and warehouse use. After the Colonel sold KFC in 1964, he and Claudia opened the Dinner House (and then sold it in 1973 to current owners Tommy and Cherry Settle). The original Dinner House burned to the ground in 1999, and the Settles rebuilt it, expanding the space while preserving the traditional look. Today, you'll enjoy a family-style meal that pays tribute to the Sanders legacy with old-fashioned Southern hospitality and elegant ambiance. There's fried chicken, of course, as well as baked chicken, sugar-cured Kentucky country ham, steaks, chops and fish. With every entrée, you get eight all-you-can-eat vegetables, including mashed potatoes, corn pudding, breaded tomatoes and creamed spinach. Plus — better loosen that belt! — there are fresh-baked biscuits, cornbread, salads and house-made desserts, including apple, chess and chocolate-pecan pies and fruit cobblers. Full bar. Serving lunch and dinner Tue–Sun. Closed Mon. 3202 Shelbyville Rd, Shelbyville, KY 40065. (502) 633-5600. www.claudiasanders.com. Go to: www.wtle.com/274. ***American Traditional, Fried Chicken. $$.***

Clifton's Pizza Company

Clifton's, which opened in 1990 in a century-old former hardware store, is noted not only for great pizza at reasonable prices but also for its casual, funky, slightly psychedelic — yet family-friendly — vibe. The hand-tossed pizzas, available on regular or wheat crusts, are generously topped. In addition to all the tried-and-true favorites, topping options include chicken, artichoke hearts, pineapple, spinach, chopped garlic, broccoli and zucchini. A half-dozen specialty pizzas include the 8 Cheese and the creamy Chicken Alfredo on thin crust. The hefty build-your-own calzones allow you to choose a generous six toppings. And Clifton's also offers a trio of pasta selections, salads and a number of sandwiches, including one with portobello on ciabatta bread with melted Asiago cheese and roasted red peppers. Beer and wine available. Serving lunch and dinner Tue–Sun. Closed Mon. 2230 Frankfort Ave, Louisville, KY 40206. (502) 893-3730. www.cliftonspizza.com. Go to: www.wtle.com/288. ***Pizza. $$.***

Club Grotto

"Southern Gothic" is one way to describe Club Grotto — Southern for the fare, which includes specialties such as corn pudding and sautéed calf's liver as well as more internationally inspired contemporary dishes, and Gothic for the décor, which features gargoyles, red walls, enigmatic black-and-white photos and other somewhat bizarre touches. But don't get the idea that the place is creepy; on the contrary, it's warm, whimsical and inviting, with an honest family touch. It's run by James and Juanita McKinney, parents of original chef/owner Jim McKinney II, whose creative vision gave birth to Club Grotto in 1993. Sadly, chef Jim died of a heart attack at age 32 in 2001. That's when his mom and dad stepped in, and they've kept the popular restaurant alive as a labor of love. The kitchen has retained such dishes as the New Orleans barbecued shrimp appetizer, the famous Vegetable Orgy (one of many vegetarian-friendly dishes) utilizing seasonal produce, blackened rare ahi, Southern-fried walleye pike and, for dessert, the fallen chocolate soufflé. Full bar. Serving dinner Tue–Sun. Closed Mon. 2116 Bardstown Rd, Louisville, KY 40205. (502) 459-5275. Go to: www.wtle.com/117. ***Bistro, Contemporary. $$.***

Come Back Inn

Situated in a working-class, urban Louisville neighborhood, this unpretentious, ultra-casual little dive (in the best sense of the word) bar and restaurant serves up hearty, Chicago-style Italian fare at inexpensive prices. The signature Italian beef sandwich features tender sliced beef stacked high on a hoagie bun; you'll need a fork to eat it. Start your meal with the fried antipasto won tons stuffed with cheeses and prosciutto or a house-made soup such as traditional Italian Wedding. And of course there's a range of pastas, with meatballs that would make Mama proud. The house-made red sauce is so good, you'll probably want to order extra to dip a breadstick in — or take a bottle of it home with you. The pizzas topped with four cheeses are also excellent. Full bar. Both locations serving dinner Tue–Sat. Swan Street location closed Sun–Mon. Jeffersonville location serving lunch Mon–Sat. Closed Sun. 909 Swan St, Louisville, KY 40204. (502) 627-1777. Two locations. www.comebackinn.net. Go to: www.wtle.com/112. ***Café, Italian, Pizza. $.***

Corbett's

Contemporary; $$$
5050 Norton Healthcare Blvd, Louisville, KY 40241
(502) 327-5058, www.corbettsrestaurant.com
Go to: www.wtle.com/24711

Cottage Inn

Fried Chicken, Home-style; $
570 Eastern Pkwy, Louisville, KY 40217
(502) 637-4325
Go to: www.wtle.com/195

Cumberland Brews

Billing itself the smallest brewery in Kentucky, this laid-back Highlands brewpub and restaurant, opened by the Allgeier family in 2000 in a former ice cream shop, is indeed tiny, seating about 40 in its main downstairs dining room. (There's also an intimate upstairs room). The menu at Cumberland Brews is fairly limited as well, but it's quality, not quantity, that matters here. Brewmaster Matt Gould always has five house beers on tap — Nitro Porter, a cream ale, a brown ale, a pale ale and mead (a malt beverage made with 75 percent honey) — plus specialty/seasonal brews such as Summer Wheat, Coffee Stout and Mocktoberfest. A chalkboard lists the beers and the daily specials. Many diners choose to make a meal of the appetizers, which include Jamaican jerk or Buffalo-style chicken wings, hand-cut potato chips with roasted garlic dip, and roasted red pepper hummus. Sandwiches include a Kentucky bison burger and a fried whitefish sandwich. And, befitting the joint's former identity as an ice cream shop, family patriarch Larry Allgeier cranks out house-made ice cream and malt cups for dessert. Beer and wine available. Serving lunch Fri–Sun, dinner nightly. 1576 Bardstown Rd, Louisville, KY 40205. (502) 458-8727. Go to: www.wtle.com/31. ***American Traditional, Brewpub. $$.***

Cunningham's

American Traditional, Burgers; $$
630 S 4th St, Louisville, KY 40202
(502) 587-0526
Go to: www.wtle.com/169

De La Torre's ~ *Best Spanish*

Louisville's lone Spanish restaurant serves the authentic flavors of Madrid and beyond in a romantic, European-style setting. Executive chef Miguel de la Torre, born and raised in Spain, owns the restaurant with wife Maggie. They moved to Louisville in 1987 and opened this restaurant, consistently ranked among the city's top spots for fine dining. De La Torre displays fluency in the dishes of the various regions of Spain, including the famed paella — his lobster paella is the house specialty. Other highlights abound, from tapas such as grilled calamari and Spanish omelets to entrées such as roasted chicken and lamb, not to mention daily specials and rich desserts. The wine list features primarily Spanish selections: If you can't decide, go with the sangria. Next door to De La Torre's is La Bodega, a tapas bar that Miguel and Maggie opened in 2004. Full bar. Serving dinner and late-night Tue–Sat. Closed Sun–Mon. 1606 Bardstown Rd, Louisville, KY 40205. (502) 456-4955. www.delatorres.com. Go to: www.wtle.com/369. ***Small Plates, Spanish. $$.***

Dooley's Bagels & Deli ~ *Best Bagels*

Dooley's Bagels & Deli is a locally based chain founded by New York native Bill Squitieri, whose success at the first Dooley's, on Long Island, prompted him to seek another city in which to set up shop. Research led him to Louisville, where he opened his first store in 1994. His bagel empire now consists of many stores in three states — most in the Louisville area. Dooley's bakes about 15 varieties of thick, chewy bagels daily — including plain, sesame, onion, garlic, tomato herb, spinach, apple walnut and chocolate chip — and offers a variety of cream cheeses. Breakfast brings cinnamon rolls, muffins and egg dishes. For lunch, choose from assorted "melted" and cold deli sandwiches, all available on a bagel, croissant or sub bun. A soup of the day and several salads are also available. Dooley's also has its own line of coffee. The stores deliver to area offices from 10 am to 2 pm weekdays. No alcohol available. Serving breakfast and lunch daily. 980 Breckenridge Ln, Louisville, KY 40207. (502) 893-3354. Multiple locations. www.dooleys.net. Go to: www.wtle.com/17. ***Bagels, Breakfast, Café. $.***

El Mundo

At first glance, the fare may appear fairly ordinary — nachos, burritos, enchiladas, tacos, quesadillas — but this funky little cantina, where you order at the counter and pick up your food when it's ready, isn't your padre's Mexican restaurant. As El Mundo's website explains, they "use many authentic ingredients but the fare is [their] twisted version of authentic Mexican." Most of the recipes come from Bea Chamberlain, who owns the restaurant. Daily specials might include such nontraditional ingredients as goat cheese, portobello mushrooms, lamb and calamari. El Mundo also uses black beans while most of its counterparts use refried. The fish tacos, featuring grilled Atlantic cod, are wonderful. Plenty of vegetarian choices are offered; beyond that, most dishes on the menu can be modified to accommodate vegans. And there's a wide selection of Mexican beers and tequilas. Serving lunch and dinner Tue–Sat. Closed Sun–Mon. 2345 Frankfort Ave, Louisville, KY 40206. (502) 899-9930. www.502elmundo.com. Go to: www.wtle.com/247. ***Mexican. $$.***

Emperor of China/Empress of China

These two longtime local favorites, owned by Ai-Ling Wang, feature nearly identical menus, but the atmosphere at the Emperor, which has an impressive balcony, is a little fancier and more reminiscent of the Big Apple's Chinatown. The Empress, which opened in 1980, is the original; it was one of Louisville's first upscale Chinese restaurants and has been nationally recognized. Both restaurants feature selections from the Hunan, Mandarin and Szechwan regions of China and are popular places to entertain out-of-town guests. Among the numerous menu highlights are Beijing duck, pot stickers, sizzling rice soup, Monk's Dream (a vegetarian dish) and cold noodles with sesame sauce, along with healthier steamed and rotisserie dishes. Full bar. Serving lunch and dinner daily. 2210 Holiday Manor Shopping Ctr, Louisville, KY 40222. (502) 426-1717. Two locations. Go to: www.wtle.com/176. ***Chinese. $$.***

English Grill

Continental, Hotel Restaurant; $$$
335 W Broadway (The Brown Hotel), Louisville, KY 40202
(502) 583-1234, www.brownhotel.com
Go to: www.wtle.com/285

Equus

In 2005, Equus celebrated 20 years of fine dining, and it appears poised to continue its tradition for decades to come. Elegant and intimate with a tasteful equestrian theme, the restaurant's interior belies its location around the corner from a St. Matthews shopping center. White tablecloths, subtle lighting, fine china and crystal set the stage for the culinary masterpieces of executive chef and owner S. Dean Corbett, who's been at the helm since the beginning. While the restaurant's website describes the fare simply as "refined American cuisine," Corbett remains endlessly inventive as he seasonally updates his menu and unveils new classic-dishes-in-the-making. Over two decades, Corbett has developed a number of signature dishes. Favored starters include crab cakes with red pepper tartar sauce, and veal sweetbreads with smoked bacon, seasonal mushrooms and Madeira wine. Signature entrées include Parmesan-crusted sea bass with lemon dill beurre blanc, and Shrimp Jenkins (fried shrimp flavored with brown sugar, Tabasco, Worcestershire, rosemary and bourbon). You'll also find the Chef's Vegetarian Whim, with the very best vegetables the season has to offer. Full bar. Serving dinner Mon–Sat. Closed Sun. 122 Sears Ave, Louisville, KY 40207. (502) 897-9721. www.equusrestaurant.com. Go to: www.wtle.com/6. ***Contemporary. $$$.***

Ernesto's Mexican Restaurant

Ernesto's, a local chain with five locations (the Middletown restaurant on Shelbyville Road is the original), specializes in fairly authentic, quick and easy Mexican fare that isn't too spicy, at prices that can't be beat. Highlights of the lengthy menu include the corn tamales, chile rellenos, fajitas and flautas. Be sure to try the tomatillo sauce. Full bar. Serving lunch and dinner daily. Hours may vary by location. 10602 Shelbyville Rd, Louisville, KY 40223. (502) 244-8889. Multiple locations. Go to: www.wtle.com/250. ***Mexican. $.***

Ferd Grisanti Restaurant

The Grisanti family is a mainstay of Italian dining in Louisville. Paul and Vincent Grisanti, sons of namesake Ferd, operate Ferd Grisanti Restaurant (with help from other family members). Paintings by various Grisantis grace the walls, and the cornice work is by Ferd himself, who died in 1993. Loyal customers come here for classic Italian dishes featuring house-made pasta — the marinara sauce is wonderful, as is the linguine with clam sauce — as well as veal dishes. Antipasto choices such as calamari and roasted garlic will kick your taste buds into high gear and prepare them for the feast to come. Ferd Grisanti draws high marks for its hospitality and ambiance, in part because the chef makes personal visits to tables. Full bar. Serving dinner Mon–Sat. Sun brunch 10:30 am–3 pm. 10212 Taylorsville Rd, Jeffersontown, KY 40299. (502) 267-0050. www.ferdgrisanti.com. Go to: www.wtle.com/211. ***Brunch, Italian. $$.***

FireFresh BBQ

Barbecue; $
6435 Bardstown Rd, Louisville, KY 40291 *(Multiple Locations)*
(502) 239-7800, www.firefreshbbq.com
Go to: www.wtle.com/22924

The Fishery

Seafood; $$
3624 Lexington Rd, Louisville, KY 40207
(502) 895-1188
Go to: www.wtle.com/360

Flabby's Schnitzelburg

German, Sports Bar/Pub Food; $
1101 Lydia St, Louisville, KY 40217
(502) 637-9136, www.flabbys.com/fcc.htm
Go to: www.wtle.com/189

Gasthaus ~ *Best German*

Even if you can't pronounce *gemutlichkeit* (German for comfortable friendliness), you can most likely say "Gasthaus," which is essentially the same thing. This authentic eatery proves the saving grace of a surprisingly barren German restaurant scene in Louisville, considering the Bluegrass State's relatively large German-American population. Decorated haphazardly with knickknacks from the owners' home in Bochum, Gasthaus radiates with a charm distinctive to family-run operations. A friendly waitstaff dressed in traditional folk costumes adds to the atmosphere as customers are guided through the menu of traditional German cuisine. Chicken, veal, beef and pork dominate the menu in the expected schnitzels, spatzles and stroganoffs, and there are a few vegetarian entrées, as well. Meatless or no, main courses disprove the bland-and-heavy stereotype often attributed to German fare, owing in part to a hint of French influence. Recommended dishes include chicken ragout, beef *rouladen* and goulash as well as excellent sides such as sauerkraut and pan-fried potatoes. The house-made desserts alone could keep Gasthaus in business, as locals often stop in for a cup of coffee and a slice of apple strudel, fallen chocolate soufflé or one of the ever-changing (and ever-delicious) assortment of rich cake rolls and tortes. Reservations suggested. Beer and German wine available. Serving dinner Tue–Sat. Closed Sun–Mon. 4812 Brownsboro Ctr, Louisville, KY 40207. (502) 899-7177. www.gasthausdining.com. Go to: www.wtle.com/190. ***Dessert, German. $$.***

Genny's Diner

It isn't fancy, and it sure isn't a place to go if you're on a diet. But if you're craving a humongous all-American burger with all the fixin's, it's hard to beat Genny's. Gargantuan appetites will be challenged by the cheese-smothered, 1.25-pound, triple-decker Sweet Daddy Burger. More moderately sized burgers are available for more reasonable appetites. The Frickled Pickles — deep-fried dill chips — are nothing short of legendary, and the fries and onion rings are also excellent. While you're pigging out, the four-foot cheeseburger mural and the fish tanks will keep the young'uns entertained. If you still have room for dessert, try the peanut butter cream pie. There's an all-you-can-eat breakfast on Saturday mornings. Full bar. Serving breakfast, lunch and dinner Mon–Sat. Closed Sun. 2223 Frankfort Ave, Louisville, KY 40206. (502) 893-0923. Go to: www.wtle.com/170. ***Breakfast, Burgers, Diner, Home-style. $.***

Havana Rumba

Caribbean/Tropical, Cuban; $$
4115 Oechsli Ave, Louisville, KY 40207
(502) 897-1959, www.myhavanarumba.com
Go to: www.wtle.com/389

Heine Brothers' Coffee ~ *Best Coffeehouse*

From its humble birth as an espresso cart in an East Louisville grocery, Heine Brothers' Coffee has slowly but steadily built a devoted following. It has grown to include seven Louisville locations cherished as neighborhood gathering places where folks can linger over outstanding espressos, cappuccinos, lattes and mochas. The coffee, roasted on site, comes from fine, organic, fair-trade beans grown in Guatemala, Nicaragua, Costa Rica, Sumatra, Mexico and Ethiopia. Heine Brothers' locations are as eclectic as their staff and customers. The first, in the Highlands neighborhood at 1295 Bardstown Road, opened in 1994. The Crescent Hill store is noted for its wooden floors and tin ceilings, and the Douglass Loop store is located at what used to be a trolley turnaround. All locations, operated by ex-copywriter Gary Heine and ex-attorney Mike Mays, also serve international teas and scrumptious Kizito cookies and muffins produced in Elizabeth Kizito's Bardstown Road bakery. Some locations also serve sandwiches. No alcohol available. Serving during breakfast, lunch and dinner hours Mon–Sat. Closed Sun. Some locations open Sun. Hours vary by location. 1295 Bardstown Rd, Louisville, KY 40204. (502) 456-5108. Multiple locations. www.heinebroscoffee.com. Go to: www.wtle.com/45. ***Coffeehouse. $.***

Homemade Ice Cream and Pie Kitchen ~

Best Dessert, Best Ice Cream

It's sugar, sugar everywhere at Homemade Ice Cream and Pie Kitchen, with eight Louisville locations offering old-fashioned flavors, old-fashioned value and even a collection of old-timey knickknacks and a free jukebox. Pies, cakes and cookies are baked from scratch daily, and the ice cream is fresh-churned with real cream, just like Grandma used to make. The signature item here is the Caramel Iced Dutch Apple Pie, but that's just one among many mouthwatering goodies. The menu is always changing to reflect seasonal offerings — autumn, for example, brings pumpkin bundt cake, pumpkin cheesecake and pumpkin ice cream — and the owners' whims. There are flaky fruit pies such as peach, cherry and apple; meringue pies, such as chocolate, butterscotch and lemon; and chess pie. As for the cakes, favorites include double chocolate and yellow cake with caramel frosting. You can also get holiday cookies and much more. No alcohol available. Serving during lunch and dinner hours daily. Hours vary by season and location. 2525 Bardstown Rd, Louisville, KY 40205. (502) 459-8184. Multiple locations. www.piekitchen.com. Go to: www.wtle.com/181. ***Bakery, Dessert, Ice Cream. $.***

The Irish Rover ~ *Best Irish/British*

Michael Reidy, a native of County Clare, and wife Siobhan serve up an atmosphere as authentic as Michael's brogue at popular gathering spot The Irish Rover. The 150-year-old building in the historic Clifton-Crescent Hill neighborhood began as a saloon and still retains that homey feel, aided by jovial service. Adding to the atmosphere are ancestral photos and recorded Irish music. The menu is rich in hearty, traditional British Isles dishes such as Guinness beef stew, smoked salmon and potato gratin, bangers and mash, and fish and chips. As you'd expect, there's a substantial selection of Irish whiskey and beer — draft selections include Irish favorites Guinness and Smithwick's, along with Irish Rover Red, a classic red ale brewed especially for the Rover by Bluegrass Brewing Co. Burgers, chicken and salads are available for die-hard Yankees. A Saturday brunch, served 11 am–2 pm, includes a traditional Irish breakfast. There's patio dining in season. Menu varies at La Grange location. Full bar. Serving lunch and dinner Mon–Sat. Late-night Fri–Sat. Closed Sun. Hours vary by location. 2319 Frankfort Ave, Louisville, KY 40206. (502) 899-3544. Two locations. www.theirishroverky.com. Go to: www.wtle.com/208. ***Brunch, Irish/British. $$.***

J. Gumbo's

The bright purples and yellows that line the walls at rapidly expanding chain J. Gumbo's (formerly Gumbo a Go-Go, with the Taylorsville Road location breaking from the franchise and keeping the original name), along with hot sauce-themed décor, get hungry customers prepared for the spicy, New Orleans-style eats. Cajun and Creole specialties include jambalaya and étouffée (choice of chicken, shrimp or crawfish), with drunken chicken (chicken in tomatoes and beer stew) another recommended entrée. And you can't go wrong with New Orleans-classic red beans and rice. Try banana pudding or peach cobbler for dessert. Now with seven Louisville locations. Beer available. Serving lunch and dinner daily. Closes 8 pm Sun. Hours vary by location. 2109 Frankfort Ave, Louisville, KY 40206. (502) 896-4046. Multiple locations. www.jgumbos.com. Go to: www.wtle.com/33. ***Cajun/Creole. $.***

Jack Fry's ~ *Best Contemporary*

The spirit of Jack Fry, the gentleman bootlegger and gambler who opened a neighborhood tavern on this spot when Prohibition ended in 1933, lives on at the Louisville landmark bearing his name. The dark, charming ambiance, excellent wine list and cocktails, and impeccable service make it an ideal destination for special occasions. Creative and savory sauces, glazes, herb crusts, compotes and purées enliven the superb chops, beef filets, veal medallions, poultry (roasted organic chicken) and seafood (pan-seared halibut and lobster tails). Full bar. Serving lunch Mon–Fri, dinner nightly. Late-night Fri–Sat. 1007 Bardstown Rd, Louisville, KY 40204. (502) 452-9244. www.jackfrys.com. Go to: www.wtle.com/4. ***Bistro, Contemporary. $$.***

Joe Huber Family Farm & Restaurant

About 20 miles from Louisville, surrounded by cornfields in the little southern Indiana town of Starlight, is Joe Huber Family Farm & Restaurant, a fully functioning farm where you can pick your own fruits and vegetables (in season) and visit a petting zoo. And, when you get hungry, you can chow down in a big, barnlike restaurant where everything is prepared from scratch using fresh ingredients, including homegrown produce. The specialty is Huber's Country Platter Dinner: fried chicken, Huber Honey Ham, fried biscuits and apple butter, country slaw, mashed potatoes and gravy, green beans, corn, and chicken and dumplings. This eye-popping feast is served family-style, which means everybody in your party shares from the platters and bowls of food at the center of the table. Appetizers include fried green tomatoes, and among entrées are grilled pork chops, farm-raised catfish filets and Black Angus rib eye. Or you may choose a country vegetable plate. Save room for house-made pie or cobbler. Huber's Orchard, Winery & Vineyards produces several varieties of wine (including peach, strawberry and blackberry). There's also a cheese factory and bakery. Full bar. Serving lunch and early dinner daily. Hours vary by season. 2421 Scottsville Rd, Starlight, IN 47106. (812) 923-5255. www.joehubers.com. Go to: www.wtle.com/193. ***Fried Chicken, Home-style. $$.***

Joe's O.K. Bayou ~ *Best Cajun/Creole*

"Welcome to the Swamp," proclaims a neon sign in the bar area of Joe's O.K. Bayou. The restaurant opened just in time for Mardi Gras in 1995 and has been serving genuine Cajun and Creole cuisine, cooked by a New Orleans native, in a festive, laid-back atmosphere ever since. The bar is reminiscent of a bayou fishing shack, while the dining room completes the theme with murals of fog-shrouded cypresses rising from murky waters. The menu offers everything you'd hope to find in a Louisiana eatery, including Cajun entrées such as étouffée (crawfish, shrimp or chicken), gumbo, and red beans and rice. Specialty dinners include soft-shell crab, gator tail, shrimp, frog legs and fried oysters — the belt-busting "Big Mamou" platter offers a generous sampling of these specialties. Or go crazy with five pounds of boiled crawfish. Nightly all-you-can-eat specials are also offered. Louisiana-brewed beers, as well as the more standard domestics, are available in bottles and on draft. Desserts include whiskey-laced bread pudding and pralines. Full bar. Serving lunch and dinner daily. 9874 Linn Station Rd, Louisville, KY 40223. (502) 426-1320. Two locations. www.joesokbayou.com. Go to: www.wtle.com/34. ***Cajun/Creole. $.***

L&N Wine Bar and Bistro

The initials stand not for the famed Louisville & Nashville Railroad but for husband-and-wife owners Len Stevens and Nancy Richards. L&N, which opened in 2003 in the Clifton/ Butchertown area, creates a warm and cozy ambiance thanks to three fireplaces, exposed brick walls and original local artwork. It's clear L&N is serious about wine: There are nearly 80 by-the-glass (or by-the-taste) options, knowledgeable servers, and the country's largest Cruvinet wine dispensing system, which keeps wines fresh for six weeks after uncorking. And there's a menu to match. Want to nibble while sampling vintages? Go for appetizers such as scallops and gnocchi or warm four-cheese fondue with apples and kielbasa. If you prefer something more substantial, dig in to a smoked pork chop, the Tuna Humphries (pepper-seared rare ahi with truffled risotto) or the blue plate special, which could be anything from gourmet meat loaf to grilled mixed sausages. Vegetable Wellington and a stuffed squash entrée satisfy the vegetarian crowd. Amid all the wine, beer drinkers will find a well-chosen list of bottled brews. For dessert, try the heavenly Belgian chocolate fondue. Full bar. Serving dinner Mon–Sat. Late-night Fri–Sat. Closed Sun. 1765 Mellwood Ave, Louisville, KY 40206. (502) 897-0070. www.landnwinebarandbistro.com. Go to: www.wtle.com/22934. ***Bistro, Contemporary, Wine Bar. $$.***

La Rosita Grill

Mexican; $$
1515 E Market St, New Albany, IN 47150 *(Multiple Locations)*
(812) 944-3620, www.larositagrill.com
Go to: www.wtle.com/24523

Le Relais ~ *Best French*

Le Relais, which translates as "the relay," is widely acclaimed as one of Louisville's finest restaurants in any category, noted for meticulous preparation, artistic presentation and world-class service. Nestled within the historic terminal at Bowman Field, where Charles Lindbergh landed the Spirit of St. Louis in 1927, it resonates with romantic atmosphere and Continental charm. The upscale-casual dining room is accentuated by 1940s art deco-style finishes and white linen-covered tables, while the outdoor deck offers a more relaxed atmosphere. The veal chop marinated in sherry and Dijon mustard is among other outstanding entrées on a short list of eight or nine. The lamb loin and the rainbow trout are also excellent choices. Full bar. Serving dinner Tue–Sun. Closed Mon. 2817 Taylorsville Rd (Bowman Field), Louisville, KY 40205. (502) 451-9020. www.lerelaisrestaurant.com. Go to: www.wtle.com/108. ***Continental, French. $$$.***

Lee's Korean Restaurant ~ *Best Korean*

Louisville's first Korean restaurant, opened a quarter-century ago, remains something of a secret. And that's just fine with locals in the know. The stone *bi bim bop* at Lee's — rice, fried egg, vegetables and beef served in a stone bowl — is a favorite, as is the *galbi jim*, a beef stew fortified with marinated charbroiled ribs. While beef dominates the menu, there are also plenty of chicken, pork, seafood and meatless options. The vegetable pancake, which you can sauce to your heart's desire using the bottles at your table, is a marvelous appetizer. Chinese dishes are available for those who are a little less adventurous. And, of course, there's kimchi (pickled vegetables), a Korean specialty. Beer available. Serving lunch and dinner Mon–Sat. Closed Sun. 1941 Bishop Ln, Louisville, KY 40218. (502) 456-9714. Go to: www.wtle.com/245. ***Korean. $.***

Lemongrass Cafe

Chinese, Thai, Vietnamese; $
1019 Bardstown Rd, Louisville, KY 40204
(502) 238-3981
Go to: www.wtle.com/384

Lilly's

Kathy Cary, who grew up on a Louisville-area farm, opened her celebrated restaurant with husband Will in 1987, naming it after their daughter. She already had made her mark as a caterer and chef in Washington, D.C., and then with a gourmet-to-go shop in Kentucky. She has been repeatedly invited to cook at New York's prestigious Beard House and has been written up in almost every major food publication. She even taped two cooking segments for Martha Stewart's TV show. So what does that mean to you, the hungry diner on a quest for the best in Louisville? Plenty. You see, Cary's proud of her roots: Her seasonally changing menu features local produce, and it showcases Kentucky and Southern flavors with her own unique spin. That means appetizers, "Kentucky Tapas," such as the Kentucky Lake catfish spring roll with Asian dipping sauce. It means dinner entrées like roasted lamb shank with Kentucky-ground grits and the God Bless Our Local Farmers vegetable plate. And it means lunch selections such as the fried green tomato BLT and Cary's gourmet chicken potpie. Special three-course, prix fixe meals are also available. Save room for the caramel cake. Reservations suggested. Full bar. Serving lunch and dinner Tue–Sat. Closed Sun–Mon. 1147 Bardstown Rd, Louisville, KY 40204. (502) 451-0447. www.lillyslapeche.com. Go to: www.wtle.com/120. ***Contemporary, Small Plates. $$$.***

Limestone Restaurant

Any questions about the regional allegiance of this establishment are quickly answered by its menu. Welcome to the South, y'all — but leave your preconceptions at home. "New Southern Cooking, Old Southern Charm" is the motto for chefs/owners Michael Cunha and Jim Gerhardt, who helped bring The Oakroom to prominence before opening the more casual and modern Limestone in 2003. They're big believers in using regional produce, meats and cheeses. Appetizers include Southern-fried chicken livers and shrimp and grits. Cunha and Gerhardt excel at seafood: roasted salmon, seared sea bass. Wherever you're from, the braised beef short ribs with smoky white beans, collard greens and hot water cornbread will bring out your inner Southerner. The Feed Me Chef option is a five-course, spontaneous tasting menu for your entire table, with optional wine pairings — the wine's free after 9 each night. Full bar. Serving lunch Mon–Fri, dinner Mon–Sat. Sun brunch 10 am–2 pm. 10001 Forest Green Blvd, Louisville, KY 40223. (502) 426-7477. www.limestonerestaurant.com. Go to: www.wtle.com/121. ***Brunch, Contemporary, Home-style. $$.***

Lonnie's Best Taste of Chicago ~ *Best Hot Dogs*
Lonnie Edwards knows a thing or two about Chicago-style hot dogs. When he and wife Diane lived in the Windy City, he owned a hot dog restaurant in addition to working a full-time job. A job transfer brought the couple to Louisville several years ago, and Lonnie decided to open a similar eatery here, thus educating locals on the pleasures of a Vienna Beef hot dog in a poppy seed bun with yellow mustard, bright green relish, tomato, cucumber, chopped onions, hot peppers and celery salt. Lonnie's original location, which opened in 2002, was replaced a year later by the current one in St. Matthews. Additional menu items include chili, Polish sausage, Italian beef sandwiches, gyros, corned beef, chicken breasts and wings, fried fish (Friday and Saturday), and soul food plates (Wednesday only). A second location was slated to open in spring 2008. No alcohol available. Serving lunch and early dinner Mon–Sat. Closed Sun. 121 St. Matthews Ave, Louisville, KY 40207. (502) 895-2380. Go to: www.wtle.com/197. ***Diner, Hot Dogs. $.***

Los Aztecas ~ *Best Mexican*
With four area locations, authentic local Mexican restaurant chain Los Aztecas specializes in fajitas — including the Azteca Fajitas, loaded with steak, chicken, shrimp and spicy chorizo sausage — and Grande Tlaloc, otherwise known as enchiladas. Los Aztecas also offers a variety of seafood selections, including several shrimp dishes, and an impressive number of combination plates and lunch specials. If you're in the mood for something a little different, try the Pechuga Azteca, a marinated and floured boneless chicken breast stuffed with ham, ground

beef and cheese. Full bar. Serving lunch and dinner daily. 530 W Main St, Louisville, KY 40202. (502) 561-8535. Multiple locations. www.losaztecas.net. Go to: www.wtle.com/259. ***Mexican. $.***

Lynn's Paradise Cafe ~ *Best Breakfast, Best Home-style*

Cross a funky diner with Pee-wee's Playhouse, and you might end up with something like Lynn's Paradise Cafe. With concrete animal statues outside and an interior characterized by "ugly lamps," brightly colored booths and a heavily decorated tree, this café is the brainchild of owner Lynn Winter, a Louisville native whose overactive imagination permeates every nook and cranny. The food is about the only thing they take seriously here. Lynn's is famed for its bountiful breakfasts — biscuits and gravy, huge omelets, French toast, and cheese grits — that are served all day long. There's also plenty of hearty comfort food like macaroni and cheese and roast turkey with cranberry sauce. Full bar. Serving breakfast, lunch and dinner daily. 984 Barret Ave, Louisville, KY 40204. (502) 583-3447. www.lynnsparadisecafe.com. Go to: www.wtle.com/194. ***Breakfast, Brunch, Diner, Home-style. $.***

Maido Essential Japanese Cuisine & Sake Bar

"Japanese home-style cooking" is how owners Jim and Toki Huie describe the cuisine at Maido, which they opened in 2004 after a couple of years spent operating a small sushi-to-go business at Seafood Connection on Bardstown Road. She grew up in a restaurant family in Osaka, Japan, while he was born and raised in Kentucky and had never eaten Japanese food before he met his future bride. Both paid their way through college by working at restaurants. Maido is not a sushi bar but rather an *izakaya*, described as the Japanese version of a Spanish tapas bar, with an informal environment that lends itself to groups of friends sharing selections from the extensive, affordable menu. Popular sushi choices include the Osaka Blue roll — a cooked tuna roll — and Dragon Breathing Fire, whose name hints it's not for the timid. The broiled eel is also top-notch. If you prefer fried foods, you'll enjoy oysters, chicken, beef and vegetables coated in *panko* (Japanese bread crumbs). In addition to the largest variety of sake (both hot and cold) in town, Maido boasts a short but diverse selection of imported beers and American microbrews carefully chosen to complement the food. Serving lunch buffet Mon–Fri, late lunch Sat, dinner Mon–Sat. Closed Sun. 1758 Frankfort Ave, Louisville, KY 40206. (502) 894-8775. www.maidosakebar.com. Go to: www.wtle.com/239. ***Japanese/Sushi. $.***

Mai's Thai

Thai; $
1411 E 10th St, Jeffersonville, IN 47130
(812) 282-0198
Go to: www.wtle.com/376

Mark's Feed Store ~ *Best Barbecue*

Thriving, locally based Mark's Feed Store has grown to several Louisville-area locations. The original, on Dixie Highway, is actually a former feed store, which accounts for the name. Mark's, a regular winner of local "best barbecue" competitions, draws rave reviews for its lean, smoky baby back ribs, which are "guaranteed fallin' off the bone," as well as for its chicken and pork. The rich, well-seasoned burgoo — a Kentucky-hallmark hearty stew of meat and vegetables — is also a winner. The spicy barbecue sauce, with a dab of mustard, is a nod to South Carolina-style barbecue, but a red version is available as well. Beer and wine available. Serving lunch and dinner daily. 10316 Dixie Hwy, Louisville, KY 40272. (502) 933-7707. Multiple locations. www.marksfeedstore.com. Go to: www.wtle.com/21845. ***Barbecue. $.***

Mike Linnig's

Open-air dining is a large part of the appeal at longtime Louisville favorite Mike Linnig's, as is the fact that you can get a lot of seafood for just a little money. This casual eatery's origins trace to 1925, when the Linnig family opened a fruit stand along the Ohio River. Although indoor seating is available, in pleasant weather most customers prefer the outdoor picnic tables shaded by beautiful, old trees. There, they can enjoy a cold brew and a range of mostly fried fare such as the signature fish sandwich, shrimp, frog legs, oysters, salmon, clam strips and onion rings. Non-fried selections include Alaskan snow crab legs and the popular turtle soup. Steaks, burgers and chicken dishes are also offered. Beer available. Serving lunch and dinner Tue–Sun. Closed Mon. Closed late-Oct to late-Jan. 9308 Cane Run Rd, Louisville, KY 40258. (502) 937-9888. www.mikelinnigsrestaurant.com. Go to: www.wtle.com/358. ***Seafood. $$.***

Napa River Grill

This homegrown tribute to Northern California wine country offers an eclectic wine list that has often earned the Award of Excellence from *Wine Spectator* magazine, and the gourmet, California-inspired cuisine beautifully complements that list. The relaxed, secluded ambiance — with seating at the bar, in the contemporary dining rooms or on a patio with a grapevine-covered fieldstone wall — will make you feel as close to the Golden State as you're likely to feel in Louisville. The well-informed staff will help you select the right wine for your meal (or vice versa). For starters, try the ancho chili-dusted calamari. A quintet of salads includes a superlative Caesar and the Hawaiian ahi, which combines sesame seared rare tuna with mixed greens and Asian vegetables. Among entrées, the Monterey pork chop is a terrific choice, but seafood lovers will relish the Thai curry scallops and the crab cakes. The baked squash ratatouille is an excellent vegetarian choice, and the aged 22-ounce rib eye or the tenderloin with jumbo lump crab and horseradish cream sauce will pacify beef eaters. Full bar. Serving lunch Mon–Fri, dinner nightly. 3938 Dupont Cir, Louisville, KY 40207. (502) 893-0141. www.napariverlouisville.com. Go to: www.wtle.com/122. ***Contemporary. $$.***

The New Albanian Brewing Co., Pub & Pizzeria ~ *Best Sports Bar/Pub Food*

A mecca for beer drinkers in the Louisville metro area, this not-so-local watering hole has earned an impressive loyal patronage despite its hard-to-find location in a remote New Albany strip mall. Proclaiming mainstream American light beer as public enemy number one, The New Albanian Brewing Co. (formerly, and still informally, referred to as Rich O's) offers a massive selection of top-shelf imports and domestic microbrews in a London pub-like atmosphere, complete with giant portraits of fellow dissenters Marx and Lenin. The management takes great pride in updating the constantly changing menu with new and eccentric brews from all over the globe, so no night at NABC is ever the same. What you can count on, however, is dozens of beers on tap and hundreds by the bottle, served at the appropriate temperature and in the proper glassware for their respective styles. NABC includes Sportstime Pizza, with its delicious pizzas, pastas and sandwiches — try the Big Ten, the Herbivore or the Carnivore. Full bar. Generally serving lunch, dinner and late-night Mon–Sat. Call for specific hours. Closed Sun. 3312 Plaza Dr, New Albany, IN 47150. (812) 949-2804. www.newalbanian.com. Go to: www.wtle.com/374. ***Pizza, Sports Bar/Pub Food, Worth the Drive. $.***

Nios at 917

Contemporary, Small Plates; $$
917 Baxter Ave, Louisville, KY 40204
(502) 456-7080, www.niosat917.com
Go to: www.wtle.com/24453

North End Cafe

Two renovated shotgun houses in Louisville's Clifton neighborhood are the setting for North End Cafe, which uses traditional cuisine as a jumping-off point for a creatively eclectic menu that emphasizes healthy cooking with fresh ingredients. (The restaurant maintains its own vegetable and herb garden in nearby Simpsonville.) The café opened in 2003 and expanded into the house next door in 2005, when a full bar and lounge were added, plus additional outdoor seating. It's a bright, homey and inviting place, the walls covered with local artwork. The breakfast menu — featuring omelets, unusual pancakes, and biscuits and gravy as well as a tofu stir-fry — is available until 3 each afternoon. From the lengthy, seasonally changing tapas menu, options can include ribs, and crab cakes with avocado purée and cucumber *fresca*. Lunch and dinner favorites include the calamari Caesar salad, rosemary roasted chicken and dumplings, and pork tenderloin with cider gravy. Vegetarian delicacies include wild mushroom lasagna and vegetable enchiladas. Full bar. Serving breakfast, lunch and dinner Tue–Sun. Closed Mon. 1722 Frankfort Ave, Louisville, KY 40206. (502) 896-8770. www.northendcafe.com. Go to: www.wtle.com/375. ***Breakfast, Contemporary, Small Plates. $$.***

The Oakroom

The Oakroom, the flagship restaurant in the glorious, century-old Seelbach Hilton hotel, has a sterling reputation. Patrons have included F. Scott Fitzgerald, John F. Kennedy and Al Capone. The cuisine, described as "international Kentucky fine dining," is exquisite — firmly based in regional ingredients, but with significant global influences. A continually changing menu revels in creative surprises, balanced flavors and gourmet twists on comfort food — such as the BLT with pork belly, tomato jam and goat cheese, and The Oakroom version of the Kentucky Hot Brown with quail breast, pancetta crisp, corn relish, grit Johnny cake and Mornay sauce. The lavish Sunday brunch buffet (10 am–2 pm) offers complimentary champagne beginning at 1 pm. Reservations suggested. Full bar. Serving dinner Tue–Sat. Closed Mon. 500 4th St (The Seelbach Hilton), Louisville, KY 40202. (502) 807-3463. www.seelbachhilton.com/hoteldining_theoakroom.html. Go to: www.wtle.com/412. ***Brunch, Contemporary, Hotel Restaurant. $$$.***

Omar's Gyro ~ *Best Greek*

Mustard yellow walls, framed local art and marble-top tables compose the upscale-funky décor of this quaint Mediterranean sandwich shop, known for its creative take on the traditional Greek pita sandwich, the gyro, a lamb and beef combination typically atop a buttered pita accompanied by various vegetables and relishes. Omar's menu is simple: a handful of gyros and hummus dip, with baklava for dessert. But with a hearty helping of deliciously marinated meat (or grilled bell peppers and onions for the vegetarian lot), fresh condiments and Omar's special yogurt sauce, lack of options isn't really a problem. In addition to classic lamb-beef, chicken and vegetable varieties, Omar's offers sweet barbecue- and Caribbean jerk-style gyros that prove as scrumptious and satisfyingly fresh as they are unique. Though gyros are made to order, service proves relatively quick and efficient. Kettle-fried potato chips make a perfectly crispy accompaniment to any sandwich. Beer available. Serving lunch and dinner Mon–Sat. Closed Sun. 969 1/2 Baxter Ave, Louisville, KY 40204. (502) 454-4888. Go to: www.wtle.com/191. ***Greek. $.***

Palermo Viejo

Palermo Viejo, which takes its name from the lively neighborhood in Buenos Aires, is a meat lover's paradise. It is owned by brothers Francisco and Federico Elbl, who were born in Louisville but raised by their Puerto Rican mother and Spanish father. Standout entrées include La Parillada, the house specialty, featuring house-made Argentine sausage, short ribs, flank steak and sweetbreads served on a special table grill. Grilled chicken and seafood are also available. In the mood for carbs rather than protein? A variety of pasta dishes showcase the influence of Argentina's Italian settlers. There's a very nice selection of Argentine wines to complement your meal. Full bar. Serving dinner Mon–Sat. Closed Sun. 1359 Bardstown Rd, Louisville, KY 40204. (502) 456-6461. www.palermoviejo.info/index3.html. Go to: www.wtle.com/35. ***Latin/South American. $$.***

The Patron

Bistro, Brunch, Contemporary; $$
3400 Frankfort Ave, Louisville, KY 40207
(502) 896-1661, www.thepatron.org
Go to: www.wtle.com/390

Pat's Steak House ~ *Best Steak House*

Truly a Louisville institution, Pat's Steak House has been family-owned and -operated since 1958, when it originally opened as Min's. It exudes Old Louisville ambiance and gracious Southern hospitality under current owner Pat Francis, who took over in the 1980s. With its 1950s-style character — dim lighting, dark-paneled walls and waiters in green jackets — more than one diner has likened it to being in a time warp. It's an especially popular spot for special occasions with friends and family. In addition to huge, tender steaks (filet mignon, New York strip and porterhouse among them), Pat's signature dishes include the oyster cocktail appetizer, crisp fried chicken, Irish meat loaf and Southern-style vegetables. Full bar. Cash or check only. Serving dinner Mon–Sat. Closed Sun. 2437 Brownsboro Rd, Louisville, KY 40206. (502) 893-2062. www.patssteakhouselouisville.com. Go to: www.wtle.com/368. ***Steak House. $$$.***

Plehn's Bakery

Bakery, Café, Dessert, Ice Cream/Confections; $
3940 Shelbyville Rd, Louisville, KY 40207
(502) 896-4438, www.yp.bellsouth.com/plehnsbakery
Go to: www.wtle.com/24556

Porcini

Trendy, Crescent Hill-area Porcini restaurant, a favorite of University of Louisville basketball coach and New York native Rick Pitino, specializes in northern Italian cuisine. It offers both patio dining, accentuated by a mural of the Tuscan countryside, and elegant indoor dining, with a fountain adding to the romantic appeal. Classic dishes such as veal scaloppini, chicken Marsala and capellini *con pesce* (with shrimp, scallops, mussels, clams and squid) are among the many standouts on a menu noted for its variety of fresh pasta, fish and veal dishes. The tender, golden fried calamari appetizer is one of the signature items. Save room for tiramisu or one of the other memorable desserts, which change daily. Full bar. Serving dinner Mon–Sat. Closed Sun. 2730 Frankfort Ave, Louisville, KY 40206. (502) 894-8686. www.porcinilouisville.com. Go to: www.wtle.com/217. ***Italian. $$.***

Primo

Italian; $$
445 E Market St, Louisville, KY 40202
(502) 583-1808, www.primorestaurant.net
Go to: www.wtle.com/218

Proof on Main

At Proof on Main, you may actually feel like part of a tableau, with the art (contemporary and culinary) surrounding you. Located on increasingly cosmopolitan West Main Street, this restaurant shares space with 21c Museum Hotel (an art museum as well as a hotel) and features a dining room full of striking mirrors, paintings and sculptures — a mischievous-looking satyr statue welcomes you to the bar. Executive chef Michael Paley blends Tuscan and closer-to-home Southern traditions with his innovative yet approachable cuisine. Commence your dining experience with a sample platter of cured meats or tender baked octopus. Featured entrées such as rock shrimp risotto and Roman-style duck illustrate Paley's artistry. Full bar. Serving breakfast and dinner daily, lunch Mon–Fri. 702 W Main St, Louisville, KY 40202. (502) 217-6360. www.proofonmain.com. Go to: www.wtle.com/22935. ***Contemporary. $$$.***

Ramsi's Cafe on the World

Cozy, unique, relaxed, fun, eclectic. These are just a few of the adjectives routinely used to describe globe-spanning Ramsi's Cafe on the World, which gets extra points for its late hours. Bar-hoppers and other denizens of the night know that at the end of the evening, they can rely on Ramsi's to satisfy just about any international craving they might have: Italian, Mediterranean, Middle Eastern, Cuban, Asian, Jamaican, and on and on. The extensive menu ranges from soups (15-bean and a soup of the day), salads and appetizers to sandwiches and more than two dozen entrées, including beef, chicken, seafood, lamb, pastas and an ample selection of vegetarian and vegan dishes. A dozen vegetarian side dishes include spinach Alfredo and fried plantains. Overall favorites include the Pollo Nuevo Havana, a Cuban-style blackened chicken dish; the grilled sea bass with a Mandarin horseradish glaze; and the CUBeAN burrito. More than likely, you'll have to wait for a table — the cozy dining room seats just 60 — but after eating here once, you won't complain. Full bar. Serving lunch Mon–Sat, dinner and late-night daily. 1293 Bardstown Rd, Louisville, KY 40204. (502) 451-0700. www.ramsiscafe.com. Go to: www.wtle.com/185. ***Contemporary, Vegetarian. $$.***

Raw Sushi Lounge

Asian Fusion, Japanese/Sushi; $$
520 S 4th St, Louisville, KY 40202
(502) 585-5880, www.rawsushilounge.com
Go to: www.wtle.com/22950

RockWall Bistro

American Traditional, Brunch; $$
3426 Paoli Pke, Floyds Knobs, IN 47119
(812) 948-1705, www.rockwallbistro.com
Go to: www.wtle.com/22937

Saffron's Restaurant ~ *Best Middle Eastern*

Authentic Persian cuisine — from the area now known as Iran, and beyond — is the order of the day at Saffron's, and it's served with genuine warmth in a comfortable atmosphere. No surprise, then, that proprietor Majid Ghavami, a former host at

Italian restaurants Casa Grisanti and Vincenzo's, is considered one of the best restaurant hosts in Louisville. The menu, while limited, is loaded with intriguing combinations of flavors. A quartet of appetizers includes sautéed eggplant flavored with onion, garlic, yogurt and mint, served with pita; grilled breast of quail; and pistachio soup enhanced with cinnamon. The specialty of the house, *sheeshleek*, more commonly known as rack of lamb, is out of this world. The rest of the menu consists of a grilled salmon dish with a saffron-barberry sauce, four varieties of kabobs (including one vegetarian), four stews (including the luscious vegetarian *fesenjoon*, made of crushed walnuts, caramelized onion, pomegranate juice and fresh vegetables) and a Greek salad. Fragrant basmati rice comes with entrées. For dessert, be sure to try the Persian ice cream, flavored with saffron, pistachio and rose water. It's unlike anything you'll find at Baskin-Robbins. Full bar. Serving lunch Mon–Fri, dinner Mon–Sat. Closed Sun. 131 W Market St, Louisville, KY 40202. (502) 584-7800. www.saffronsrestaurant.com. Go to: www.wtle.com/254. ***Middle Eastern. $$.***

Sapporo Japanese Grill and Sushi ~ *Best Japanese/Sushi*

Sapporo Japanese Grill and Sushi, a hip, locally owned Japanese steak house, distinguishes itself from national Japanese steak house chains in a number of ways, most notably its exquisite sushi bar. You'll be drawn in immediately by the high-tech, industrial appearance, which makes great use of steel, glass, black marble and neon. There's an area with large tabletop *teppanyaki* grills for those who enjoy slice-and-dice theatrics with their Japanese-American cuisine. The teppanyaki menu, which includes chicken, steak and seafood, is excellent. But Sapporo really gets high marks with its sushi bar, the largest in town in terms of seats (two dozen) as well as selection (about 75 sushi and sashimi choices, all fresh and attractively presented). One of the many standouts is the lobster roll, a wonderful combination of lobster, crab, avocado and asparagus wrapped in rice and seaweed with a creamy mayo sauce enlivened by wasabi and citrus. Elsewhere on the menu, the miso soup, baked mussels, udon (noodles in broth), bento boxes and tempura dishes are also very good. Full bar. Serving dinner nightly. Late-night Thu–Sat. 1706 Bardstown Rd, Louisville, KY 40205. (502) 479-5550. www.sapporojapanese.com. Go to: www.wtle.com/242. ***Japanese/Sushi. $$.***

Seviche: A Latin Restaurant ~ *Best Latin/South American*

For much-lauded chef/owner Anthony Lamas, Seviche represents both a new beginning and the continuation of a fine Nuevo Latino dining tradition. As the name of the enterprise indicates, the house specialty is ceviche, a South American dish consisting of raw seafood marinated in a mixture of spices and citrus juices that "cook" it. Rock shrimp, ahi and crawfish are among the dozen varieties. Signature dishes include feijoada — a Brazilian dish of smoked meats, sausage and black beans, served over rice, with braised greens — and macadamia-crusted sea bass. A sister restaurant, Seviche: A Latin Bistro, opened in 2007 on Goose Creek Road. Full bar. Serving dinner nightly. 1538 Bardstown Rd, Louisville, KY 40205. (502) 473-8560. Two locations. www.sevicherestaurant.com. Go to: www.wtle.com/36. ***Latin/ South American, Seafood. $$.***

Shalimar Restaurant ~ *Best Indian*

A trio of immigrant cousins — Sukh Bains, Gurmukh Pandher and Tirath Pandher — opened Shalimar more than a decade ago, and it has been around longer than any other Indian restaurant in Louisville. Obviously the cousins are doing something right with their northern Indian cuisine. Shalimar, which anchors a strip mall, has a subdued elegance highlighted by a wall of mirrors at the back and Indian-themed prints. The savory fried turnovers known as samosas, stuffed with potatoes, peas and spices, are particularly worthy. Chicken wing aficionados should try the tandoori wings, well seasoned and cooked in the clay oven for a smoky flavor that you won't find at a "regular" wing spot. The lamb *saag*, featuring tender chunks of meat cooked with spinach and spices, is fantastic, as is the chicken *tikka masala*, boneless breast meat cooked in tomato and butter sauce. And the fiery chicken or lamb vindaloo will definitely open your sinuses. Vegetarians and vegans have a bounty of options. The *nav rattan korma* is a rich and textured garden delight featuring an assortment of nine fresh vegetables sautéed in herbs with cashews and raisins. Mango or pistachio ice cream and *kheer* (rice pudding) are among the fine desserts. A lunch buffet is served daily. Full bar. Serving lunch and dinner daily. 1820 S Hurstbourne Pkwy, Louisville, KY 40220. (502) 493-8899. www.shalimarlouisville.com. Go to: www.wtle.com/111. ***Indian. $$.***

Stan's Fish Sandwich

When you name your restaurant after a single sandwich, it had better be a good one, and a lot of folks swear that Stan's has the best fish sandwich in town. Stan and Lelia Gentle, who opened the retail St. Matthews Seafood Co. in 1979, started the restaurant later that year after frequent suggestions from the market's customers. Over the years, Stan's has gradually expanded its menu to include offerings such as crab cakes; New England clam chowder and Louisiana seafood gumbo; and grilled tuna, swordfish and salmon platters. But the original fish sandwich remains the calling card. (The Gentles closed the market in 2004, although they provide limited retail sales at the restaurant and online.) Beer available. Serving lunch and early dinner Mon–Sat. Closed Sun. 3723 Lexington Rd, Louisville, KY 40207. (502) 896-6600. www.stansfish.com. Go to: www.wtle.com/356. ***Seafood. $.***

Stevens & Stevens Deli ~ *Best Deli*

New York-style Stevens & Stevens Deli, which shares space with Ditto's Grill, serves it up fresh and fast. While it does a heavy takeout business, especially at lunch, booth and table seating are available. There's a full menu with some creative variations on typical deli food in addition to essentials such as piled-high pastrami and corned beef sandwiches, soups, and salads, with plenty of vegetarian, vegan and kosher options. Many menu items bear whimsical or celebrity names (Me Turkey - You Jane, the Woody Allen, and Isabella Tortellini pasta salad). The filling Stevens Salad combines spiced pecans, golden apples and crumbled blue cheese over mixed greens with balsamic vinaigrette dressing. And the bakery produces to-die-for chocolate chip cookies, chess bars and other exquisite desserts. No alcohol available. Serving lunch until 4 pm Mon–Sat. Closed Sun. 1114 Bardstown Rd, Louisville, KY 40204. (502) 584-3354. www.stevensandstevensdeli.com. Go to: www.wtle.com/408. ***Deli. $.***

Thai-Siam ~ *Best Thai*

The first Thai restaurant in the Louisville area, Thai-Siam in the Gardiner Lane Shopping Center serves a good-value menu of slightly Americanized fare known for its heat and detailed attention to flavor. Since 1990, locals have depended on this local mainstay for staples with a kick: spicy green curry, pad thai and a peanut sauce-enhanced chicken satay appetizer that has been known to put hair on the chest. But Thai-Siam boasts an extensive menu to suit all thresholds for heat, so if you love Thai but not the fire, this is the place for you. Vegetarian options abound, as do the expected noodle dishes, curries and rice plates. Beer and wine available. Serving lunch and dinner Mon–Sat. Closed Sun. 3002 1/2 Bardstown Rd, Louisville, KY 40205. (502) 458-6871. www.thaisiam-ky.com. Go to: www.wtle.com/378. ***Thai. $.***

Third Avenue Cafe ~ *Best Vegetarian*

"Good food – good karma" is the motto at Third Avenue Cafe,

a cozy and funky little neighborhood restaurant that still bears traces of its former life as a pharmacy. Third Avenue Cafe is acclaimed for its "v"-studded menu — which stands not for "victory" but for dishes that are vegan or can be made vegan on request. You can even get a vegan Reuben sandwich or BLT. Meatless entrées include the savory Portobella Napoleon, a marinated and grilled mushroom cap layered with feta, roasted veggies and provolone; curry roasted veggies; and a black bean burger. Meat eaters will be satisfied, too, as the menu also offers burgers, steak, pork chops, chicken and fish. The Seafood Hot Brown, with pan-seared grouper, garlic tiger shrimp, bacon and tomato slices on house-made focaccia and topped with Mornay sauce, is a creative variation on the local tradition. The luscious desserts, like everything on the menu, are house-made. Sidewalk patio dining is available. Trivial Pursuit cards on the tables help pass time 'til your food arrives. Live entertainment Fri and Sat nights. Full bar. Serving lunch and dinner Mon–Sat. Closed Sun. 1164 S 3rd St, Louisville, KY 40203. (502) 585-2233. www.thirdavecafe.com. Go to: www.wtle.com/380. ***Café, Vegetarian. $$.***

Toast on Market

Breakfast, Café; $
736 E Market St, Louisville, KY 40202
(502) 569-4099, www.toastonmarket.com
Go to: www.wtle.com/24589

Tony Boombozz Pizzeria

According to owner Tony Palombino, the "Boombozz" name comes from Italian slang meaning wild, crazy and fun. "Gourmet," on the other hand, is a word often used to describe his pies. Palombino, whose father opened Louisville's original wood-fired pizza restaurant in 1987, offers a variety of traditional pies and "famous creations," including several national and international award winners. The Pollotate, which has followed Palombino around from restaurant to restaurant and city to city over the years, is based on a family recipe and features marinated chicken, roasted potatoes and red onions on a garlic-olive oil glazed crust with Asiago and mozzarella cheeses. The Tuscan Chicken pizza consists of garlic sauce, grilled chicken, portobello mushrooms, sweet red onions, Roma tomatoes and three cheeses, and the D'Sienna is fresh spinach with tomato cream sauce. Oven-baked panini sandwiches are another option. Although Boombozz primarily focuses on takeout and delivery, dine-in seating is available. Beer and wine available. Generally serving lunch and dinner daily. Hours vary by location. 1448 Bardstown

Rd, Louisville, KY 40204. (502) 458-8889. Multiple locations. www.tonyboombozz.com. Go to: www.wtle.com/291. ***Pizza. $$.***

Twig and Leaf ~ *Best Diner*

Not much has changed at the Twig and Leaf since 1941. The vintage neon sign out front has earned near-iconic status over the years, pointing locals to this neighborhood retro diner, affectionately referred to as "The Twig." The classic black, white and chrome color scheme still dominates the tiny dining room, while a curmudgeonly staff — decidedly more tattooed and pierced than their 1950s equivalents — still serves up a traditional diner-style menu of highly affordable blue plate specials and always-available breakfast items. Whether brunching on weekend mornings or calling it a night after a Friday or Saturday on the town (when the place is open 24-hours), locals pack in for endless cups of coffee and fixtures such as country-fried steak, catfish po-boys and quarter-pound burgers. Lunch and dinner, however, take a back seat to the outstanding list of American breakfast favorites, served all day long. From country ham to breakfast quesadillas, all the standards are there, with omelets sized by a two- or three-egg criterion and "twig taters," aka hash browns, as addictive as ever. À la carte pancakes, eggs and bacon make super-sizing breakfast easy and affordable. No matter what time of day, don't forget to stop by the dessert and ice cream bar for malts, shakes and, of course, sundaes. No alcohol available. Serving breakfast, lunch and dinner daily. Open nearly 24 hours Fri–Sat. Closes 5 pm Sun. 2122 Bardstown Rd, Louisville, KY 40205. (502) 451-8944. Go to: www.wtle.com/409. ***American Traditional, Breakfast, Burgers, Diner. $.***

Uptown Cafe ~ *Best Bistro*

Uptown Cafe, the more casual and budget-conscious sister of Café Metro — both owned by the charming Nancy Shepherd — has, like its across-the-street sibling, been delighting Louisville diners for about a quarter-century. The upscale-casual café ambiance includes tall windows looking out onto Bardstown Road, and awning-covered sidewalk dining is available during pleasant weather. The menu features an array of tantalizing beef, poultry, seafood and pastas. (Try the duck ravioli.) Seafood selections include the ever-popular salmon croquettes and outstanding shrimp bisque, as well as a number of seafood-and-pasta combinations. Vegetarians, and others, love the vegetarian stir-fry and the black bean cakes appetizer. There are also burgers, sandwiches and salads. Be sure to save room for one of the tempting and affordable desserts (raspberry trifle, a Napoleon with fresh fruit, or white chocolate mousse), which are prepared across the street at Café Metro. Full bar. Serving lunch and dinner Mon–Sat. Closed Sun. 1624 Bardstown Rd, Louisville, KY 40205. (502) 458-4212. www.uptownlouisville.com. Go to: www.wtle.com/168. ***Bistro, Contemporary, Dessert. $$.***

Vietnam Kitchen ~ *Best Vietnamese*

It's been said that a number of Louisville's Asian chefs eat at Vietnam Kitchen on their days off. The restaurant is a fixture in Louisville's thriving Asian-American community that also includes Annie Café, less than a mile away. And the owner makes regular trips to Vietnam to stay abreast of culinary developments. Vietnam Kitchen is small but boasts an impressive menu that makes it difficult to choose. For an appetizer, try the sliced beef with shrimp crackers or the dumplings. Among main courses, on a menu rife with fine seafood choices, the catfish cooked in a clay pot with fish sauce is out of this world. *Pho*, or noodle soup, is a specialty at Vietnam Kitchen, which also takes justifiable pride in its selection of rice vermicelli dishes. *Bahn mi*, or loaded Vietnamese-style sub sandwiches on toasted baguettes, are a real bargain. Many dishes are designated spicy, but aren't unbearably hot. End your meal with some Vietnamese iced coffee. Beer available. Serving lunch and dinner Thu–Tue. Closed Wed. 5339 Mitscher Ave, Louisville, KY 40214. (502) 363-5154. Go to: www.wtle.com/385. ***Vietnamese. $.***

Vince Staten's Old Time Barbecue

Vince Staten, a freelance writer, *Courier-Journal* columnist and author of nearly a dozen books, has ably demonstrated his knowledge of all things smoked by writing not one but two books on the subject — *Real Barbecue: The Only Barbecue Book You'll Ever Need* (with Greg Johnson) and *Jack Daniel's Old Time Barbecue Cookbook*, the latter packed with almost 300 recipes. His restaurant in Prospect proves he is perfectly capable of putting theory into practice. You can choose from an amazing array of six sauces to adorn your savory pulled pork and ribs, and Staten's unique coleslaw, based on an old family recipe, gets its sweetness from a surprise ingredient: whipped cream. Full bar. Serving lunch and dinner daily. 13306 W Hwy 42, Prospect, KY 40059. (502) 228-7427. www.statensbbq.com. Go to: www.wtle.com/27. ***Barbecue. $.***

Vincenzo's ~ *Best Italian*

Visitors routinely use the words "luxurious," "elegant" and "romantic" to describe this fantastic Italian restaurant situated in a graceful, old bank building. The excellent European-style cuisine coupled with the Old World charm and service of Vincenzo's, owned by chef Agostino Gabriele and brother Vincenzo, make it one of the top restaurants in Louisville, period. The preparation of many dishes, including the Caesar salad and several appetizers, is completed tableside. The wide-ranging menu includes a variety of pasta dishes as well as seafood such as swordfish and pine nut-encrusted salmon. It's a veal lover's delight, with no fewer than seven *vitello* options. Full bar. Serving lunch Mon–Fri, dinner Mon–Sat. Closed Sun. 150 S 5th St, Louisville, KY 40202. (502) 580-1350. www.vincenzositalianrestaurant.com. Go to: www.wtle.com/220. ***Italian. $$.***

Volare

Italian; $$
2300 Frankfort Ave, Louisville, KY 40206
(502) 894-4446, www.volare-restaurant.com
Go to: www.wtle.com/238

Wagner's Pharmacy

Breakfast, Diner; $
3113 S 4th St, Louisville, KY 40214
(502) 375-3800
Go to: www.wtle.com/410

Westport General Store

Burgers, Contemporary, Home-style; $$
7008 Main St, Westport, KY 40077
(502) 222-4626, www.westportgeneralstore.com
Go to: www.wtle.com/22936

Wick's Pizza ~ *Best Pizza*

Since opening their first Wick's Pizza in 1991, Michael and Meredith Wickliffe have expanded to four Louisville locations. The Highlands site on Baxter Avenue is the original. While it mainly caters to a younger, collegiate crowd with its colorful, tie-dyed, classic-rock atmosphere, families won't feel threatened. Mountains of toppings weigh down the hearty pizzas. Specialty pies include the popular Big Wick (with tomatoes, onions, Italian sausage, beef, ham, pepperoni, green and black olives, mushrooms, and green peppers), the Mighty Meaty Wick, Wick's Veggie Delight, Wick's Cajun BBQ Chicken, Grilled Fajita Chicken and Wick's Bacon & Ranch — the latter two have a base of ranch dressing rather than the traditional tomato sauce. Pasta lovers can choose from lasagna, several varieties of spaghetti, and ravioli. The extensive sandwich menu offers no fewer than 16 options, including a BLT with provolone. There are also salads and, if you need 'em, appetizers. For dessert, try the unusual Tye-Dye Cheese Cake, with swirls of raspberry, kiwi and mango toppings. Full bar. Serving lunch and dinner daily. Late-night Fri–Sat. 975 Baxter Ave, Louisville, KY 40204. (502) 458-1828. Multiple locations. www.wickspizza.com. Go to: www.wtle.com/295. ***Italian, Pizza. $$.***

W.W. Cousins ~ *Best Burgers*

W.W. Cousins' in-house bakery turns out marvelous, buttery buns for its gigantic, cooked-to-order burgers. You can dress the burgers yourself at the mind-blowing, 40-item burger-topping bar, which features not only all the condiments and fixings you'd expect, but also adventurous (even outrageous) items such as sauerkraut, peanuts and shredded coconut. Steaks, chicken and seafood dishes, as well as a great grilled cheese sandwich, are also on the menu. And the in-house bakery means the desserts are fabulous. No alcohol available. Serving lunch and dinner daily. 900 Dupont Rd, Louisville, KY 40207. (502) 897-9684. Go to: www.wtle.com/175. ***American Traditional, Burgers, Diner. $.***

Yang Kee Noodle

Asian Fusion; $
7900 Shelbyville Rd, Louisville, KY 40222
(502) 426-0800, www.yangkeenoodle.com
Go to: www.wtle.com/22921

Zen Garden

Asian Fusion, Vegetarian, Vietnamese; $
2240 Frankfort Ave, Louisville, KY 40206
(502) 895-9114, www.zengardenrestaurant.org
Go to: www.wtle.com/381

Z's Oyster Bar & Steakhouse ~ *Best Seafood*

The best of land and sea unite at Z's Oyster Bar & Steakhouse, where proprietor Mehrzad Sharbaiani has quickly built a reputation that has spread well beyond Louisville since Z's opened in 2000. The atmosphere exudes class, with polished wood and brass, dim lighting, and old-school supper club ambiance. Z's features prime steaks aged for a month on-site and fresh seafood flown in daily from locales including (but not limited to) Hawaii, Maine and Washington state. A half-dozen varieties of oysters are offered, and the signature "Best Filet in Town" and the live Maine lobster highlight the extensive à la carte menu. Full bar. Serving lunch Mon–Fri, dinner nightly. 101 Whittington Pkwy, Louisville, KY 40222. (502) 429-8000. www.zoysterbar.com. Go to: www.wtle.com/364. ***Oysters, Seafood, Steak House. $$$.***

While ***top-echelon contemporary restaurants****, steak houses and some of the South's top Asian eateries garner press clippings, the chili dogs and orange drinks at The Varsity keep winning the hearts and stomachs of Atlanta diners.*

Bacchanalia ~ *Best Contemporary*

Housed in a former meatpacking plant on the west side of Midtown, industrial-chic Bacchanalia remains an Atlanta favorite for contemporary haute cuisine. Consistently ranked as one of the city's top restaurants by the *Atlanta Journal-Constitution*, this DiRoNA restaurant is also a frontrunner on the national culinary scene. (It has been named No. 39 on *Gourmet* magazine's America's Top 50 Restaurants list.) Husband-and-wife team and chefs/owners Clifford Harrison and Anne Quatrano promote locally grown, organic ingredients with their daily changing, prix fixe menus of pan-roasted fish, exceptional pastas and succulent meat dishes. Appropriately, as Bacchanalia is named for the annual festival celebrating the Roman god of wine, the superb wine pairings make each meal at Bacchanalia a near-divine experience. Jacket and tie required. Reservations required. Full bar. Serving dinner Mon–Sat. Closed Sun. 1198 Howell Mill Rd. N.W., Atlanta, GA 30318. (404) 365-0410. Go to: www.wtle.com/6542. ***Contemporary. $$$.***

Bone's Restaurant ~ *Best Steak House*

Since 1979, Atlanta's — and perhaps the South's — premier steak house, Bone's Restaurant, has been welcoming diners with its beginning-to-end old-fashioned sensibility. But its supper club-like atmosphere and top-rate chops prove forever-hip, as this spot on the bustling corner of Peachtree and Piedmont remains the acme of business dining among the city's movers and shakers. Oversized prime steaks, chops and fresh seafood are as flavorful and tender as anywhere in the country. From the 10-ounce "petite" filet to the massive 28-ounce T-bone, it's difficult to go wrong. Top it all off, if you can, with the Mountain High Pie. Full bar. Serving lunch Mon–Fri, dinner nightly. 3130 Piedmont Rd. N.E. Atlanta, GA 30305. (404) 237-2663. Go to: www.wtle.com/8534. ***Steak House. $$$.***

The Dining Room at The Ritz-Carlton, Buckhead

With the distinguished luxury that has become synonymous with the exclusive hotel chain's name, The Ritz-Carlton, Buckhead, brings world-class dining to Atlanta's toniest neighborhood. The Dining Room is one of an elite handful of restaurants across the country to receive the highly prestigious Mobil Five-Star Award, and it has been named No. 24 on *Gourmet* magazine's America's Top 50 Restaurants list. The formula is simple: true, Southern hospitality in a sophisticated setting with top-notch, progressive Continental cuisine. From seared monkfish to sweetbread kabobs, each dish achieves the superior Ritz-Carlton standard. The award-winning wine cellar ensures a comprehensively first-class experience. Jacket required. Reservations required. Full bar. Serving dinner Tue–Sat. Closed Sun–Mon. 3434 Peachtree Rd. N.E., Atlanta, GA 30326. (404) 237-2700. Go to: www.wtle.com/8311. ***Contemporary. $$$.***

Joël ~ *Best French*

James Beard award-winning chef Joël Antunes had already made a name for himself in top kitchens across Europe — earning a few coveted Michelin stars along the way — before arriving at The Ritz-Carlton, Buckhead, nearly a decade ago. It was no surprise, then, when Atlanta gourmands willingly followed this undeniably gifted yet refreshingly humble Frenchman to his eponymous brasserie when it opened downtown in 2001. In a space as sleek as his menu, Antunes resides over his custom, 62-foot stainless steel stove, preparing contemporary French cuisine with Asian and Mediterranean accents. Just ask one of the two on-duty sommeliers to help pair one of over 5,000 wines with anything, from the excellent seared scallops to tender Kobe beef. Full bar. Serving lunch Tue–Fri, dinner Tue–Sat. Closed Sun–Mon. 3290 Northside Pkwy. N.W., Atlanta, GA 30327. (404) 233-3500. Go to: www.wtle.com/8291. ***Contemporary, French. $$$.***

Kyma ~ *Best Greek*

Buckhead Life Restaurant Group founder and CEO Pano Karatassos gives a nod to his Greek heritage with Kyma, one of the group's latest red-hot dining concepts. In a blue-and-white décor reminiscent of the beautiful Aegean Islands, diners may choose to enjoy a glass of wine under the stars on the year-round patio, or nibble on Greek tapas under the faux constellations on the dining room's elegant vaulted ceilings. Fresh fish and seafood are the way to go here, with an impressive array of catches from across the globe, but any of the classic Greek specialties — from lamb shank to slow-cooked eggplant stew — will likely make your stomach shout, "oopah!" Full bar. Serving dinner Mon–Sat. Closed Sun. 3085 Piedmont Rd. N.E., Atlanta, GA 30305. (404) 262-0702. Go to: www.wtle.com/8305. ***Contemporary, Greek, Seafood. $$$.***

MF Sushibar ~ *Best Japanese/Sushi*

The name Chris "Magic Fingers" Kinjo has quickly become synonymous with superlative sushi in Atlanta. Designed by brother and co-founder Alex, the chic establishment fills with an urban clientele that enjoys the contrast of traditional Japanese art and modern techno beats. The sushi bar packs in patrons intently watching Magic Fingers — the nickname from which the restaurant's name is derived — at work, as he prepares his assembly of colorful sashimi and creatively designed sushi rolls. Ask about special fish selections and unique delicacies from Japan that are not on the menu. A sister restaurant, MF Buckhead, was opened in fall 2007. Beer, wine and sake available. Serving lunch Mon–Fri, dinner nightly. 265 Ponce De Leon Ave. N.E., Atlanta, GA 30308. (404) 815-8844. Two locations. Go to: www.wtle.com/8385. ***Japanese/Sushi. $$.***

Nam ~ *Best Vietnamese*

The Kinjo brothers, also of MF Sushibar, have put much effort into creating a simultaneously authentic and sexy Vietnamese restaurant. Locals have responded with overwhelming turnout, prompting the *Atlanta Journal-Constitution* to name Nam one of the city's 10 best overall restaurants. Located in the Midtown Promenade, the chic atmosphere makes an ideal setting for sampling the spectacular nouvelle Vietnamese cuisine. From sweet-and-sour fish soup to banana leaf-steamed halibut, the affordable and highly approachable menu offers an array of choices boasting only the finest ingredients, reflecting varied and exotic flavors. Beer and wine available. Serving lunch Tue–Fri, dinner Mon–Sat. Closed Sun. 931 Monroe Dr. N.E., Atlanta, GA 30308. (404) 541-9997. Go to: www.wtle.com/8563. ***Vietnamese. $$.***

Rathbun's

One of the most lauded restaurants in the American South, Rathbun's has enjoyed quite a reign atop the Atlanta fine-dining scene since respected restaurateur/chef Kevin Rathbun opened it in May 2004. But the industrial-chic eatery, located in The Stove Works building at the edge of Inman Park, refuses to rest on its laurels. The atmosphere remains casual; the regionally influenced menu is relatively affordable; and a walk-ins-only policy on the exquisite patio makes last-minute dinner plans possible. Small plates such as Thai rare beef and onion salad scan Rathbun's global sensitivity, while entrées may concurrently include sea scallops on country ham grits, and Asian-inspired seared yellowfin tuna with ginger pineapple. Full bar. Serving dinner Mon–Sat. Closed Sun. 112 Krog St. N.E., Atlanta, GA 30307. (404) 524-8280. Go to: www.wtle.com/8293. ***Contemporary. $$$.***

The Varsity ~ *Best Hot Dogs*

As iconic an Atlanta entity as Coca-Cola, the original Varsity has been downtown's two-block incarnation of Southern diner Americana since 1928. Here, chili dogs topped with yellow mustard form the base of the nutritional pyramid; the hometown team draws twice the crowd on game days (go Jackets!); and variations on the words "coca cola" encompass all drink options. (Orange soda, for example, becomes "orange co-cola." If befuddled, just order the specialty frozen orange slushie drink known as the FO.) Be familiar with the lingo of the primarily burger-and-dog menu by the time your server asks, "What'll ya have?" or the charmingly short-tempered waitstaff might turn redder than the large "V" on the eatery's sign. No alcohol available. Serving lunch and dinner daily. 61 North Ave., Atlanta, GA 30308. (404) 881-1706. Multiple locations. Go to: www.wtle.com/6566. ***Burgers, Diner, Hot Dogs. $.***

Watershed

Watershed restaurant has been blurring the line between home cooking and fine dining since opening in a converted service station in suburban Decatur. The funky-chic space proves the ideal location for indulging in a seasonal menu with Southern flair. Tuesday's Southern Fried Chicken Night is a particular treat at Watershed, and from-scratch desserts, including one of the area's best chocolate cakes, are an absolute must. Country ham with red-eye gravy, banana fritters, and omelets with roasted new potatoes make Sunday brunch (10 am–3 pm) one of the best times to visit. Full bar. Serving lunch and dinner Mon–Sat. 406 W. Ponce De Leon Ave., Decatur, GA 30030. (404) 378-4900. Go to: www.wtle.com/8560. ***Brunch, Contemporary. $$.***

AUSTIN TEXAS

10 LOCAL FAVORITES

Befitting a progressive capital city, *Austin's time-tested chicken-fried steak and chile con queso have made room for some of the country's best sushi offerings.*

Castle Hill Cafe ~ *Best Contemporary*

For Austin dwellers seeking fine contemporary dining with a Southwestern twist, Castle Hill Cafe offers expertly prepared dishes that are as flawless as the service. And the regionally influenced menu, which changes every two weeks, is as extensive as the wine list. This *Austin American-Statesman* Four-Star, Top-50 restaurant serves up plenty of fresh flavors, from Asian duck spring rolls to the Southwestern Caesar salad, offering several vegetarian options in the mix. Like the wine list, desserts are considered house specialties, from the rich peanut butter mousse pie to the New Orleans-style bread pudding. Full bar. Serving lunch Mon–Fri, dinner Mon–Sat. Closed Sun. 1101 W. 5th St., Austin, TX 78703. (512) 476-0728. Go to: www.wtle.com/8901. ***Contemporary. $$.***

Doña Emilia's South American Bar & Grill ~ *Best Latin/South American*

Downtown's Doña Emilia's South American Bar & Grill is the ideal lunch spot for the business crowd seeking wireless access and sports TV. At night, it's a dream date destination: drinks, dinner and dancing in a tropical paradise setting. Doña Emilia herself oversees the preparation of traditional South American and New Latin cuisine with influences from Columbia, Brazil and Argentina. Work off your decadent meal on the dance floor at the upstairs tropical Atrium Bar that features some of the best mojitos in town, along with Mexican and South American beers, specialty tequilas, and 50 Latin and four Texas wine selections. Full bar. Serving breakfast and lunch Tue–Sat, dinner Tue–Sun. Sun brunch 11 am–2:30 pm. Closed Mon. 101 San Jacinto Blvd., Austin, TX 78701. (512) 478-2520. Go to: www.wtle.com/8996. ***Breakfast, Brunch, Latin/South American. $$.***

Eddie V's Edgewater Grille ~ *Best Seafood*
The go-to spot for Austin seafood connoisseurs seeking fresh fish, subtle sauces and stellar service, Eddie V's Edgewater Grille offers upscale dining and ambiance without pretension. The brainchild of restaurant gurus Larry "Eddie" Foles and Guy "Mr. V." Villavaso, Eddie V's offers two Austin locations as well as a Scottsdale, Ariz., branch. Every morsel of seafood is shipped in fresh, and the menu includes a number of steak, veal and chicken options. Eddie V's has claimed numerous local awards, including best seafood in *The Austin Chronicle* readers' poll, Three-Star/Top-50 honors in the *Austin American-Statesman*'s Dining Guide, and a spot on Tom Horan's Top Ten Texas Steakhouses list. Full bar. Serving dinner nightly. 301 E. 5th St., Austin, TX 78701. (512) 472-1860. Two locations. Go to: www.wtle.com/9702. ***Seafood, Steak House. $$.***

Fonda San Miguel ~ *Best Brunch, Best Mexican*
A favorite with locals and tourists for more than 30 years — President George W. Bush is said to have proposed to wife Laura here — Fonda San Miguel offers authentic Mexican décor with a menu that lives up to its beautiful interior. This *Austin American-Statesman* Four-Star/Top-50 restaurant features a range of delectable entrées, from traditional chile con queso to creative renditions of old favorites, such as the chile relleno. On Sunday, enjoy a brunch buffet reputed to be one of the best in the city, packed with cold appetizers, salads, hot side dishes, entrées and desserts. Full bar. Serving dinner Mon–Sat. Sun brunch 11 am–2 pm. 2330 W. North Loop Blvd., Austin, TX 78756. (512) 459-4121. Go to: www.wtle.com/9379. ***Brunch, Mexican. $$.***

Freddie's Place ~ *Best Diner*
The baby blue building housing owner Fred Nelson's Freddie's Place on trendy South First Street welcomes adults, kids and

even their dogs to come inside and play or to frolic outside on the huge patio underneath the trees. Enjoy an old-fashioned outdoor barbecue, including free brisket, at 6 pm Tuesday through Thursday, from March until October. Or step inside for made-from-scratch sandwiches, burgers, salads and hearty entrées. For dessert, sample the rich house-made cheesecake or hot apple pie. Live music on the patio most Thu–Sat evenings. Full bar. Serving lunch and dinner daily. 1703 S. 1st St., Austin, TX 78704. (512) 445-9197. Go to: www.wtle.com/9218. ***American Traditional, Diner. $.***

Mirabelle Restaurant ~ *Best Bistro*

At Mirabelle Restaurant, it's all about the flavor, thanks to the creative sauces, chutneys and coarsely chopped salsas that offer the perfect combination of texture and taste for the meat, seafood and vegetarian creations. Sister restaurant to Castle Hill Cafe in the Central District, this eclectic bistro offers a similar upscale-yet-relaxed atmosphere, with fusion dishes from the Middle East, the Southwest, the Pacific Rim, Italy and other regions. Just save room for dessert: This *Austin American-Statesman* Four-Star/Top-50 restaurant offers a tempting array of sweet finishes, from fruit cobblers to tiramisu to specialty cheesecakes. Live jazz Tue nights. Full bar. Serving lunch Mon–Fri, dinner Mon–Sat. Closed Sun. 8127 Mesa Dr., Austin, TX 78759. (512) 346-7900. Go to: www.wtle.com/8842. ***Bistro, Contemporary. $$.***

Threadgill's ~ *Best Home-style*

With a rich history and some of the best Southern, soul and Creole food in Austin, it's no wonder Threadgill's is the place locals bring out-of-town friends for down-home cooking and service with a smile. Even before Kenneth Threadgill became famous for his culinary talents, he was known for bringing live music to North Austin, and he received the first beer license in the area. He mentored Janis Joplin, who in the 1960s often played at the original Threadgill's on North Lamar. Menu favorites include Threadgill's renowned chicken-fried steak as well as Creole-style meat loaf with a choice of 27 side items. On Sunday, hit the Gospel Brunch Buffet (10 am–1 pm) for Belgian waffles and omelets cooked to order (South location only). The full bar features an extensive beer selection and specialty Texas-style margaritas. Serving lunch and dinner daily. 6416 N. Lamar Blvd., Austin, TX 78752. (512) 451-5440. Two locations. Go to: www.wtle.com/8755. ***American Traditional, Brunch, Home-style. $.***

Uchi ~ *Best Japanese/Sushi*

Austin's wildly popular Japanese fusion restaurant, Uchi, — "house" in Japanese — is elegant enough for that little black dress, yet casual enough for your inked and multi-pierced date. Uchi offers the perfect menu for experiencing high-quality sakes and new kinds of sushi in the romantic ambiance of a refurbished home. Only a sushi master like Tyson Cole — mentioned on *Food & Wine* magazine's 2005 Best New Chefs list — could invent such eclectic combinations of fresh fish, veggies and fruit. Full bar. Serving dinner nightly. 801 S. Lamar Blvd., Austin, TX 78704. (512) 916-4808. Go to: www.wtle.com/9355. ***Japanese/Sushi. $$.***

Vespaio ~ *Best Italian*

When you step into highly acclaimed veteran chef/owner Alan Lazarus' Vespaio, there's little doubt you've entered an authentic Italian eatery. This beloved Austin culinary destination — an *Austin American-Statesman* Four-Star/Top-50 restaurant and named best Italian restaurant in readers' polls — is hip enough for the trendy while catering to families as well. The impeccably trained staff is knowledgeable about food and wine pairings, occasionally offering samples of the bar's extensive wine list, with more than 30 varieties available by the glass. Just as impressive as the wine selection is Vespaio's authentic menu — think daily risottos, Toscana pizzas and veal ravioli — with much of the daily fare provided by the restaurant's own garden. Full bar. Serving dinner Tue–Sun. Closed Mon. 1610 S. Congress Ave., Austin, TX 78704. (512) 441-6100. Go to: www.wtle.com/9347. ***Italian. $$.***

Zoot

For more than 15 years, Zoot has been serving some of Austin's finest contemporary cuisine prepared with local ingredients. Each visit brings a new culinary adventure, with more than 38 wines sold by the glass for pairing with dinner. Zoot offers an extensive, seasonally rotating, à la carte menu with game, seafood and vegetarian options, but it is the tasting menus that separate this cottage-style bistro from other upscale restaurants. Desserts may range from a rich chocolate cake with zinfandel-infused cherries to a European-style cheese plate paired with a selection of dessert wines and ports. Named one of the best overall restaurants in Austin by the *Austin American-Statesman*. Full bar. Serving dinner Tue–Sun. Closed Mon. 509 Hearn St., Austin, TX 78703. (512) 476-7649. Go to: www.wtle.com/9229. ***Contemporary. $$$.***

BALTIMORE MARYLAND

10 LOCAL FAVORITES

***There's much, much more to cosmopolitan Baltimore** cuisine than crab cakes. Still, you won't want to leave the city without devouring several of them, including the award-winning specialties at G & M Restaurant & Lounge.*

The Black Olive ~ *Best Greek*

Many time-tested recipes from generations of Spiliadis family establishments in Istanbul and their native Greece are served today at their Fells Point eatery, The Black Olive. The Spiliadis family believes in simple preparation and organic ingredients realized in traditional Greek small plates and the restaurant's specialty: fresh fish, prepared whole and fileted tableside. Sushi-grade tuna, lamp chops and beef tenderloin are other top entrée options. The bread pudding isn't your usual sweet treat — it's prepared with house-made olive bread — and is one of the restaurant's must-haves. A substantial wine list includes Greek varieties. Full bar. Serving lunch and dinner daily. 814 S. Bond St., Baltimore, MD 21231. (410) 276-7141. Go to: www.wtle.com/5935. ***Greek. $$$.***

Blue Sea Grill ~ *Best Seafood*

Noted Baltimore restaurateur Steve de Castro sets the local seafood standard with his Blue Sea Grill on downtown Power Plant district's restaurant row. The menu spotlights fresh seafood from local waters and from all over the world. Winning entrées include whole fish, steaks, steamed or tempura lobster, and flounder stuffed with crabmeat. Full bar. Serving dinner Mon–Sat. Closed Sun. 614 Water St., Baltimore, MD 21202. (410) 837-7300. Go to: www.wtle.com/6119. ***Clams, Crab Cakes, Seafood. $$$.***

The Brass Elephant ~ *Best Contemporary*

Old-fashioned glamour glistens from every corner of Baltimore culinary stalwart The Brass Elephant, from the original Tiffany skylights to the elegant sconces that give the restaurant its name. (Word is that the wife of one of the building's former owners adored elephants.) This *Baltimore* magazine Top 50 Restaurant offers a menu of classic entrées with a contemporary twist, such as the cioppino with house-made spinach linguine or duck breast with fig tartlet. *Wine Spectator* has recognized the establishment's top-notch, albeit affordable, wine list. In the upstairs Tusk Lounge, the after-work crowd relaxes in a laid-back atmosphere, with classic cocktails and more casual crab cakes-and-burgers fare. Full bar. Serving lunch Mon–Fri, dinner nightly. 924 N. Charles St. Baltimore, MD 21201. (410) 547-8485. Go to: www.wtle.com/5527. ***Contemporary. $$$.***

The Brewer's Art ~ *Best Brewpub*

It's not every day that you find such eclectic, upscale contemporary cuisine at a brewpub — but then, The Brewer's Art isn't your ordinary pub. Specializing in Belgian-style microbrews, from the award-winning Resurrection to the dark, lusty Proletary Ale, The Brewer's Art elevates the brewpub experience in everything from its vats of beer to the top-notch kitchen. (After all, the restaurant has been named one of *Baltimore* magazine's Top 50 Restaurants.) From the steamed mussels to the Frogmore stew, the fare here is anything but typical. The list of desserts prepared by the pastry chef rotates, but get the chocolate crème brûlée when available. Full bar. Serving dinner nightly. 1106 N. Charles St., Baltimore, MD 21201. (410) 547-6925. Go to: www.wtle.com/5706. ***Brewpub, Contemporary. $$.***

Charleston

Even with the numerous fine-dining options in the Fells Point/Harbor East area, Baltimore foodies can't get enough of chef/owner Cindy Wolf's Charleston, named after the city whose kitchens taught her the ins and outs of Southern cooking. This James Beard Foundation nominee for Best Chef: Mid-Atlantic splits her time between Petit Louis Bistro and this Mobil Four-Star eatery, where the "improvisational" menu features Wolf's unique blend of French and Low Country technique, as in the Charleston shellfish bisque, for example, or the salad of grilled local peaches. The highly praised wine list earns *Wine Spectator*'s Best of Award of Excellence year after year. Full bar. Serving dinner Mon–Sat. Closed Sun. 1000 Lancaster St., Baltimore, MD 21202. (410) 332-7373. Go to: www.wtle.com/5529. ***Contemporary, Home-style. $$$.***

G & M Restaurant & Lounge ~ *Best Crab Cakes*
To inspire the kind of devotion that this Linthicum Heights eatery receives from its patrons is no easy feat. The crab cakes, which have also been lauded by *The Washington Post*, *Baltimore* magazine and others, are available by mail order. But there's nothing like having them served to you in the dining room — fresh, large and golden brown, on a platter or a sandwich. A modest wine list accompanies the first-rate mix of other American, Italian and Greek cuisine. Full bar. Serving lunch and dinner daily. 804 N. Hammonds Ferry Rd., Linthicum Heights, MD 21090. (410) 636-1777. Go to: www.wtle.com/5867. ***American Traditional, Crab Cakes, Seafood. $$.***

The Helmand ~ *Best Middle Eastern*
One of *Baltimore* magazine's Top 50 Restaurants, acclaimed Afghan restaurant The Helmand is named for both the longest river in Afghanistan and the owners' first-born son. The casual upscale eatery offers a plethora of meatless options alongside traditional lamb and chicken kabobs and stews, satisfying vegetarians and carnivores alike. Specialties include *chopendez* (marinated tenderloin of beef) and ginger-infused sea bass. And with reasonable entrée prices, you can afford to sample one of the intriguing desserts. Full bar. Serving dinner nightly. 806 N. Charles St., Baltimore, MD 21201. (410) 752-0311. Go to: www.wtle.com/6110. ***Middle Eastern. $$.***

Matsuri ~ *Best Japanese/Sushi*
Repeatedly acclaimed for its traditional Japanese cuisine, artisanal sushi and extensive sake selection, Matsuri remains a Baltimore staple for Japanese eats. Family-owned and -operated, this quaint Federal Hill cornerstone evokes the tiny local sushi bars of Tokyo, although the upstairs private dining room often remains more true to the restaurant's name (which translates as "festival"). Matsuri is all about

variety. The menu is one of the most expansive in the area, featuring a long list of appetizers plus the classic teriyakis, tempuras and noodle dishes familiar to the American palate. But the chefs keep things creative, particularly with their exotic sushi selection. Beer, wine and sake available. Serving lunch Mon–Fri, dinner nightly. 1105 S. Charles St., Baltimore, MD 21230. (410) 752-8561. Go to: www.wtle.com/6067. ***Japanese/Sushi. $$.***

The Oregon Grille ~ *Best Brunch*

At first glance, elegant Hunt Valley establishment The Oregon Grille seems from another era — a time when dinner jackets were a must for gentlemen and ladies never picked up the tab. But at Sunday brunch (11:30 am–3 pm), the equestrian-themed restaurant, recipient of the coveted Mobil Four-Star rating, cultivates a more casual vibe with astute diners taking advantage of reduced prices for the top-flight cuisine. Enjoy dining in the 19th-century stone farmhouse or the lush garden for both classic and creative brunch specialties, such as the Hangtown Fry or the lobster-and-macaroni casserole. At dinner, expect a top-notch Continental menu, with dry-aged prime steaks sharing menu space with crab cakes. Jacket required after 5 pm. No jeans permitted. Substantial wine list and full bar. Serving lunch Mon–Sat, dinner nightly. Sun brunch. 1201 Shawan Rd., Hunt Valley, MD 21030. (410) 771-0505. Go to: www.wtle.com/5711. ***Brunch, Contemporary, Steak House. $$$.***

The Prime Rib ~ *Best Steak House*

One of Baltimore's most elegant restaurants — named Most Romantic as well as a Top 50 by *Baltimore* magazine — The Prime Rib bills itself as "The Civilized Steakhouse" and is sometimes known locally as simply "The Bone." It opened to rave reviews in 1965 and has since added two equally lauded locations in Washington, D.C., and Philadelphia. Winner of a *Wine Spectator* award, the steak house was inspired by Manhattan's tony supper clubs of the 1940s. Its tuxedo-clad waiters and piano entertainment set a sophisticated mood, as does the classic steak house menu, including succulent prime rib, filet mignon and flat iron steak. Jacket required. Extensive wine list and full bar. Serving dinner nightly. 1101 N. Calvert St., Baltimore, MD 21202. (410) 539-1804. Go to: www.wtle.com/6145. ***Steak House. $$$.***

BIRMINGHAM ALABAMA

10 LOCAL FAVORITES

***Beyond the time-honored barbecue** and fried green tomatoes, award-winning Southern restaurateur Frank Stitt has helped put Birmingham on the national restaurant map.*

Bottega Restaurant and Café ~ *Best Italian*

Tucked in the historic Bottega Favorita building near the Five Points South neighborhood, Bottega and its adjacent casual café are the inventions of Birmingham restaurant guru Frank Stitt. Opened in 1988, Bottega is a romantic, European-style retreat that attracts a well-dressed crowd seeking an elegant meal before heading to the theater or another special destination. While several of Bottega's dishes come from across the Mediterranean, the menu's focus is Italian provincial with an ever-changing selection of appetizers, pastas, seafood, steak, veal and desserts. Don't miss the signature Parmesan soufflé or the upside-down honey cheesecake if available. The full bar features more than 180 red, white and sparkling wines with 16 available by the glass. Café serving lunch and dinner Mon–Sat. Restaurant serving dinner Mon–Sat. Closed Sun. 2240 Highland Ave. S., Birmingham, AL 35205. (205) 939-1000. Go to: www.wtle.com/7637. ***Italian. $$.***

Chez Fonfon ~ *Best French*

Chez Fonfon is the destination for sophisticated Birmingham foodies who want to indulge in French cuisine without purchasing a plane ticket to Paris. Frank Stitt opened this intimate bistro in 2000, next door to his award-winning Highlands Bar and Grill in the Five Points South neighborhood. Like the chef/owner's other successful establishments, Chez Fonfon features a unique wine list, complete with several French vintages. If tapas-style dining fits your mood, there's an ample selection of appetizers, such as country pâté, but meat-and-potato lovers shouldn't miss the extensive selection of hearty entrées or one of the best burgers in town. Reservations not accepted. Full bar. Serving lunch Tue–Fri, dinner Tue–Sat. Closed Sun–Mon. 2007 11th Ave. S., Birmingham, AL 35205. (205) 939-3221. Go to: www.wtle.com/7551. ***Bistro, Burgers, French. $$.***

Cobb Lane Restaurant ~ *Best American Traditional*
Almost like a scene from *Driving Miss Daisy*, Birmingham institution Cobb Lane Restaurant has been pleasing the ladies who lunch there — and most everyone else — since its 1948 inception. The oak-shaded outdoor patio, which ranks among the area's most lovely, provides a perfect setting to dine on upscale-traditional Southern fare including the likes of fried green tomatoes, chicken salad, fried chicken, catfish and steak Oscar. A resplendent Sunday champagne brunch (11 am–2:30 pm) includes classic luncheon entrées such as shrimp and grits, and eggs Benedict. Leave room for chocolate roulage, the signature dessert. Full bar. Serving lunch and dinner Tue–Sat. Sun brunch. Closed Mon. 1 Cobb Ln. S., Birmingham, AL 35205. (205) 933-0462. Go to: www.wtle.com/7377. ***American Traditional, Brunch, Home-style. $$.***

The Fish Market Restaurant ~ *Best Seafood*
Birmingham-area seafood lovers owe many thanks to George Sarris for creating The Fish Market, now with several franchise locations, boasting inexpensive, quality ocean bounty. Supplied by the town's oldest and largest fishery, Empire Seafood (recently acquired by the restaurant), more than 17 varieties of fish and shellfish, served fried, grilled or baked, accompany a formidable list of pastas, salads and other Greek-influenced cuisine. For dessert, choose from lemon or lime pie, numerous cheesecakes and decadent baklava. Full bar. Serving lunch and dinner daily. 5407 Hwy. 280, Birmingham, AL 35242. (205) 980-8600 Multiple locations. Go to: www.wtle.com/7717. ***Seafood. $.***

Highlands Bar and Grill ~ *Best Contemporary*
With his rural Alabama roots, a philosophy degree from Berkeley and a culinary education from the French countryside, James Beard award-winner and chef/owner Frank Stitt has been

making waves across the country's restaurant scene. Stitt's gourmet creations have earned him *Bon Appétit*'s Legends of the Decade award, while his flagship restaurant, Highlands Bar and Grill, has been placed fifth on *Gourmet* magazine's list of the country's top eateries. Locals with discerning tastes flock to this intimate dinner hot spot for its charming décor as well as its ever-changing menu, including a signature oyster bar and seasonal delights such as fresh strawberry sorbet. Jacket suggested, and no shorts allowed in the dining area. Full bar. Serving dinner Tue–Sat. Closed Sun–Mon. 2011 11th Ave. S., Birmingham, AL 35205. (205) 939-1400. Go to: www.wtle.com/7368. ***Contemporary. $$$.***

Hot and Hot Fish Club

With perhaps the most intriguing name on the Birmingham restaurant scene, the Hot and Hot Fish Club is also turning out some of the city's top dishes. Chef Chris Hastings' stylish yet casual Southside eatery — named after his great-grandfather's epicurean gentlemen's club — focuses on local organic produce and farm-raised meats rather than seafood and spicy flavors, as one might think. But the surprises don't end there: Sit at the chef's counter and observe Hastings in action in Birmingham's only completely open kitchen as he whips up his daily changing menu of exceptional and creative contemporary Southern cuisine. If available, try the house-made sausage. Honors include Hastings' nomination for the James Beard Foundation's Best Chef: South award in 2007. Specialty martinis and a *Wine Spectator* award-winning wine list round out the full bar. Serving dinner Tue–Sat. Closed Sun–Mon. 2180 11th Ct. S., Birmingham, AL 35205. (205) 933-5474. Go to: www.wtle.com/7371. ***Contemporary. $$$.***

Jim 'N Nick's Bar-B-Q ~ *Best Barbecue*

Fun and casual, steadily growing Birmingham-based chain Jim 'N Nick's Bar-B-Q serves some of the South's best barbecue — pork, ribs, brisket, chicken and burgers, all cooked over a hickory wood fire. Hometown fans fill the place, not only for the barbecue, but also for the beloved house-made cheese biscuits and other pre-dinner munchies. There's an ample selection of salads, but the hand-pulled pork barbecue sandwich on sourdough with coleslaw may be your best bet. Top it all off with fresh-baked pie. Consistently voted Best Barbecue in *The Birmingham News* readers' poll. Full bar. Serving lunch and dinner daily. 1908 11th Ave. S., Birmingham, AL 35205. (205) 320-1060 Multiple locations. Go to: www.wtle.com/7442. ***Barbecue. $.***

Niki's West Steak & Seafood ~ *Best Home-style*
Since 1957, Birmingham staple Niki's West Steak & Seafood has been packing them in as much for the plentiful vegetable selection as for the creative seafood dishes and inexpensive steaks. There are often as many as 40 available veggies on the old-fashioned meat-and-three buffet, including anything from mashed potatoes to sometimes four varieties of beans, to pair with an entrée such as country-fried steak. Don't miss the house fish special, prepared fried, broiled or Greek-style. The restaurant has received numerous local and national accolades, including a mention in *Gourmet* magazine for its extensive veggie selection. Full bar. Serving breakfast, lunch and dinner Mon–Sat. Closed Sun. 233 Finley Ave. W., Birmingham, AL 35204. (205) 252-5751. Go to: www.wtle.com/7465. ***American Traditional, Buffet/Cafeteria, Home-style, Seafood. $.***

Sneaky Pete's ~ *Best Hot Dogs*
Founded by Greek immigrant Pete Graphos in 1966, Birmingham-based chain Sneaky Pete's has earned its popularity thanks to fabulous hot dogs and its special house sauce. Traditionalists love the original Sneaky Pete with mustard, kraut, onions and house sauce, while the Junkyard Dog takes that combo one step further by adding cheddar cheese, relish and slaw. Each restaurant opens bright and early at 6:30 am with a hearty Southern breakfast selection, while the Vestavia Hills location also serves lunch and dinner with wine and beer selections. Other Sneaky Pete's are open daily for breakfast and lunch and serve no alcohol. 1919 Kentucky Ave., Birmingham, AL 35216. (205) 822-5558 Multiple locations. Go to: www.wtle.com/7599. ***Breakfast, Diner, Hot Dogs. $.***

Sol y Luna ~ *Best Mexican*
Historic Seventh Avenue's smartly decorated Sol y Luna features masterfully prepared traditional Mexican tapas, some of the city's best margaritas and more than 60 premium tequilas. Mexican native and local restaurant veteran Guillermo Castro serves as chef/owner, preparing such delights as tomatillo lobster tacos, iron-skillet mussels, shredded-beef flautas and chicken crêpes. Try a goat's milk caramel crêpe for dessert if available. Full bar. Serving lunch Mon–Fri, dinner Mon–Sat. Sun brunch 11 am–3 pm. 2811 7th Ave. S., Birmingham, AL 35233. (205) 322-1186. Go to: www.wtle.com/7477. ***Brunch, Mexican, Southwestern. $$.***

BOSTON MASSACHUSETTS

10 LOCAL FAVORITES

Like the famed city itself, gastronomic history blends comfortably with cutting-edge contemporary in Beantown, from time-honored Irish pubs and sports bars to award-winning French and French-inspired spots.

Harvard University

Abe & Louie's ~ *Best Steak House*

Boston loves steak houses — something about the elegant conventionality of the time-honored archetype appeals to locals' reverence for tradition. But Boston adores the cozy, upscale Abe & Louie's, opened in 1999 by Back Bay Restaurant Group. Big booths and oversized leather chairs provide the support and space needed to work through a pound of porterhouse or a succulent bone-in filet mignon. Top-notch steaks aren't the only draw. Old-timey lobster Savannah, as well as lump crabmeat cocktails, juicy veal and the special swordfish chop prove equally tempting. The restaurant has gained recognition for its wine list, too, which is as broad as the menu. Full bar. Serving lunch and dinner daily. Sat–Sun brunch 11 am–3 pm. 793 Boylston St., Boston, MA 02116. (617) 536-6300. Go to: www.wtle.com/13423. ***Brunch, Steak House. $$$.***

Aujourd'hui ~ *Best French*

Aujourd'hui at the Four Seasons Hotel in Back Bay is the kind of legendary restaurant diners dream about; the kind of place one's parents went on very special occasions; the place where couples go to get engaged. For most, the exquisite, ornate setting makes for a milestone dining experience to remember forever. The well-seasoned kitchen designs exciting contemporary menus anchored in French technique and tied to Boston through the use of local ingredients. One early summer menu included such choices as roasted cod with shellfish ragout, organic Vermont rack of lamb and juicy pork tenderloin. The Sunday brunch buffet (11 am–2 pm) features raw and sushi bars, carving stations, and decadent breakfast items such as chocolate waffles. Jacket required. Full bar. Serving dinner nightly. Sun brunch. 200 Boylston St. Boston, MA 02116 (617). 338-4400. Go to: www.wtle.com/12384. ***Brunch, Contemporary, French, Hotel Restaurant. $$$.***

Brown Sugar Cafe ~ *Best Thai*

When Brown Sugar Cafe opened in Boston's Fenway neighborhood in 1996, its sophisticated flavors quickly seduced many local students and residents. Now with a third location, the three comfortable eateries offer menus so extensive that diners have long lists of reasons to return. Brown Sugar's chefs have a solid handle on the contrast of flavors that define Thai cuisine: Sweet, salty, spicy and sour notes fill most dishes, such as the *na-tang* (minced pork and shrimp with mint, coconut milk and crushed peanuts). Any of the chef's many specialties, as well as deep-fried whole fish, are recommended. Beer and wine available. Serving lunch and dinner daily. 129 Jersey St., Boston, MA 02215. (617) 266-2928. Multiple locations. Go to: www.wtle.com/13436. ***Thai. $$.***

Cask 'n Flagon ~ *Best Sports Bar/Pub Food*

Directly in the shadow of Fenway Park's outfield wall known as the Green Monster, the Cask 'n Flagon remains the gastronomic antidote — er, more like catalyst — for Red Sox fever. This beer-soaked dive has been the quintessential Boston sports bar ever since it opened in 1969 as a neighborhood joint called Oliver's, which hosted now-famous musicians Jimi Hendrix, Bruce Springsteen and classic rockers Boston. A recent remodeling added 60 high-definition televisions, spiffier décor and an expanded menu headed by a culinary school grad. The Sox's most diehard fans now enjoy gourmet pub fare to the tune of Sloppy Joe burgers with house-made chili, grilled meat loaf and crab cakes. Full bar. Serving lunch and dinner daily. 62 Brookline Ave., Boston, MA 02215. (617) 536-4840. Go to: www.wtle.com/13408. ***American Traditional, Burgers, Sports Bar/Pub Food. $$.***

Legal Sea Foods ~ *Best Seafood*

Legal Sea Foods is, quite simply, a local seafood legend.

What began in 1950 as a quaint Cambridge fish market grew to become one of the most highly regarded seafood chains in America, with locations up and down the East Coast. The flagship Park Square location features blue-toned décor, aquariums and a state-of-the-art wine cellar holding 10,000 bottles. Choose from the fish-friendly wines by the glass at the bar, and peruse the lengthy menu of Boston's freshest catches held to Legal's hallmark quality standard. The clam chowder and the lobster bake have earned celebrity of their own. But from raw to fried and everything in between, this celebrated restaurant sets the East Coast mark. Full bar. Serving lunch and dinner daily. 26 Park Pl., Boston, MA 02116. (617) 426-4444. Multiple locations. Go to: www.wtle.com/13265. ***Seafood. $$.***

L'Espalier

L'Espalier is known as the first restaurant to receive four stars from *Boston Globe* critic Alison Arnett. Perhaps even more impressive, though, is this elegant Back Bay eatery's local reputation as one of Boston's favorite and most consistent spots for special-occasion dining since its 1978 opening. Today, chef/proprietor Frank McClelland, the James Beard Foundation's 2007 Best Chef: Northeast, offers a menu featuring several-course, prix fixe options that change nightly to showcase local artisanal ingredients and French technique. Lunch includes à la carte items in addition to a tasting menu. Jacket and tie suggested. Full bar. Serving lunch Mon–Fri, dinner nightly. 30 Gloucester St., Boston, MA 02115. (617). 262-3023. Go to: www.wtle.com/12387. ***French. $$$.***

Locke-Ober ~ *Best Continental*

Officially founded in 1875, Locke-Ober remains a hub for Boston's most powerful movers and shakers to deal and dine. James Beard award-winning chef Lydia Shire purchased the restaurant in 2001 to restore the dining rooms and update the menu, working to maintain the restaurant's legacy while infusing it with her own modern style. The menu retains some of the old standards, such as lobster bisque and baked Alaska, while at the same time opening the door to more inventive dishes, such as barbecued bluefish with toasted corn arepas. Shire's blend of tradition and creativity has prevailed, as *Gourmet* magazine has, in the past, named Locke-Ober No. 18 on its America's Top 50 Restaurants list. Jacket required. Full bar. Serving lunch Mon–Fri, dinner Mon–Sat. Closed Sun. 3 Winter Pl., Boston, MA 02108. (617) 542-1340. Go to: www.wtle.com/12338. ***Contemporary, Continental. $$$.***

Matt Murphy's Pub ~ *Best Irish/British*

Throughout the day, Matt Murphy's Pub pours pints of hearty beer to accompany the Irish farmhouse-style food from its quaint Brookline Village setting. The close quarters inspire strangers to share friendly conversation over ploughman's platters (spiced beef, pickles, bread and cheese), shepherd's pie, and fish and chips. Late in the evening, the place morphs from a cozy Irish stopover into a buzzing live music venue, while Sunday brunch (11 am–3:30 pm) offers plentiful traditional Irish breakfasts to grateful families. Full bar. Serving lunch and dinner daily. 14 Harvard St., Brookline, MA 02445. (617) 232-0188. Go to: www.wtle.com/12419. ***Brunch, Irish/British. $$.***

Oleana

In opening Oleana in 2001, chef/owner Ana Sortun created a neighborhood restaurant that is, in a word, beautiful. A romantic dining room, filled during the winter months with a cozy blaze from the wood stove, along with the vine-wrapped patio make an ideal setting for indulging in the belly-warming, gourmet Middle Eastern menu. Seasonal dishes with Arabic and Mediterranean influences, particularly the cuisine of Turkey, might include crab- and pea-stuffed *kibbeh* (minced meat), pomegranate-glazed pork ribs, or cabbage leaf-wrapped bluefish. Dessert is a must at Oleana: The accomplished and inventive pastry chef puts together sophisticated selections, such as the signature baked Alaska and house-made seasonal ice creams. Full bar. Serving dinner nightly. 134 Hampshire St., Cambridge, MA 02139. (617) 661-0505. Go to: www.wtle.com/13152. ***Contemporary, Middle Eastern. $$.***

Union Bar and Grille ~ *Best Contemporary*

The Aquitaine Group's burgeoning local restaurant empire added one more jewel to its crown when chef/owner Seth Woods opened Union Bar and Grille in 2003. Helping to revitalize the up-and-coming SoWa area in the South End, this sophisticated converted-warehouse space draws crowds from the neighborhood, the suburbs and beyond. See and be seen among Boston's beautiful people, sipping chilled cocktails at the posh bar and munching on Woods' creative fare. The bold, accessible menu includes regional dishes, such as smoked Long Island duck breast, as well as gourmet American favorites, from burgers topped with andouille sausage to roasted rack of lamb. Full bar. Serving dinner nightly. Sat–Sun brunch 10 am–3 pm. 1357 Washington St., Boston, MA 02118. (617) 423-0555. Go to: www.wtle.com/11760. ***Brunch, Contemporary. $$$.***

BUFFALO NEW YORK

10 LOCAL FAVORITES

***Like a culinary Galápagos Islands**, Buffalo has spawned a number of indigenous foodstuffs, including beef on weck sandwiches, frozen custard and the Anchor Bar's now-ubiquitous spicy chicken wings.*

Buffalo City Hall

Anchor Bar ~ *Best Wings*

Buffalo is so famous for its spicy chicken wings that its name will forever be linked with this finger-licking-good bar food. If you want to try the wings that started it all, head to Anchor Bar, where local lore claims that original owner Teressa Bellissimo created this snack late one night in 1964 for her son and his hungry friends. Four decades later, tourists flock here to consume the incomparable wings by the plate or bucketful, prompting the prestigious James Beard Foundation to give the bar its America's Classics Award in 2003. Choose between mild, medium, hot, spicy barbecue or "suicidal" sauce. The otherwise extensive menu consists of bar standards, sandwiches and home-style Italian dishes. Full bar. Serving lunch and dinner daily. 1047 Main St., Buffalo, NY 14209. (716) 884-4083. Go to: www.wtle.com/15474. ***American Traditional, Beef on Weck, Italian, Sports Bar/Pub Food, Wings. $.***

Anderson's Custard ~ *Best Ice Cream*

Home to two Buffalo specialties, frozen custard and beef on weck sandwiches, Anderson's Custard got its start in New York City in 1946. By 1947, homesick founders Carl and Greta

Anderson had moved their custard stand to Buffalo, where it became a beloved local franchise. The hearty side of the menu features the savory local tradition of roast beef on a kummelweck roll. Then there's the custard — a sublime soft-serve concoction with a silky egg-rich base that's sold by the cone or dish, or used in sundaes and banana splits. Special flavors are produced daily to supplement the 19 regular varieties on the menu. No alcohol available. Serving lunch and dinner daily. 2634 Delaware Ave., Buffalo, NY 14216. (716) 873-5330. Multiple locations. Go to: www.wtle.com/15366. ***Beef on Weck, Ice Cream. $.***

Charlie the Butcher's ~ *Best Beef on Weck*

The standard-bearer for Buffalo's unique beef on weck sandwiches for nearly a century, Charlie the Butcher's has morphed from a family-run butcher shop to a restaurant and catering company with many area locations. Following in the footsteps of his grandfather, who started the business in 1914, owner Charles W. Roesch is quickly becoming a local — and maybe even national — celebrity after TV appearances with Regis Philbin and Bobby Flay. Charlie's famed beef on weck begins with roast beef cooked for 18 hours, then carved by hand and piled an inch thick on a kummelweck roll. One side of the bun is slathered with house-made horseradish, and the other dipped in juice. No alcohol available. Serving lunch and dinner daily. 1065 Wehrle Dr., Williamsville, NY 14221. (716) 633-8330. Multiple locations. Go to: www.wtle.com/15458. ***Beef on Weck, Diner. $.***

Chef's Restaurant ~ *Best Italian*

Open since 1923, Chef's Restaurant offers great Italian food in a casual family atmosphere. Family-run since 1954, it retains a retro feel with its red-and-white checked tablecloths and unpretentious menu. Staple starters include fried ravioli and the local favorite, sweet Palermo peppers stuffed with sausage, pepperoni, salami and cheese. The Spano Special (rigatoni with ricotta and meat sauce) and the Irv Special (spiral pasta with sautéed mushrooms, pepperoncini and onions) remain pasta favorites when available. Dishes such as veal cacciatore and chicken-broccoli Alfredo may also be offered occasionally. Full bar. Serving lunch and dinner Mon–Sat. Closed Sun. 291 Seneca St., Buffalo, NY 14204. (716) 856-9187. Go to: www.wtle.com/15390. ***Italian. $.***

The Left Bank ~ *Best Contemporary*

The dim lighting and exposed brick walls in this 1800-era restored building create an upscale-yet-casual setting for foodies and trendsetters who frequent The Left Bank. Since there are only 20 or so tables, and an outdoor patio, be sure to make reservations well in advance, particularly for weekend dining. The innovative menu fuses European and Asian flavors and techniques, confidently uniting such ingredients as tilapia and won tons. Light meals and entrées include six versions of focaccia and a variety of ambitious seafood and pasta dishes. The String Quartet Brunch is served Sundays from 11 am–2:30 pm. Full bar. Serving dinner nightly. Late-night Fri–Sat. 511 Rhode Island St., Buffalo, NY 14213. (716) 882-3509. Go to: www.wtle.com/15247. ***Bistro, Contemporary. $$.***

Pano's on Elmwood ~ *Best Greek*

Once distinguished by the big blue bison perched atop its roof — it will be removed as the restaurant completes its redesign — Pano's on Elmwood is not only the favorite Greek restaurant in Buffalo, it's also one of the city's most popular 24-hour diners. A previous expansion didn't shorten the lines much, especially for late-night meals when the year-round patio becomes a prime post-bar-hopping destination. Breakfast specialties include the bargain-priced Two-Two-Two (two pancakes, two eggs and two pieces of bacon, ham or sausage), omelets and Belgian waffles. Gyros and souvlaki are available as breakfast sides and for lunch, while an extensive dinner menu features heavier Mediterranean fare and various steaks. Pano's offers a fish fry every Friday from 11 am–10 pm. Beer and wine available. Serving breakfast, lunch, dinner and late-night daily. 1081 Elmwood Ave., Buffalo, NY 14222. (716) 886-9081. Go to: www.wtle.com/15344. ***Breakfast, Diner, Fish Fry, Greek. $$.***

Rue Franklin ~ *Best French*

Boasting the look and feel of an intimate Parisian café, Buffalo's premier French eatery, Rue Franklin, has garnered high praise from the likes of *Esquire* magazine and *The New York Times*. Located in a converted row house, Rue Franklin was perhaps the city's first restaurant to offer seasonal menus. The list of appetizers may include sea scallops with saffron sauce and lime polenta, and past entrées have featured Arctic char with lightly creamed leeks, and squab with Moroccan spices. If you're willing to try Rue Franklin midweek, you can dine in style for less with the three-course, prix fixe menu offered Tuesday through Thursday. Jacket suggested. Full bar. Serving dinner Tue–Sat. Closed Sun–Mon. 341 Franklin St., Buffalo, NY 14202. (716) 852-4416. Go to: www.wtle.com/15333. ***French. $$$.***

Saigon Bangkok ~ *Best Thai*

Saigon Bangkok is truly a place of beauty, with its richly furnished interior of deep red carpet, mustard yellow walls and greenery galore. Its equally elegant menu offers extensive choices in both Vietnamese and Thai cuisines. Lunch focuses on steamed rice dishes, noodle dishes and several vegetarian specialties. On the Thai dinner menu, you'll find starters such as satay, tempura and a variety of soups. House specialties tamarind duck and grilled salmon should not be missed, when available. The Vietnamese menu features asparagus crabmeat soup, pho and numerous stir-fries. Beer and wine available. Serving lunch and dinner daily. 512 Niagara Falls Blvd., Buffalo, NY 14223. (716) 837-2115. Go to: www.wtle.com/15470. ***Thai, Vietnamese. $$.***

Schwabl's Restaurant ~ *Best German*

Known as much for its roast beef sandwiches as for its top-notch German food, tiny and dimly lit Schwabl's has been in business since 1837 and at its present location since 1946, with longtime employee Cheryl Staychok and husband Gene now at the helm. The focal point in the little white house is the meat carver at the end of the bar, which slices roast beef for the beef on weck sandwiches. Sample a variety of aged cheeses to start. German specialties include goulash, dumplings, and fried haddock or yellow pike. The local-favorite winter cocktail, the hot Tom & Jerry, is available Thanksgiving through St. Patrick's Day. Full bar. Serving lunch and dinner daily. 789 Center Rd., West Seneca, NY 14224. (716) 674-9821. Go to: www.wtle.com/15335. ***Beef on Weck, German. $$.***

Ted's Hot Dogs ~ *Best Hot Dogs*

In 1927, Greek-born Theodore Spiro Liaros invested $100 — a small fortune for a struggling immigrant — in a former tool shed at the foot of Massachusetts Avenue under the newly constructed Peace Bridge. Over the years, the humble hot dog shed has grown into a mini-chain, with locations across western New York. Today, Ted's dogs come in three sizes: regular, jumbo and foot-long. Toppings include cheese, chili and Ted's "secret sauce." Italian or Polish sausage, fish sandwiches, and various burgers round out the menu. Picnic tables make for pleasant outdoor eating in nice weather. No alcohol available. Serving lunch and dinner daily. 6230 Shimer Rd., Lockport, NY 14094. (716) 439-4386 Multiple locations. Go to: www.wtle.com/15350. ***Burgers, Hot Dogs. $.***

CHARLOTTE NORTH CAROLINA

10 LOCAL FAVORITES

***Charlotte's a culinary-rich and diverse city**, from fried chicken to fried lobster tails, and shrimp and grits to Eastern Carolina-style barbecue — meaning the whole hog, with a vinegar-based sauce.*

Baoding ~ *Best Chinese*

As sister cities, Charlotte and Baoding, China, enjoy a relationship based on the mutual exchange of ideas and culture. Luckily, for residents of the Queen City, that includes food. Opportunely located in the Sharon Corners retail center, this sophisticated bistro packs in locals seeking a cut above the average Chinese chow. The chic décor offsets a more conventional, authentic menu of sesame chicken, steamed sea bass and Singaporean rice noodles. Many a Baoding duck (the house specialty) grace the tables, while soft-shell crab and Rainbow Shrimp provide much-needed pick-me-ups for shoppers stopping in for a bite. Full bar. Serving lunch and dinner daily. 4722-F Sharon Rd., Charlotte, NC 28210. (704) 552-8899. Go to: www.wtle.com/4678. ***Chinese. $$.***

Bill Spoon's Barbecue ~ *Best Barbecue*

This family-owned barbecue joint is nothing fancy to look at, inside or out, but customers have been packing in for quality lunches of down-home 'cue since 1963. Until his death in 2007, at age 78, Bill Spoon himself greeted guests at the door. His Southern hospitality lives on, though. Hushpuppy baskets and tall glasses of sweet tea are kept full, and pork is prepared Eastern Carolina-style (the whole pig, with a vinegar-based sauce). Whether you're there for a small or large plate, a sandwich or a combo, the meat is seasoned enough as is, though the house hot sauce is worth sampling if you like more zing. No alcohol available. Serving lunch Mon–Sat. Closed Sun. 5524 South Blvd., Charlotte, NC 28217. (704) 525-8865. Go to: www.wtle.com/4126. ***Barbecue. $.***

Bonterra Dining & Wine Room ~ *Best Contemporary*

Housed in a historic converted Methodist church in the South End district, Bonterra Dining & Wine Room is making some history of its own on the Charlotte fine-dining scene. Owner, veteran restaurateur and avid wine connoisseur John "J.D." Duncan successfully combines the charm of the old with the luxury of the new, his cozy eatery having earned prestigious honors from AAA, DiRoNA and *Wine Spectator*. Bonterra has become the place for Queen City movers and shakers to enjoy a glass of wine after work or a fine meal. The seasonal, contemporary menu spans the cuisines of France and Italy, but some of the best dishes — such as the signature fried lobster tail appetizer — exemplify the restaurant's Southern roots. Full bar. Serving dinner Mon–Sat. Closed Sun. 1829 Cleveland Ave., Charlotte, NC 28203. (704) 333-9463. Go to: www.wtle.com/4097. ***Contemporary, Wine Bar. $$$.***

Carpe Diem

After several moves, Carpe Diem has finally found a home in the picturesque Elizabeth neighborhood. Sisters/proprietors Tricia Maddrey and Bonnie Warford credit the 1989 Robin Williams film *Dead Poets Society* for providing name recognition with its eponymous tag line. But perhaps they are downplaying the draw of the sleek dining room and their affordable, outstanding cuisine. The nightly evolving, contemporary American menu features everything from pistachio-crusted trout to a vegetable crêpe. And there's no time like the present to indulge in house-made desserts. Full bar. Serving dinner Mon–Sat. Closed Sun. 1535 Elizabeth Ave., Charlotte, NC 28204. (704) 377-7976. Go to: www.wtle.com/4098. ***Contemporary. $$.***

Mama Ricotta's ~ *Best Italian*

When a young Frank Scibelli saw a noticeable shortage of exceptional Italian restaurants in his university town, he did what any typical undergrad in a bind would do: He called his mother. Gradually, crash-course cooking lessons via the telephone evolved into a newfound appreciation for the authentic cuisine served during his childhood in Springfield, Mass. When he opened his first Mama Ricotta's restaurant in 1993, he brought these traditional family recipes to a tiny 39-seat establishment. Today, his exceptionally popular King's Pointe eatery offers extra-large portions of the same from-scratch pizzas, lasagnas and signature penne alla vodka. Just don't fill up — ha! — without saving room for the sinfully delicious chocolate Nutella pie. Beer and wine available. Serving lunch Mon–Fri, dinner nightly. 601 S. Kings Dr., Charlotte, NC 28204. (704) 343-0148. Go to: www.wtle.com/5155. ***Italian. $$.***

Penguin Drive-In ~ *Best Burgers, Best Diner*

Defiantly perched in the trendy Plaza-Midwood district sits the Penguin Drive-In, paying homage to the gods of unconventionality and contradiction. This Charlotte landmark attracts all kinds of folks who drag stools up to the cozy bar or squeeze just one more friend into the big, comfy booths for a basket of fried pickles and other typical diner fare. Well, nothing about the Penguin is typical, really. Where else could you order a glass of Ferrari-Carano merlot with your Full Blown Hemi (triple cheeseburger with everything), or a cold PBR to wash down your soy dog and black bean hummus? The restaurant's greatest secret might be the chef's experience cooking in top-flight, mainstream restaurants. Full bar. Serving lunch, dinner and late-night daily. 1921 Commonwealth Ave., Charlotte, NC 28203. (704) 375-6959. Go to: www.wtle.com/4741. ***Burgers, Diner, Sports Bar/Pub Food. $.***

Pewter Rose Bistro ~ *Best Brunch*

Long before the industrial South End neighborhood was cool, the pleasantly eclectic Pewter Rose Bistro functioned as a textile warehouse. Today, many a power lunch transpire in the sun-drenched dining room, and romantic dates take a sophisticated yet mellow turn for the better among the intimately clustered tables. From bananas Foster French toast to crab cake Benedict, Saturday and Sunday brunches (10 am–2:30 pm) draw loyal morning and afternoon crowds, while superior gourmet bistro fare, such as pan-braised chicken, and small plate offerings (low country shrimp with fried green tomatoes, for example) keeps patrons climbing the unforgettably steep staircase every night of the week. Pewter Rose Bistro has won several honors from *Wine Spectator* magazine. Full bar. Serving lunch and dinner Mon–Sat. Sat–Sun brunch. 1820 South Blvd., Charlotte, NC 28203. (704) 332-8149. Go to: www.wtle.com/4668. ***Bistro, Brunch, Contemporary, Small Plates. $$.***

Price's Chicken Coop ~ *Best Fried Chicken, Best Home-style*

It's understated. It's greasy. It's absolutely some of the best fried chicken you'll ever taste. Since 1962, Price's Chicken Coop has drawn a steady lunchtime crowd to its nondescript brick hut in South End. At first glance, it doesn't seem like much: Diners carry takeout-only orders in cardboard boxes accompanied by copious stacks of napkins. And, though the menu offers several options, you won't see much besides deep-fried chicken breasts, tater rounds, coleslaw and hushpuppies. But just one bite, and you'll experience the difference when whole chickens are prepared in-house, kept overnight in a secret marinade, and then hand-dipped in flour spiced with a top-secret recipe. Just remember — breaking the no-cell phone policy will demonstrate what happens when modern technology comes between Southerners and their fried chicken. No alcohol available. Cash only. Serving lunch and early dinner Tue–Sat. Closed Sun–Mon. 1614 Camden Rd., Charlotte, NC 28203. (704) 333-9866. Go to: www.wtle.com/5541. ***Fried Chicken, Home-style, Soul Food. $.***

Upstream ~ *Best Seafood*

Don't fight the current leading you toward Upstream: There's a reason local foodies are heading in schools to the posh Phillips Place location in South Park. Harper's Restaurant Group's Charlotte venture has gained recognition from some of the most prestigious national culinary organizations — including DiRoNA and *Wine Spectator* — for its constantly evolving, top-notch menu of Pacific Rim cuisine with West Coast flair. Wacky appetizers such as Tuna Tuna Tuna (three varieties of tuna served in a martini glass) precede creative seafood specialties such as crab ravioli or sake-marinated sea bass with lobster dumplings. The stainless steel oyster bar and an impressive stand-alone sushi menu offer excellent raw alternatives. For dessert, the Sweet Bento Box, with warm chocolate cake, a banana spring roll, five-spice ice cream and "forbidden" rice pudding may be impossible to resist. Full bar. Serving lunch Mon–Sat, dinner nightly. Sun brunch 10:30 am–2:30 pm. 6902 Phillips Pl. Ct., Charlotte, NC 28210. (704) 556-7730. Go to: www.wtle.com/4669. ***Brunch, Japanese/Sushi, Seafood. $$$.***

Village Tavern ~ *Best American Traditional*

So much more than a tavern, Village Tavern has been a neighborhood staple for all-occasion dining since its 1984 conception in nearby Winston-Salem, N.C. South Park proves the perfect backdrop for this traditional American restaurant's popular patio on which twenty- and thirty-somethings enjoy live music and sip cold draft microbrews or glasses of one of the more than 100 wine varieties. On any given day, you're sure to find a booth of hot wings and draft beers adjacent to a table of filets and fine wine. Sunday brunch (10 am–3 pm) swarms with the after-church crowd seeking Belgian waffles or shrimp and grits. Whatever the occasion, make sure to indulge in a basket of the signature house-made potato chips. Village Tavern has won the coveted *Wine Spectator* Award of Excellence for several years running. Full bar. Serving lunch and dinner daily. Late-night Fri–Sat. 4201 Congress St., Charlotte, NC 28209. (704) 552-9983. Go to: www.wtle.com/4114. ***American Traditional, Brunch, Sports Bar/Pub Food. $$.***

CHICAGO ILLINOIS

10 LOCAL FAVORITES

Chicago's restaurant scene boasts some of the nation's top contemporary and French-inspired fine dining, but the Windy City remains the epicenter of steak houses, hot dogs, deep-dish pizza and Italian beef sandwiches.

Alinea

This Lincoln Park establishment opened in 2005 and has already acquired accolades, including being named the No. 1 restaurant in America by *Gourmet* magazine. The environment is unmistakably modern, with mahogany furniture, a steel staircase separating the three dining rooms, and a reflecting pond. Gastronomic mad scientist/visionary chef Grant Achatz breaks food down to a molecular level using various techniques to maximize flavors in his contemporary American cuisine. You may not immediately understand the arrangement of the food that appears before you, but the waitstaff is more than happy to explain what you're looking at and how you should go about consuming it. Alinea offers seasonally changing degustation menus of 12 and 24 courses to be enjoyed over the course of several hours. Full bar. Serving dinner Wed–Sun. Closed Mon–Tue. 1723 N. Halsted St., Chicago, IL 60614. (312) 867-0110. Go to: www.wtle.com/23444. ***Contemporary. $$$.***

Blackbird

With a strikingly luminescent and minimalist dining room, wildly popular Blackbird has packed diners elbow-to-elbow at its sleek, shiny tables since 1998. Chef/partner Paul Kahan crafts his seasonally changing contemporary menus based upon the freshest available ingredients. Like the décor, less is more with his cuisine. You won't find architectural monstrosities here, but the richness of flavors makes the dishes far from simplistic. Past entrées have included braised pork belly and slow-roasted baby lamb. Full bar and award-winning wine list. Serving lunch and dinner Mon–Fri, dinner Sat. Closed Sun. 619 W. Randolph St., Chicago, IL 60606. (312) 715-0708. Go to: www.wtle.com/23447. ***Contemporary. $$$.***

Charlie Trotter's ~ *Best Contemporary*

In addition to his show on PBS, a couple of cookbooks and multiple philanthropic endeavors, Charlie Trotter continues to advance the cause of culinary artistry at his Lincoln Park dining room. Located in a turn-of-the-century townhouse, this internationally acclaimed restaurant set the precedent for fine dining in Chicago. Charlie Trotter's offers three ever-changing degustation menus of contemporary fare, ranging from seven to 12 courses. Though the numbers may sound overwhelming, the philosophy here is small portions: Chef Trotter says, "I want [guests] to feel stimulated and alert. ... Food doesn't have to be rich to taste good." Wine pairings accompany the tasting menus, but there's also a non-alcoholic beverage sampling menu for health enthusiasts. Jacket required. Full bar. Serving dinner Tue–Sat. Closed Sun–Mon. 816 W. Armitage Ave., Chicago, IL 60614. (773) 248-6228. Go to: www.wtle.com/23442. ***Contemporary. $$$.***

Everest

Visit Everest to experience new heights in romance, culinary excellence and literal altitude, as it is located on the 40th story of the Chicago Stock Exchange. With floor-to-ceiling windows to enhance the view, white columns, and bronze sculptures on each table, the atmosphere epitomizes decadent dining. Chef/proprietor Jean Joho's Alsatian roots are apparent in his progressive French cuisine and on the wine list. Diners may choose from three- or four-course, prix fixe menus, the chef's eight-course degustation menu, or the seven-course vegetarian menu. Though menus change seasonally, favorite dishes include the house-smoked salmon appetizer and entrées such as filet of venison and roasted Maine lobster. Full bar. Serving dinner Tue–Sat. Closed Sun–Mon. 440 S. LaSalle St., Chicago, IL 60605. (312) 663-8920. Go to: www.wtle.com/23454. ***Contemporary, French. $$$.***

Frontera Grill ~ *Best Mexican*

With six cookbooks, his own TV show and two wildly successful restaurants, Rick Bayless's efforts to showcase authentic Mexican cuisine in the United States are immeasurable. His first restaurant, Frontera, has provided a contemporary take on flavors from south of the border to Chicago since 1987, and it won the 2007 Outstanding Restaurant Award from the James Beard Foundation. The monthly changing menu, inspired by Mexican traditions from many regions, features moles, chile-thickened braises, and organic and often custom-grown vegetables. When available, try the duck enchiladas with roasted tomato-serrano sauce or select from the Marisqueria, the "sustainable seafood bar" featuring fresh oysters as well as fish and shrimp entrées. Full bar. Serving lunch and dinner Tue–Sat. Sat brunch 10:30 am–2:30 pm. Closed Sun–Mon. 445 N. Clark St., Chicago, IL 60610. (312) 661-1434. Go to: www.wtle.com/23575. ***Brunch, Contemporary, Mexican, Seafood. $$.***

Gibsons Bar & Steakhouse ~ *Best Steak House*

Whether famous and seeking a private meal, single and looking to mingle, or carnivorous and hungry for a quality cut of meat, locals crowd this Gold City institution where bigger is always better. While waiting for a table, you may want to dive headfirst into an oversized martini and befriend cigar smokers at the bar. If elementary school failed to teach you the value of sharing — even the servers recommend it — the portions here likely will. To accompany classic favorites such as London broil, 24-ounce porterhouses and two different sizes of filet mignon, there are double (in size) baked potatoes and sautéed mushrooms and spinach. Enormously large lobster tails are available for palates that need surf to balance their turf selections. A second location opened in Rosemont in 2000. Full bar. Serving dinner nightly. 1028 N. Rush St., Chicago, IL 60611. (312) 266-8999. Go to: www.wtle.com/23650. ***Steak House. $$$.***

Lou Malnati's Pizzeria ~ *Best Pizza*

Chicago is known for art, architecture, da Bears, da Bulls and the Blues Brothers, but perhaps the greatest cultural contribution of the city is the Chicago-style pizza. Lou Malnati, using the family recipe dating from the '40s, opened his flagship restaurant in Lincolnwood in 1971. Now with over 25 restaurants statewide, Lou Malnati's Pizzerias serve their signature buttery, deep-dish crust (deep because the dough is stretched high to fit the pan, but not technically thick as is often assumed) filled with a California plum tomato sauce and copious amounts of vegetables. The thin-crust pizza draws rave reviews as well, as do the stuffed spinach bread and the chicken sandwiches. Beer and wine available. Hours and delivery vary by location. 439 N. Wells St., Chicago, IL 60610. (312) 828-9800. Multiple locations. Go to: www.wtle.com/23585. ***Italian, Italian Beef, Pizza. $$.***

Manny's Coffee Shop & Deli ~ *Best Deli*

Leave your diet at the door and nosh nostalgically at Manny's Coffee Shop & Deli, a Chicago tradition for more than 50 years. At its current location since 1964, the interior and exterior have seen few changes, but the pastrami and corned beef are enough of an attraction to keep politicians, police and area workers coming back. Wisecracking employees and the pace of the cafeteria-style counter may seem intimidating for first-time diners, so having an idea of what you're going to order helps. Grab a crispy potato pancake to accompany your monstrous cured-meat sandwich of choice, and don't plan on any rigorous afternoon activity. No alcohol available. Serving breakfast and lunch daily. 1141 S. Jefferson St. Chicago, IL 60607. (312) 939-2855. Go to: www.wtle.com/23553. ***Breakfast, Deli. $.***

Red Light ~ *Best Asian Fusion*

At Red Light, you will be greeted by a neon-flamed rooftop and an avant-garde interior full of wrought iron, lanterns and tropical trees. In spite of the distractingly fun décor, executive chef Jackie Shen's inspired Asian Fusion cuisine is what provides the real fireworks. Appetizers that illustrate her culinary prowess are foie gras and pork steamed dumplings or five-spice ribs. The entrées range from traditional fare such as pad thai and *kung pao* chicken to more complex dishes such as the signature Shanghai-style catfish — an enormous fish prepared tableside and topped with a red vinegar sweet-and-sour sauce. Hotheads will be pleasantly surprised and tongue-torched by dishes marked spicy or "intense sweating." Full bar. Serving lunch Mon–Fri, dinner nightly. 820 W. Randolph St. Chicago, IL 60607. (312) 733-8880. Go to: www.wtle.com/23506. ***Asian Fusion. $$.***

Tru

"Whimsy is serious business at Tru," the restaurant advertises, and never will you find another establishment where fine dining is as much fun. With purse-holding stools at each table, aesthetically complex bathrooms and one of Andy Warhol's Marilyn Monroes on the wall, the atmosphere is playful while refined. The extremely accommodating and unpretentious staff ensures that absolutely every detail is handled smoothly. Executive chef Rick Tramonto and partner/executive pastry chef Gale Gand engineer progressive French fare available on a three-course, prix fixe menu or the nine-course "collections" menus. Entrées may include poached striped bass with duck consommé, or braised beef short rib with eel and Thai eggplant. Gand's desserts are exquisite. Jacket required. Full bar. Serving dinner Mon–Sat. Closed Sun. 676 N. St. Clair St., Chicago, IL 60611. (312) 202-0001. Go to: www.wtle.com/23468. ***Contemporary, French. $$$.***

CINCINNATI OHIO

10 LOCAL FAVORITES

***French and French-inspired** fine dining have long claimed the top rungs of Cincinnati cuisine, although the city remains best known for its signature five-way chili.*

John A. Roebling Bridge

Beluga ~ *Best Japanese/Sushi*

Ultra-hip Beluga can be a serene Japanese sushi restaurant or a thumping nightclub, depending upon your arrival time. The clean-cut minimalist décor features a rock garden, comfy couches and contemporary light fixtures under open rafters. Young professionals come later at night to grab a bite at the traditional sushi bar and then dance to the high-volume DJ-chosen music playing in the lounge. In the early evening, however, diners of all ages share big platters of mixed sushi or enjoy steaks, roasted lamb or duck, or seafood. Creative rolls include the American Dream (shrimp tempura topped with barbecued eel and avocado), Dynamite (minced tuna, salmon and red snapper in a spicy sauce), and French (crabmeat, cucumber and cream cheese wrapped in an egg crêpe). Full bar. Serving dinner Mon–Sat. Closed Sun. 3520 Edwards Rd., Cincinnati, OH 45208. (513) 533-4444. Go to: www.wtle.com/4786. ***Asian Fusion, Japanese/Sushi. $$$.***

BOCA ~ *Best Italian*

Relocated to Oakley from its former Northside neighborhood, contemporary Italian restaurant BOCA draws a comfortably eclectic crowd with its artistically presented dishes. Diners sit at well-lit, closely packed tables with a view of the bustling kitchen and wood-fired oven. Chef/owner David Falk offers two dining experiences. In the trattoria, you'll find basic antipasti, pastas and meat dishes, while the larger casual-chic dining room focuses on more sophisticated cuisine, with weekly changing, prix fixe dinners. If available, try sensuous entrées such as scallops with caramelized Brussels sprouts or beef filet with Alaskan king crab. Full bar. Serving dinner Tue–Sat. Closed Sun–Mon. 3200 Madison Rd., Cincinnati, OH 45209. (513) 542-2022. Go to: www.wtle.com/4772. ***Contemporary, Italian. $$$.***

The BonBonerie ~ *Best Bakery, Best Dessert*

The BonBonerie is both a wonderful bakery bursting with specialty cakes, cookies and pastries, as well as a tearoom fit for a queen's breakfast or lunch. Mismatched china and brightly painted walls set the scene. The tearoom's breakfast menu features an ever-changing array of scones and coffeecakes, while the lunch menu is composed of tea sandwiches, fresh fruits and pastries. Recommended desserts include hand-cut cookies, raspberry shorties and cappuccino brownies, while numerous teas, coffees, lemonade and Italian ices make up the beverage menu. Reservations must be made at least 24 hours in advance for the popular afternoon tea. No alcohol available. Serving breakfast and lunch Mon–Sat. Closed Sun. 2030 Madison Rd., Cincinnati, OH 45208. (513) 321-3399. Go to: www.wtle.com/3770. ***Bakery, Breakfast, Café, Dessert. $.***

Daveed's at 934

While cooking at Cincinnati's well-known French restaurant Maisonette, chef/owner David Cook picked up the nickname "Daveed," a moniker he has carried over to his own fine-dining establishment. He opened Daveed's at 934 with his wife and general manager, Liz Cook, in 1999. The small, eclectic menu changes frequently, but adventurous specials may include seared venison with sweet potato spatzle or seared Chilean sea bass with Israeli couscous. Enjoy the chocolate malt molten cake or the almond and roasted pear cheesecake in the outdoor wine garden: a brick-walled courtyard, where light-strung trees, wrought iron furniture and a bubbling fountain create an idyllic alternative to the small interior dining rooms. Full bar. Serving dinner Tue–Sat. Closed Sun–Mon. 934 Hatch St., Cincinnati, OH 45202. (513) 721-2665. Go to: www.wtle.com/4532. ***Contemporary. $$$.***

Jean-Robert at Pigall's ~ *Best French*

In 2002, former Maisonette chef Jean-Robert de Cavel rekindled a Cincinnati tradition by opening Jean-Robert at Pigall's at the former site of the renowned and beloved French restaurant Pigall's. Inside the circa-1825 Greek revival building, diners are seated either in the spacious main dining room or in smaller, more private corners. If you like to be where the action is, make reservations to sit at the chef's table overlooking the kitchen. The menu changes seasonally, but the French-American cuisine may include culinary delights such as roast Cornish hen, filet of tenderloin with blue cheese ravioli, and slow-cooked pork chops with apple and endive. Full bar. Serving lunch Thu–Fri, dinner Tue–Sat. Closed Sun–Mon. 127 E. 4th St., Cincinnati, OH 45202. (513) 721-1345. Go to: www.wtle.com/4545. ***Contemporary, French. $$$.***

Montgomery Inn ~ *Best Barbecue*

When the Montgomery Inn was opened by Ted Gregory in 1951, it was more of a neighborhood watering hole than a beacon for barbecue lovers. However, his wife, Matula Gregory, changed all of that when she took a dinner of pork ribs smothered in her secret sauce to the bar for her husband, who shared the over-generous helpings with his buddies. Soon, word of Matula's delicious cooking spread, and barbecue was added to the menu. Today, the Gregory children run all three Montgomery Inn locations. Not surprisingly, ribs remain the specialty and come in four sizes, from petite to king slab, and are served with a salad and choice of potatoes. Full bar. Serving lunch Mon–Fri, dinner nightly. 9440 Montgomery Rd., Montgomery, OH 45242. (513) 791-3482. Multiple locations. Go to: www.wtle.com/3732. ***American Traditional, Barbecue. $$.***

The Precinct ~ *Best Steak House*

Constructed in 1901 as one of the country's first police patrol stations, The Precinct's distinctive Romanesque building, with its gabled roof and arched windows, was remodeled into a restaurant in 1981 by owner Jeff Ruby. The supper club-like dining room was once the stable for the horses that pulled early patrol wagons. Today, the feeding troughs have been replaced with intimate tables, where patrons bask in the warm light of individual lamps. Signature steaks bear the names of Cincinnati sports stars and include: The Carson Palmer (filet mignon), The Oscar Robertson (sirloin) and Steak Munoz (blackened sirloin). Standard steak house sides range from creamed spinach to sweet potato fries. Full bar. Serving dinner nightly. 311 Delta Ave., Cincinnati, OH 45226. (513) 321-5454. Go to: www.wtle.com/4969. ***Steak House. $$$.***

Skyline Chili ~ *Best Chili*

So distinctive is Cincinnati-style chili — thinner and sweeter than Southwestern versions and traditionally served over spaghetti with a mound of finely shredded cheddar cheese — that it's in a category all its own. Although many consider

Empress Chili to be the original purveyor of Cincinnati chili, it was former Empress cook and Greek immigrant Nicholas Lambrinides who elevated the chili to regional-specialty status when he opened Skyline Chili in 1949. It has grown into a multi-state chain with more than 100 takeout and dine-in restaurants (including three in downtown Cincinnati). Menus include classic chili three-way (with spaghetti, chili and shredded mild cheddar); four-way (add diced onions or red beans); and five-way (add onions *and* red beans). Oyster crackers and hot sauce are obligatory sides. No alcohol available. Serving lunch and dinner daily. 254 E. 4th St., Cincinnati, OH 45202. (513) 241-4848. Multiple locations. Go to: www.wtle.com/4317. ***Chili. $.***

Teller's of Hyde Park ~ *Best American Traditional*
Housed in the former Hyde Park Savings and Loan building, swanky American Traditional dining spot Teller's of Hyde Park features tall pillars and cocktail tables that mimic old teller windows. Young urban professionals predominate on the mezzanine overlooking the bar downstairs as well as on the outdoor patio that features a fireplace, brick bar and wrought iron tables. Even the former vault is open for seating, with cushions and heavy curtains offsetting the giant metal entrance. The menu changes seasonally, but recommended constants include crab cakes, hand-tossed pizza, raspberry and goat cheese salad, and rosemary chicken with penne pasta. The well-stocked full bar has more than 50 bottled beers and 30 on tap, with 23 wines by the glass and more than 100 by the bottle. Serving lunch and dinner daily. Sat–Sun brunch 10 am–2 pm. 2710 Erie Ave., Cincinnati, OH 45208. (513)321-4721. Go to: www.wtle.com/3748. ***American Traditional, Brunch. $$.***

Trio ~ *Best Contemporary*
Bare brick walls with copper accents add a modern industrial feel to the upscale-casual Trio restaurant. Owned by Gregg Pancero, Trio is consistently rated one of Cincinnati's top American contemporary restaurants. An open-air veranda added in 2004 boasts two stone fireplaces to warm patrons during the colder months. Pancero began his career working in his father's pizza joints, so you can feel confident in trying his innovations like the moo shu pork pizza or the smoked salmon pizza (the perfect blend of Norwegian salmon, capers and three cheeses). Other winning entrées include the pan-seared sea bass and Black Angus meat loaf. Cleanse your palate with the banana cream pie or the Desperate Housewives martini (caramel vodka splashed with Godiva chocolate cream liqueur). Full bar. Serving lunch and dinner daily. 7565 Kenwood Rd., Cincinnati, OH 45236. (513) 984-1905. Go to: www.wtle.com/3749. ***Contemporary, Pizza. $$.***

CLEVELAND OHIO

10 LOCAL FAVORITES

***Cleveland's eclectic restaurant scene** includes nationally renowned, chef-owned contemporaries as well as one of the country's most historic and cherished Polish eateries, Sokolowski's University Inn.*

The Baricelli Inn ~ *Best Continental*

Despite its location in Cleveland's Little Italy, the much-acclaimed Baricelli Inn specializes in American contemporary dining. Third-generation restaurateur and regular James Beard Award nominee Paul Minnillo is chef/owner of this small hotel/restaurant housed in a beautiful 19th-century brownstone mansion. His starters may include cured Italian meats and Baricelli's own artisanal cheeses, while entrée choices feature strong European and American influences, as in the rosemary and garlic flavored organic chicken with pan sauce or the ricotta and spinach ravioli. Full bar with extensive wine list. Serving dinner Mon–Sat. Closed Sun. 2203 Cornell Rd., Cleveland, OH 44106. (216) 791-6500. Go to: www.wtle.com/19206. ***Contemporary, Continental, Hotel Restaurant. $$$.***

Blue Point Grille ~ *Best Seafood*

Specializing in fresh fish and shellfish, Blue Point Grille ranks as one of Cleveland's very best restaurants overall and perennially captures local media awards for best seafood, as well. Housed in a magnificently renovated Warehouse District building dating back to 1875 (think high ceiling, chandeliers and dark woods), Blue Point offers an extensive menu that includes oysters, seafood and steaks. Ceviche or seafood chowder is the way to start, while specialties like grouper, bouillabaisse and stuffed trout make excellent main-course choices when available. Full bar. Serving lunch Mon–Fri, dinner nightly. 700 W. St. Clair Ave., Cleveland, OH 44113. (216) 875-7827. Go to: www.wtle.com/19368. ***Oysters, Seafood. $$$.***

Heck's Cafe ~ *Best Burgers*

With its warm, homey atmosphere and romantic, flower-filled atrium, Heck's Cafe doesn't exactly scream burger joint. But this converted brick townhouse nestled in the heart of Cleveland is where locals and visitors have been coming for years to get their hands — yes, both of them — on one of the famed gourmet Heck Burgers. The half pound of premium ground beef, grilled to order and served on a hand-knotted roll, is the base for a plethora of elaborate toppings, from mushrooms and peppers sautéed with garlic and white wine, to sour cream and crushed peppercorns. Otherwise, the American Traditional menu offers a nice variety of sandwiches, salads, steaks and seafood. Full bar. Serving lunch and dinner daily. Sun brunch 10:30 am–3 pm. 2927 Bridge Ave., Cleveland, OH 44113. (216) 861-5464. Go to: www.wtle.com/19073. ***American Traditional, Brunch, Burgers. $.***

Hyde Park Prime Steakhouse ~ *Best Steak House*

Hyde Park Prime Steakhouse has earned its reputation as one of Ohio's top steak houses through top-notch service and stellar cuts of beef. Started in Cleveland in 1988 and now with many other area and state locations, Hyde Park competes with high-end national chains, but maintains the character of an independently owned establishment. With a New York-chophouse décor of dark woods and dim lighting, local flavors abound, as do menu items named after Ohio sports stars. But those seeking the traditional steak house experience needn't worry: The extensive menu includes seafood, steaks and chops, including the house-specialty bone-in filet, and an array of side dishes, including creamed spinach, asparagus Béarnaise and potatoes gratin. Full bar. Serving lunch Mon–Fri at downtown Prospect Avenue location only. Serving dinner nightly. 123 W. Prospect Ave., Cleveland, OH 44115. (216) 344-2444. Multiple locations. Go to: www.wtle.com/19390. ***Steak House. $$$.***

Lola ~ *Best Contemporary*

A meal at chef/owner Michael Symon's Lola should certainly be included on the list of things not to miss during a visit to Cleveland. This native talent earned his degree from the Culinary Institute of America and returned to his Cleveland stomping grounds to capture the vibrancy of the city he loves with a progressive menu of creative bistro fare. Symon's sexy Tremont district eatery has recently gained much national attention, earning him a regular spot on the Food Network as well as a 2007 James Beard Foundation nomination for Best Chef: Great Lakes. Just remember, you're in mushroom country, so do try the wild mushroom appetizer or the bone-in rib eye with morels and ramps, when available. Full bar. Serving lunch Mon–Fri, dinner nightly. 2058 E. 4th St., Cleveland, OH 44115. (216) 621-5652. Go to: www.wtle.com/22045. ***Contemporary. $$$.***

Mallorca ~ *Best Spanish*

Known for attentive service and its seafood-centric Spanish and Portuguese menu, Warehouse District standout Mallorca invites diners to enjoy a leisurely, multi-course meal. Despite the white tablecloths and formally attired waitstaff, the mood remains casual at this hot spot and at each of the handful of regional sister locations. You're invited to linger over the lengthy cocktail menu, extensive wine list and after-dinner drink menu while indulging in an array of authentic dishes. Standout starters include gazpacho and broiled Spanish sausage. For your main course, sample the paella Valenciana, twin lobster tails or the filet of sole when available. Tiramisu makes a fantastic finish. Full bar. Serving lunch Mon–Sat, dinner nightly, with dinner menu beginning at 1 pm on Sun. 1390 W. 9th St., Cleveland, OH 44113. (216) 687-9494. Go to: www.wtle.com/19379. ***Seafood, Spanish. $$.***

Pearl of the Orient ~ *Best Asian Fusion*

Pearl of the Orient has been the leader of the pack among Cleveland-area Chinese and Asian Fusion restaurants for years. Often voted Best Chinese Restaurant by *Cleveland Magazine* and *Northern Ohio Live*, the two locations are operated by sister-brother combo Rose Wong and George Hwang. Both spots offer upscale Americanized Chinese food to a well-dressed clientele. The rather extensive menu of meat, seafood and vegetarian options, including scallion pancakes, pot stickers and Peking duck in three courses, remains assuredly MSG-free. The West Side (Detroit Road) location offers a new sushi list filled with classic favorites. Full bar. Serving lunch Mon–Sat, dinner nightly. 19300 Detroit Rd., Cleveland, OH 44116. (440) 333-9902. Two locations. Go to: www.wtle.com/18987. ***Asian Fusion, Chinese, Japanese/Sushi. $$.***

Sokolowski's University Inn ~ *Best Polish*

Time stands still at Sokolowski's University Inn, virtually unchanged since its 1923 opening on a hill overlooking

Cleveland's Industrial Flats. Now under the third generation of family ownership, the restaurant's Polish and American traditional home-style specialties — including pierogies, smoked kielbasa, bratwurst sausages and Salisbury steak dinners — are still served cafeteria-style. Bowls of mushroom barley and beef noodle soups make hearty starters, while entrée house specialties such as the Lake Erie perch and stuffed cabbages further warm the soul. Try the rice pudding or a slice of pie for dessert. Live piano music Wed–Fri at lunch and Fri–Sat at dinner. Full bar. Serving lunch Mon–Fri, dinner Mon–Sat. Closed Sun. 1201 University Rd., Cleveland, OH 44113. (216) 771-9236. Go to: www.wtle.com/19320. ***American Traditional, Home-style, Polish. $$.***

Tommy's ~ *Best Vegetarian*

Opened by one-time soda jerk Tommy Fello in 1972, this Cleveland Heights institution attracts most of the area's vegetarians and vegans, though the award-winning 20-ounce milkshakes draw a crowd with diverse dietary preferences. Tommy's extensive Middle Eastern-influenced menu begins with a full page of breakfast options, including numerous egg scrambles and the Elvis-worthy Mr. Stress (BLT, house-made peanut butter, mayo and American cheese on white toast). Lunch and dinner menus spotlight a host of substantial salads as well as vegetarian stalwarts such as black bean chili, baba ganoush and spinach pies. Delicious corned beef sandwiches and meat pies keep the carnivorous clientele coming back. No alcohol available. Serving breakfast, lunch and dinner daily. 1824 Coventry Rd., Coventry, OH 44118. (216) 321-7757. Go to: www.wtle.com/19413. ***Breakfast, Café, Middle Eastern, Vegetarian. $$.***

Yours Truly Restaurant ~ *Best Breakfast*

Owned and operated by the Shibley family since 1981 and now with several Cleveland-area locations, Yours Truly Restaurant specializes in all-day breakfasts, great stick-to-your-ribs diner fare, and a quaint, homey atmosphere. The local chain's numerous awards — including Best Breakfast, Best Hamburger, Best Cheap Eats and Best Place For Family Dining in local readers' polls — confirm this gem's status as an established Cleveland morning, noon and night tradition. Don't miss the signature medley of pita triangles stuffed with fried eggs, bacon and two kinds of cheese. Beer and wine available at Mayfield Village, Chagrin Falls, Hudson and Mentor locations. Serving breakfast, lunch and dinner daily. 25300 Chagrin Blvd., Beachwood, OH 44122. (216) 464-4848. Multiple locations. Go to: www.wtle.com/19051. ***Breakfast, Burgers, Diner. $.***

COLUMBUS OHIO

10 LOCAL FAVORITES

***Long a Midwest magnet** for restaurant chains, Columbus also boasts spectacular Spanish, scintillating sushi and some of the country's very best German cuisine.*

Barcelona ~ *Best Spanish*

Widely acclaimed as one of Columbus' premier restaurants, Barcelona brings a sense of Old World romance to the former Diebel's building in historic German Village. Many have called the outdoor terrace the best in the city, but whether you're sipping a glass of vino from the award-winning wine list on a nice night or enjoying live music in the intimate dining room, the food steals the show. Barcelona's cuisine tours the fine flavors of Europe, paying particular homage to the restaurant's Spanish namesake with a weekly changing selection of eclectic Mediterranean tapas and entrées. One early summer menu included such diverse selections as chilled spiced peach soup, cumin-crusted scallops and braised lamb shank. Don't miss the paella, when available. Full bar. Serving lunch Mon–Fri, dinner nightly. 263 E. Whittier St., Columbus, OH 43206. (614) 443-3699. Go to: www.wtle.com/2381. ***Contemporary, Small Plates, Spanish. $$.***

Handke's Cuisine

The vaulted stone ceilings and dim lighting of this former Schlee Bavarian Brewery building forge quite the dramatic, intimate setting at favorite special-occasion spot Handke's Cuisine. As the area's only Certified Master Chef — the American Culinary Federation's honor recognizing the highest level of culinary achievement —

German-native and chef/owner Hartmut Handke is easily one of the most accomplished of his profession in Columbus. Handke draws upon his cosmopolitan experience in creating his global cuisine, which may include anything from roasted Chilean sea bass to duck three-ways. The chef's penchant for mushrooms and veal makes dishes featuring these ingredients particularly praiseworthy. Full bar with extensive wine list. Serving dinner Mon–Sat. Closed Sun. 520 S. Front St., Columbus, OH 43215. (614) 621-2500. Go to: www.wtle.com/2387. ***Contemporary. $$$.***

Katzinger's Delicatessen ~ *Best Deli*

Since 1984, Katzinger's Delicatessen has been better educating customers raised on generic brands of olive oil, Bunny Bread and Kraft Singles. From the edge of German Village, Diane Warren imparts a passion for gourmet goods at her New York-style deli and specialty foods store. A range of soups and salads, traditional Jewish specialties and breakfast items (served all day!) are available. But locals know Katzinger's best for its cleverly named, overstuffed sandwiches. With more than 70 varieties from which to choose, quarter- or half-pound sandwiches are composed of house-baked breads, imported aged cheeses, quality meats, and house-made spreads and chutneys. Don't forget to dip into the serve-yourself pickle barrel. Beer available. Serving breakfast, lunch and dinner daily. 475 S. 3rd St., Columbus, OH 43215. (614) 228-3354. Go to: www.wtle.com/2410. ***Breakfast, Deli. $.***

Kihachi Japanese Restaurant ~ *Best Japanese/Sushi*

Numerous local foodies insist that Kihachi Japanese Restaurant not only serves some of Columbus' best traditional Japanese cuisine, but that it also ranks as one of the top two or three best restaurants of any genre. In this northwest suburban Dublin strip mall setting, many diners leave the ordering to convivial chef/owner Ryuji "Mike" Kimura, with his knowledge of the day's freshest fish. (He's been known to actually call up regulars to alert them of unusual catches.) The sublime sashimi and appetizers draw a near-fanatical following, so reservations are highly recommended. Full bar. Serving dinner Mon–Sat. Closed Sun. 2667 Federated Blvd., Dublin, OH 43235. (614) 764-9040. Go to: www.wtle.com/3266. ***Japanese/Sushi. $$.***

Lindey's ~ *Best Contemporary*

Bravo! Development, Inc.'s inaugural masterstroke, Lindey's, has remained the definitive spot for local power lunches, gatherings of friends and romantic nights on the town for more than 25 years. The original German Village spot enjoys high-energy ambiance and sleek upscale décor, invoking an Upper East Side New York bistro-like charm. From sautéed Cajun duck to braised short ribs with pasta, the contemporary menu offers an excellent selection of gourmet entrées. The popular Saturday and Sunday brunches (11 am–3 pm) boast a decadent house-made brioche French toast as well as a rotating selection of omelets, waffles and quiches. Full bar. Serving lunch and dinner daily. Sat–Sun brunch. 169 E. Beck St., Columbus, OH 43206. (614) 228-4343. Go to: www.wtle.com/2390. ***Brunch, Contemporary, Dessert. $$.***

The Old Mohawk ~ *Best American Traditional*

Photographs on the walls chronicling the more than 70 years of The Old Mohawk's history show the historic German Village neighborhood and the loyal customers who love this local favorite, as the daily out-the-door lunch lines can attest, for its classic food and comfy atmosphere. Known for its horseshoe-shaped bar, The Old Mohawk serves as an after-work watering hole, but the classic American comfort food remains a cut above casual pub fare. The beef stew fills a warm sourdough bread bowl with chunks of beef and veggies, and the Mother Mohawk sandwich (half chicken salad, half roast beef on grilled rye) is one of a kind. Full bar. Serving breakfast Sun, lunch and dinner daily. 819 Mohawk St., Columbus, OH 43206. (614) 444-7204. Go to: www.wtle.com/2398. ***American Traditional, Brunch, Burgers. $.***

Refectory Restaurant & Bistro ~ *Best French*

In true French fashion, the Refectory Restaurant & Bistro combines a deep respect for its history with a love for living life fully in the present. A restored 19th-century church and adjacent schoolhouse set the scene: *La bonne vie* echoes in the antique sanctuary, where savoring the moment is the practice and fine food, the religion. Good wine is a large part of that good life, and in this, the Refectory excels, with its extensive award-winning wine list. The rotating menu features a blend of classic and contemporary French cuisine. The chefs do particularly well with wild game in addition to house-made pâtés, rack of lamb and a number of freshly prepared seafood dishes. Jacket suggested. Full bar. Serving dinner Mon–Sat. Closed Sun. 1092 Bethel Rd., Columbus, OH 43220. (614) 451-9774. Go to: www.wtle.com/2601. ***Bistro, French. $$$.***

R.J. Snappers ~ *Best Seafood*

In landlocked Columbus, it is geographically impossible to sell seashells by the seashore, but at least R.J. Snappers sells shellfish in the Short North. This restaurant has provided fresh "seafood with imagination" to the hip, gallery-laden district since 1997. If the name and logo (a snapper — fancy that!) don't convince you that they're serious about seafood here, the 300-gallon fish tank inside should drive the point home (though the exotic fish are for decorative purposes only: You will not come face to face with your dinner while walking by). Inventive shellfish dishes include caramelized sea scallops and pesto grilled tiger prawns, while fish offerings such as potato-encrusted Florida grouper, sake marinated Chilean sea bass and Hawaiian bigeye tuna display the creative flair with which seafood is prepared here. Landlubbers will enjoy a tender Szechwan pepper-seared filet or one of the gourmet pizzas. Full bar. Serving dinner nightly. 700 N. High St., Columbus, OH 43215. (614) 280-1070. Go to: www.wtle.com/3537. ***Contemporary, Seafood. $$.***

Schmidt's Restaurant and Sausage Haus ~ *Best German*

Appropriately tucked into the heart of German Village, Schmidt's Restaurant and Sausage Haus was the original location of German-expatriate J. Fred Schmidt's meat packinghouse when he immigrated to Columbus in 1886. Five generations later, his ghost is said to haunt the restaurant (it was converted in 1976) that retains the family's meat-focused culinary history with their legendary sausages. Female servers balancing steins of German brews sport traditional dress while, on many evenings, the "haus" band, Schnickelfritz, oom-pah-pahs in the background. Spatzles and krauts aside, it's hard to stray from Schmidt's trademark sausage sandwiches and platters, the most popular of which is The Bahama Mama, a spicy ground beef and pork brat on a toasted bun. Full bar. Serving lunch and dinner daily. 240 E. Kossuth St., Columbus, OH 43216. (614) 444-6808. Go to: www.wtle.com/2602. ***German. $.***

The Worthington Inn Restaurant ~ *Best Brunch*

With certain sections dating back as far as 1816, The Worthington Inn stands out as a historic landmark in the quaint little town of Worthington. Longstanding charm and a reputation for refinement pervade the homey dining rooms that make up the restaurant, a place with a reputation that easily lives up to the hotel's standards of excellence. Contemporary cuisine with distinct French and Italian influences emphasizes seasonal and locally grown ingredients in dishes like lobster ravioli with petite vegetables and local pork tenderloin with a dried cherry and Marsala sauce. The popular Sunday brunch (10 am–2 pm) offers a buffet selection of made-to-order omelets, carved prime rib, smoked salmon and peel-and-eat shrimp. Award-winning wine list and full bar. Serving lunch and dinner Mon–Sat. Sun brunch. 649 High St., Worthington, OH 43085. (614) 885-2600. Go to: www.wtle.com/2472. ***Brunch, Contemporary. $$.***

DALLAS TEXAS

10 LOCAL FAVORITES

***Nationally acclaimed chefs** such as Kent Rathbun and Stephan Pyles, as well as one of the top French restaurants in the United States, fit nicely alongside the cherished Texas-style barbecue, fried chicken and thick steaks in Dallas.*

Abacus ~ *Best Contemporary*

Dallas dining landmark Abacus has earned singular praise from local and national media alike, including a 2005 induction into the Fine Dining Hall of Fame (*Nation's Restaurant News*). From the sleek Knox-Henderson neighborhood establishment, chef/ part-owner Kent Rathbun serves a seafood-dominated world-tour menu that proves to be less fusion cuisine and more of a side-by-side presentation of multicultural fare. Mediterranean, Cajun, Southwestern and Pacific Rim influences stand out. The signature lobster scallion shooters, served with red chile coconut sake, are the menu's most popular item. The eight- to 12-seat chef's table allows a peek into one of Dallas' first European-style theater kitchens and a sample of the chef's constantly evolving tasting menu. Full bar. Serving dinner Mon–Sat. Closed Sun. 4511 McKinney Ave., Dallas, TX 75205. (214) 559-3111. Go to: www.wtle.com/3091. ***Contemporary. $$$.***

Arcodoro & Pomodoro ~ *Best Italian*

Artfully designed to resemble an indoor Italian villa, Uptown's Arcodoro & Pomodoro represents the pinnacle of Italian cuisine in Dallas and, more specifically, the rustic and traditional comfort foods of the island of Sardinia. There are two adjacent and distinct dining areas: the more formal Pomodoro, which launched in 1988, and the hip and more casual bar scene of Arcodoro, which joined its sister space under one roof in 2000. Brothers and chefs/owners Efisio and Francesco Farris share menus, with the exception of excellent wood oven-fired pizzas, only available on the Arcodoro side. Specialties of the house include house-made ravioli, osso buco and paella for two. Full bar. Serving lunch Tue–Fri, dinner Tue–Sat. Closed Sun–Mon. 2708 Routh St., Dallas, TX 75201. (214) 871-1924. Go to: www.wtle.com/5259. ***Italian. $$.***

Bob's Steak & Chop House ~ *Best Steak House*

Though this 1993 Dallas original has been replicated at additional locations, Bob's Steak & Chop House maintains its neighborhood feel as well as owner Bob Sambol's good ol' boy personality. Masculinity reigns in every facet of the restaurant's character, although patrons of both genders praise Bob's for all-around excellence. The cigar menu and strategically placed TV screens enhance already virile steak house mainstays, from the supper club décor to the huge hunks of meat, emphasis on "huge." Fourteen-ounce veal chops, 20-ounce rib eyes and the massive 28-ounce porterhouse are garnished with the restaurant's signature glazed carrots and are accompanied by smashed, baked or skillet fried potatoes and other classic Southern sides. A high-end wine list and single malt Scotch menu are also available. Full bar. Serving dinner Mon–Sat. Closed Sun. 4300 Lemmon Ave., Plano, TX 75219. (214) 528-9446. Multiple locations. Go to: www.wtle.com/5457. ***Steak House. $$$.***

Bread Winners Cafe and Bakery ~ *Best Bakery, Best Breakfast*

Bread Winners Cafe and Bakery has been bringing home the bacon, Benedicts and bread since 1994. With locations in Uptown, Inwood Village and Plano, this local favorite offers a comfortably upscale atmosphere laden with as much personality as carb-loaded goodness. The breakfast menu boasts favorite variants on omelets, French toast and breakfast casseroles, while lunch extends to include excellent sandwich/salad/soup fare. Seasonal dinner menus have offered nut-crusted tilapia, chile-lime ribs and chicken potpie. Make sure to grab a divine oatmeal toffee cookie or some warm banana nut bread on the way out. Full bar. Serving breakfast and lunch daily, dinner Tue–Sun. 3301 McKinney Ave., Dallas, TX 75204. (214) 754-4940. Multiple locations. Go to: www.wtle.com/24653. ***Bakery, Breakfast, Café. $$.***

Bubba's ~ *Best Home-style*

From an unassuming building in Dallas' University Park comes what *Southern Living* magazine has designated some of the best fried chicken in the South. This no-nonsense, Southern-to-the-core diner says long live the days when vegetables simmer to their breaking points and when the deep fryer gets more action than the steamer, microwave and broiler combined. Pick your breast, drumstick or thigh, and slather on a pile of baked beans, candied yams and green beans. Cactus-shaped jalapeño cornbread effectively soaks up juice from the pot roast, while mashed potatoes and fluffy biscuits accompany such Southern staples as fried catfish and chicken-fried steak. No alcohol available. Serving breakfast, lunch and dinner daily. 6617 Hillcrest Ave., Dallas, TX 75205. (214) 373-6527. Go to: www.wtle.com/19727. ***American Traditional, Breakfast, Diner, Fried Chicken, Home-style. $.***

Cafe Madrid ~ *Best Spanish*

At the corner of Old World Europe and modern America lies Cafe Madrid, serving the authentic Spanish answer to hors d'oeuvres for more than 15 years. On any given night, this humble tapas eatery —with locations in Uptown and Bishop Arts—offers nearly three dozen small plates in addition to a list of daily blackboard specials. Paella is a house favorite, but everything from the Andalucian meatballs in almond sauce to the oxtail stew is delicious. The *Wine Spectator* award-winning, all-Spanish wine list deserves attention, as well, with a handful of beers, ports, sherries and sangrias also available. Travis Street serving lunch Fri–Sat, dinner Mon–Sat. Bishop Avenue serving lunch Mon–Sat. Both closed Sun. 4501 Travis St., Dallas, TX 75205. (214) 528-1731. Two locations. Go to: www.wtle.com/3945. ***Small Plates, Spanish. $$.***

Café Pacific ~ *Best Seafood*

For more than 25 years, Café Pacific has proven itself a first-class seafood restaurant à la epicurean San Francisco in the tony Highland Park Village. Often considered the dining destination for Parkies and Dallas foodies in the know, expect the 75205 treatment: A maitre d' greets you at the door; starched white linen covers tables and waitstaff alike; and Hermes scarves and Versace sunglasses abound. Although the elegance of it all evokes 1940s New York, the menu remains forward-thinking in its combinations and presentation. Imagine the likes of short-smoked salmon, ancho-chile lamb chops and brandy-and-black pepper filet mignon. The rather extensive wine list boasts notably low markups that keep locals coming back for special-occasion dining. Full bar. Serving lunch and dinner Mon–Sat. Closed Sun. 24 Highland Park Village., Dallas, TX 75205. (214) 526-1170. Go to: www.wtle.com/5402. ***Contemporary, Seafood. $$.***

The French Room ~ *Best French*

If King Louis XIV of France were to dine in the modern era, he might very well choose The French Room at The Adolphus Hotel in downtown Dallas. With food, service and atmosphere truly fit for a king, this five-star dining establishment has earned top critical acclaim from the nation's leading food experts. While the room itself appears to be straight out of 16th-century Versailles (King Louis' palace), the cuisine favors a more general European flavor: exotic caviars, spiced duck breast over foie gras, and veal tenderloin medallions. And let them eat cake. (Yes, we know that Marie Antoinette was actually Louis *XVI*'s ill-fated wife.) Or crème brûlée. Or a French soufflé. An extensive wine list includes some of the world's rarest, most expensive finds. Jacket and tie required. Full bar. Serving dinner Tue–Sat. Closed Sun–Mon. 1321 Commerce St., Dallas, TX 75202. (214) 742-8200. Go to: www.wtle.com/5029. ***Continental, French, Hotel Restaurant. $$$.***

Sonny Bryan's Smokehouse ~ *Best Barbecue*

A Dallas institution for nearly a half-century, Sonny Bryan's Smokehouse puts the plain-and-simple back into some of Big D's favorite barbecue. The tiny, 40-year-old wooden building housing the original Inwood location retains the family-run charm instituted by Sonny's grandfather, who opened the family's first restaurant in 1910. (The Bryans no longer own the now-multiple locations.) From pulled pork or chicken, to beef brisket and "vegetables," such as mac and cheese and some of Texas' best fried onion rings, the food can only get better when dipped in the thick, red house sauce for which Sonny Bryan's is known. Beer available. Hours vary by location. 2202 Inwood Rd., Dallas, TX 75235. (214) 357-7120. Multiple locations. Go to: www.wtle.com/19659. ***Barbecue. $.***

Stephan Pyles

One of Dallas' most successful chefs/restaurateurs, *Esquire* magazine's 2006 Chef of the Year and a founding father of Southwestern cuisine, Stephan Pyles opened his namesake restaurant in 2005 after his five-year sabbatical left local palates craving his trademark big, bold flavors. The classy, modern space in the Dallas Arts District proves the ideal location for indulging in Pyles' "New Millennium Southwestern Cuisine," which calls for global influences on Mexican flavors and classical techniques in Southwestern cooking. Starter selections from the ceviche menu are a must, but save room for heavy-duty entrées to the tune of barbecued short ribs, coconut-serrano lobster and chile-braised osso buco. Full bar. Serving lunch Mon–Fri, dinner Mon–Sat. Closed Sun. 1807 Ross Ave., Dallas, TX 75201. (214) 580-7000. Go to: www.wtle.com/22255. ***Contemporary, Southwestern, Spanish. $$$.***

DENVER COLORADO

10 LOCAL FAVORITES

Mile High dining has achieved lofty heights *thanks to increasingly sophisticated Denver kitchens, including Restaurant Kevin Taylor, Strings, Barolo Grill and Richard Sandoval's Tamayo.*

Passenger terminal at Denver International Airport

Barolo Grill ~ *Best Italian*

Owner Blair Taylor and his Barolo Grill are almost as well known for the staff's annual trip to Italy as for the restaurant's stellar Italian food and extensive wine list. Northern Italian cuisine is the theme, and the well-traveled staff can describe each dish's ingredients upon request as well as suggest appropriate wine pairings. The menu changes seasonally, and the specials reflect what's fresh that day, with an emphasis on sauces, fresh produce and handmade pastas. Elegant desserts range from lemon cake to panna cotta. Try to score the table next to the fireplace if romance is on your mind. Full bar. Serving dinner Tue–Sat. Closed Sun–Mon. 3030 E. 6th Ave., Denver, CO 80206. (303) 393-1040. Go to: www.wtle.com/6174. ***Italian. $$.***

Benny's Restaurante y Tequila Bar ~ *Best Burritos*

Though renowned Denver restaurateur Benny Armas has owned many local Mexican eateries over the past several decades, Benny's Restaurante y Tequila Bar is the most beloved. It's a tradition for many who swing by for the menu's star — a stuffed-to-the-brim sirloin burrito — or any of the other solid Mexican and Tex-Mex fare (tacos, carnitas, enchiladas). Enjoy a margarita at the hopping bar or on the large, enclosed patio. Weekend brunch (9 am–2 pm) includes drink specials to accompany breakfast burritos, omelets, carnitas and eggs, and menudo (tripe and hominy), the Mexican specialty/acquired taste. Full bar. Serving lunch and dinner daily. 301 E. 7th Ave., Denver, CO 80203. (303) 894-0788. Go to: www.wtle.com/5973. ***Brunch, Burritos, Mexican. $.***

Brook's Steak House & Cellar ~ *Best Steak House*

Since its 1996 launch, Brook's Steak House has been one of the Denver area's most lauded independently owned steak houses, continually winning over diners with its top-flight steaks, sides and service. Though the Greenwood Village staple resembles an Austrian château from afar, the interior décor evokes the expected supper club elegance of a shrine to all-things beef. The menu, also, follows first-rate steak house rules with its exceptional list of appetizers, salads and huge cuts of filet, porterhouse, rib eye and the like. Brook's Steak House has received awards from DiRoNA and *Wine Spectator* and has been named one of the *Rocky Mountain News'* Top Five Steak Houses. Full bar. Serving dinner nightly. 6538 S. Yosemite St., Greenwood Village, CO 80111. (303) 770-1177. Go to: www.wtle.com/6445. ***Steak House. $$$.***

Jax Fish House ~ *Best Seafood*

Respected local restaurateur Dave Query's two Jax Fish Houses, each with its own chef, are classics in a landlocked state hungry for quality seafood. The Boulder site is a narrow, bustling location that fills early with families seeking fresh ocean bounty, while young hipsters squeeze in for oyster shooters during daily drink specials. In Denver, the space is similarly packed with diners flocking to enjoy such items as cornmeal fried oysters, the lobster BLT and the white chocolate cupcake with red berry sauce. Full bar. Serving dinner nightly. 1539 17th St., Denver, CO 80202. (303) 292-5767. Two locations. Go to: www.wtle.com/6429. ***Contemporary, Seafood. $$.***

Le Central ~ *Best French*

Le Central is always packed and for good reason: Solid French fare is not only priced reasonably here but also served efficiently.

The French onion soup, escargots, pâtés — all are exemplary, and the atmosphere in this bustling eatery is anything but stuffy. Desserts are *magnifique*! Look for gateaux au *chocolat* or tarte Tatin for two. And the affordable wine list is, as one would expect, very French. Saturday and Sunday brunch (11 am–2 pm) is worth squeezing in, particularly for the Provençal-style egg dishes. Full bar. Serving lunch and dinner daily. 112 E. 8th Ave., Denver, CO 80203. (303) 863-8094. Go to: www.wtle.com/6089. ***French. $$.***

Racines ~ *Best Breakfast*

The second incarnation of the 1983 original, Racines still offers a neighborhood feel despite its snazzy new digs and increasing customer base flocking from all over the city. The enormous, mostly Southwestern menu features fantastic salads, pastas, sandwiches and burgers, though many stop by simply to snack on The Mile High Nachos at the bar as they sip on one of the award-winning margaritas. And everyone knows this is the place to go for a wide variety of breakfasts — omelets, smoked salmon Benedict, gingerbread pancakes and Belgian waffles included. There's almost always a morning line, but don't worry, an abbreviated breakfast menu is served all day. Full bar. Serving breakfast, lunch and dinner daily. Sat–Sun brunch 8 am–3 pm. 650 Sherman St., Denver, CO 80203. (303) 595-0418. Go to: www.wtle.com/5834. ***American Traditional, Breakfast, Brunch, Southwestern. $$.***

Restaurant Kevin Taylor ~ *Best Dessert*

Nationally lauded Kevin Taylor's luxury dining room in the boutique Hotel Teatro is a place that makes any occasion immediately special. Everything about the restaurant is beautiful, from the lush décor and fabulous table settings to the artfully arranged fusion of French, Southwestern and Asian food. The seasonal menu has included such items as Colorado lamb sirloin and green tea-poached tuna with house-made buckwheat noodles. The best indulgences of all might be Taylor's heavenly desserts such as the pineapple and mascarpone Napoleon. All this plus the exceptional wine list help make Restaurant Kevin Taylor one of *Rocky Mountain News*' Top 20 Restaurants. Full bar. Serving dinner Mon–Sat. Closed Sun. 1106 14th St., Denver, CO 80202. (303) 820-2600. Go to: www.wtle.com/6058. ***Contemporary, Dessert, Hotel Restaurant. $$$.***

Strings ~ *Best Contemporary*

Nationally recognized for his efforts to stop world hunger, owner Noel Cunningham has fed Denver well, too, at his uptown contemporary bistro, Strings. The menu offers elegant, updated American fare that doesn't trip over its own ingredients. Sautéed crab cakes with chutney and cranberry ketchup and the crispy veal sweetbreads, when available, are great starters, while the half-dozen pasta entrées have always been a big draw. For dessert, try the Belgian chocolate mousse cake or house-made ice cream. (The chef will take kids into the kitchen for an ice cream-making lesson.) Full bar. Serving lunch Mon–Fri, dinner nightly. 1700 Humboldt St., Denver, CO 80218. (303) 831-7310. Go to: www.wtle.com/5741. ***Contemporary. $$.***

Sushi Den ~ *Best Japanese/Sushi*

Sushi Den owners and brothers Toshi and Yasu Kizaki have figured out the smartest way to run a sushi restaurant in the United States: own a seafood-export business in Japan. This way, they're assured of knowing firsthand the quality of the fish presented to their customers. Certainly, Sushi Den's sushi and sashimi are of the finest quality, impeccably fresh and flavorful, and often served with a twist. The menu of cooked dishes follows traditional lines with a few surprises, such as roasted chicken with cilantro rice. Toshi's wife, Michiko, makes the exquisite desserts. Full bar. Serving lunch Mon–Fri, dinner nightly. 1487 S. Pearl St., Denver, CO 80210. (303) 777-0826. Go to: www.wtle.com/6198. ***Japanese/Sushi. $$.***

Tamayo ~ *Best Latin/South American*

As owner of some of the country's top Mexican and Nuevo Mexican eateries, Richard Sandoval has earned national name recognition. His staff expertly executes his contemporary versions of gourmet south-of-the-border dishes such as grilled chipotle Colorado lamb and filet mignon tacos. Try to snag a table on the second-floor patio, offering one of the best mountain views as well as taste tests of the popular tequila flights from the restaurant's extensive roster. Full bar. Serving lunch Mon–Fri, dinner nightly. 1400 Larimer St., Denver, CO 80202. (720) 946-1433. Go to: www.wtle.com/5990. ***Latin/South American, Mexican. $$.***

DETROIT MICHIGAN

10 LOCAL FAVORITES

Like the tradition of its Motown-fueled music scene, *Detroit has soul to spare in its restaurants, including the appropriately named Beans & Cornbread, Seldom Blues, and Sweet Lorraine's Cafe & Bar.*

Belle Isle Bridge

Beans & Cornbread ~ *Best Soul Food*

Self-proclaimed "soulful bistro" Beans & Cornbread reconciles its upscale atmosphere and down-home menu with the quality of its meals, often called "as good as Grandma's!" Southern soul food favorites such as gumbo and meat loaf, along with new creations such as the Harlem Burrito (made with collard greens, black-eyed peas, and tomato and cilantro salsa), pair with divine sides (think candied sweet potatoes and macaroni and cheese) to achieve a sort of food heaven. The Sunday Gospel Brunch (12 pm–1:30 pm) may be even closer to the real thing. Full bar. Serving lunch Mon–Fri, dinner nightly. 29508 Northwestern Hwy., Southfield, MI 48034. (248) 208-1680. Go to: www.wtle.com/1034. ***Brunch, Home-style, Soul Food. $$.***

Mon Jin Lau ~ *Best Asian Fusion*

One of the trendiest Asian restaurants in the Detroit area, Mon Jin Lau attracts diners from the Troy area and beyond. The swank ambiance, full bar and innovative dishes are a few of the reasons patrons don't mind waiting for a table — even with a reservation. Often voted Best Chinese by the *Metro Times*, Mon Jin Lau's food has been touted as consistently exquisite for more than 20 years. The menu includes traditional Chinese dishes, sushi and unique house specialties referred to as "nu-Asian," such as steamed mussels with black bean and garlic sauce. The sake sampler is perfect for those who can't pick a favorite cocktail. Full bar. Serving lunch Mon–Fri, dinner nightly. 1515 E. Maple Rd. Troy, MI 48084. (248) 689-2332. Go to: www.wtle.com/650. ***Asian Fusion, Chinese, Japanese/Sushi. $$.***

Rochester Chop House ~ *Best Steak House*

Located downtown in the Detroit suburb of Rochester, Rochester Chop House features first-class steaks, chops and seafood in an inviting, two-level structure that includes an expansive oyster bar and regular live piano music. The winning menu and service showcase the professional qualities of founders and restaurateurs Bill Kruse and the late Chuck Muer (of the local Kruse & Muer eateries), and either Kruse or his co-proprietor Vince Clark routinely greets diners at the door. The featured cut of beef is the classic sirloin, and the house-made coleslaw and broiled hash browns with blue cheese are great sides. Full bar with well-chosen wine list. Serving lunch Mon–Fri, dinner nightly. 306 S. Main St., Rochester, MI 48307. (248) 651-2266. Go to: www.wtle.com/1015. ***Oysters, Seafood, Steak House. $$$.***

Roma Cafe ~ *Best Italian*

Still in its original location, Detroit's oldest Italian restaurant, Roma Cafe, began serving in 1890 the same recipes they do today. Italian hospitality is the norm here as knowledgeable, tuxedo-clad waiters accomodate patrons, sometimes giving regular visitors special treatment. Not surprisingly, the menu features traditional Italian dishes, including pastas, seafood, broiled steak and veal. After-dinner treats are held in high regard, especially tiramisu and cannoli, which can be paired with cappuccino and other Italian coffees. Don't miss the Monday night buffet. Free shuttle service to Detroit Red Wings hockey games. Beer and wine available. Serving lunch and dinner Mon–Sat. Closed Sun. 3401 Riopelle St., Detroit, MI 48207. (313) 831-5940. Go to: www.wtle.com/924. ***Italian. $$.***

Russell Street Deli ~ *Best Breakfast, Best Deli*

This shotgun-style restaurant isn't for diners who want a quiet meal alone. Detroit dines together at increasingly jammed tables as the lunch hour picks up, and strangers seated next to each other begin to dive deep into conversation, which may include anything from movies to metaphysics. Even the waitstaff joins in the dialogue, and locals often joke that a degree is required to be a busboy at Russell Street Deli. During the week, Russell Street serves up classic deli sandwiches (Reubens, chicken salad, salami, etc.), salads and a rotating selection of soups. On Saturdays, a spectacular and wildly popular breakfast features more unusual dishes such as French toast made from raisin bread, and Havarti, asparagus and dill omelets. No alcohol available. Serving lunch Mon–Fri, breakfast and lunch Sat. Closed Sun. 2465 Russell St., Detroit, MI 48207. (313) 567-2900. Go to: www.wtle.com/699. ***Breakfast, Deli. $.***

Seldom Blues ~ *Best Contemporary*

Launched in 2004, Seldom Blues regularly features national jazz and blues acts from its location in the elegant GM Renaissance Center downtown. In addition to picturesque views of the Detroit River and live music every night of the week, Seldom Blues also offers outstanding contemporary Continental cuisine to the tune of champagne-butter twin lobster tails, braised short ribs and veal tenderloin medallions. A highlight of the dessert menu is the Rhythm and Blues Cake, a devil's food and chocolate mousse cake, served with Earl Grey ice cream. Full bar. Serving lunch Mon–Fri, dinner Mon–Sat. Sun brunch 11 am–4 pm. 400 Renaissance Ctr., Detroit, MI 48243. (313) 567-7301. Go to: www.wtle.com/616. ***Brunch, Contemporary, Continental, Seafood. $$$.***

Sindbads ~ *Best American Traditional*

Sindbads has come a long way since 1949, when the Blancke and VanHollebecke brothers-in-law bought the original tiny shack now housing just the restaurant's bar. The prime location allows patrons to dine by land (in the polished 430-seat dining room) or by sea, docking at tables over the scenic Detroit River, and the unassuming atmosphere and laid-back presentation have stayed consistent through the more than 50 years of growth and remodeling. The restaurant serves quality meats and simple sides, with traditional dishes such as surf and turf, king crab legs, and perch from the Great Lakes. Live music during the summer. Full bar. Serving lunch and dinner daily. Sun brunch 11:30 am–2:30 pm. 100 St. Clair Ave. Detroit, MI 48214. (313) 822-8000. Go to: www.wtle.com/1072. ***American Traditional, Brunch, Seafood. $$.***

Sweet Lorraine's Cafe & Bar ~ *Best Café*

Dishes inspired by cultures from around the globe make the cuisine at Sweet Lorraine's Cafe & Bar difficult to categorize, though the restaurant refers to itself as "world beat." From vegetarian jambalaya to yellowfin tuna over salade Niçoise, you never know what to expect from daily specials — except that they'll be outstanding. Breakfast classics, along with inventive options such as cinnamon-stuffed French toast, are served daily. The decadent cheesecake is a testament to chef/owner Lorraine Platman's beginnings as a pastry chef, while the multiple *Wine Spectator* Awards of Excellence speak for the outstanding wine list. Live jazz Tuesday nights at the Southfield location. Full bar. Serving breakfast, lunch and dinner daily. 333 E. Jefferson Ave., Detroit, MI 48226. (313) 223-3933. Multiple locations. Go to: www.wtle.com/744. ***Café, Contemporary. $$.***

Traffic Jam & Snug ~ *Best Brewpub*
In the 1960s, Cass Corridor's Traffic Jam was a standard bar named after its unfortunate parking situation, and Snug was a nearby ice cream parlor. In the 1990s, the combined Traffic Jam & Snug began brewing its own beer, and though the ice cream parlor is gone, the restaurant continues to brew up to five original varieties of beer at a time in addition to making its own cheese and baking breads in-house. The menu offers atypically light bar fare — including salads, broiled fish and the popular cheese platter — along with burgers and a variety of sandwiches. For dessert, the house-made ice cream and hot fudge is a nod to the establishment's heritage. Full bar. Serving lunch and dinner daily. 511 W. Canfield St., Detroit, MI 48201. (313) 831-9470. Go to: www.wtle.com/670. ***Bakery, Brewpub. $$.***

The Whitney ~ *Best Contemporary, Best Dessert*
Located in the historic Romanesque-style Whitney mansion, The Whitney comprises a number of ornately decorated dining rooms over three floors, each room maintaining a unique décor. Dining options are as opulent as the ambiance, with offerings such as in-house smoked salmon, blue cheese soufflé salad and the signature Old Detroiter, a 24-ounce porterhouse. The elegant Sunday brunch (11 am–2 pm) is a prix fixe meal in four courses, starting with light pastries and juices and ending with a selection of the restaurant's highly touted sweets such as the Whitney Chocolate Ugly Cake. (These treats have made The Whitney a popular spot for dessert alone.) Garden parties featuring an hors d'oeuvres buffet and live entertainment occur on Thursdays during the summer. Jacket and tie suggested. Reservations required. Full bar. Serving lunch Wed–Fri, dinner nightly. 4421 Woodward Ave., Detroit, MI 48201. (313) 832-5700. Go to: www.wtle.com/620. ***Brunch, Contemporary, Continental, Dessert. $$$.***

FORT LAUDERDALE
FLORIDA

10 LOCAL FAVORITES

Once known mainly for its spring break beach scene, *Fort Lauderdale has become quite the culinary center, with much-lauded contemporaries such as Johnny V, Max's Grille and The River House.*

Blue Moon Fish Co. ~ *Best Seafood*

On the east side of the Intracoastal Waterway sits one of Fort Lauderdale's finest restaurants, Blue Moon Fish Co., where the fresh seafood specialties are as spectacular as the view. This nautical nirvana, along with its sister location in Coral Springs, hails from the genius of nationally renowned chefs/owners Baron Skorish and Bryce Statham, who bring their gourmet cuisine to these sophisticated and tranquil settings. Ocean fare is flown in two to three times daily, and the raw bar is an excellent place to start — try the chilled selection of half-shell oysters. The seasonal menu includes some incredible desserts by the in-house pastry chef. Try the Sunday brunch (11:30 am–3 pm), which includes sample sizes of signature entrées. Full bar. Serving dinner nightly. Lauderdale-by-the-Sea location also serving lunch daily. 4405 W. Tradewinds Ave., Lauderdale-by-the-Sea, FL 33308. (954) 267-9888. Two locations. Go to: www.wtle.com/10162. ***Brunch, Dessert, Oysters, Seafood. $$$.***

Grill Room on Las Olas ~ *Best Continental*

With the same elegance as its host, the historic Riverside Hotel, the Grill Room on Las Olas shines like a colonial British officer's club room. Exceptional service that is consistently recognized by AAA with the prestigious Four Diamond Award includes the formal presentation of each dish by tuxedoed waiters and the tableside preparation of such Continental dining standards as Caesar salad and Châteaubriand. A well-heeled clientele enjoys top-shelf martinis, single-malt Scotches or glasses of one of the more than 1,500 selections from the *Wine Spectator* award-winning wine cellar. A premium cigar list is also available. Full bar. Serving dinner Mon–Sat. Closed Sun. 620 E. Las Olas Blvd., Fort Lauderdale, FL 33301. (954) 467-2555. Go to: www.wtle.com/10551. ***Contemporary, Continental, Hotel Restaurant. $$$.***

Il Mulino ~ *Best Italian*

Il Mulino has become a regular stop for Fort Lauderdale's most discriminating diners. The open kitchen and cozy, casual dining room are always buzzing with activity and familial warmth. A no-reservations policy means customers begin pouring in well before the 7 o'clock dinner hour, and the bar remains alive and packed throughout the night. Patrons don't mind waiting for Mulino's generous portions of consistently superb pasta-and-red-sauce fare. Loyals swear by the hearty basics: From the excellent garlic bread to the house-made pasta such as gnocchi with marinara sauce, every detail, both simple and complex, receives ample attention from the kitchen. Full bar. Serving lunch and dinner daily. 1800 E. Sunrise Blvd., Fort Lauderdale, FL 33304. (954) 524-1800. Go to: www.wtle.com/10788. ***Italian, Pizza. $$.***

Johnny V ~ *Best Dessert*

South Florida's most recognizable chef, Johnny Vinczencz, lives up to his "Caribbean Cowboy" nickname by bringing bold flavors and daring imagination to every dish. His Las Olas eatery, Johnny V, enjoyed immediate success — earning four stars from both *The Miami Herald* and the *Sun-Sentinel* — upon premiering in 2003. Today, Florida meets the Caribbean meets Latin America meets the world under his direction. Dessert proves the kind of creations you'd never have dreamed of but can't help dreaming of afterward, such as the mascarpone peach cheesecake. Full bar. Serving lunch and dinner daily. 625 E. Las Olas Blvd., Fort Lauderdale, FL 33301. (954) 761-7920. Go to: www.wtle.com/9496. ***Contemporary, Dessert. $$$.***

Mai-Kai ~ *Best Asian Fusion*

Since 1956, locals and tourists alike have been escaping to

Mai-Kai, a true Fort Lauderdale institution. The almost Epcot-like Polynesian village setting — complete with tiki torches, waterfalls and a thatch roof — remains one of the few authentic tiki restaurants, popularized post-World War II, still in existence. With appetizers from sushi to barbecued baby back ribs and entrées from Tahitian vanilla lobster to pad thai, the incredibly extensive menu covers the best of Asian, Pacific Islander and American cuisines. More than 50 varieties of frosty tropical drinks run the gamut of fruitiness and potency, from non-alcoholic to the tried-and-true "whoa!" Don't miss the Islander Revue, the popular Polynesian dance performance, featured twice nightly. Full bar. Serving dinner nightly. 3599 N. Federal Hwy., Fort Lauderdale, FL 33308. (954) 563-3272. Go to: www.wtle.com/10118. ***Asian Fusion, Chinese. $$$.***

Max's Grille

Max's Grille has begun a new era of dining sovereignty in local restaurateur Dennis Max's empire. His Boca Raton venture features his proven formula for success: upscale-casual dining in a metropolitan atmosphere, complete with a see-and-be-seen patio and swanky signature cocktail menu. But the food is the real secret behind Max's popularity. The list of American favorites spices up the expected, featuring such items as chicken wings in a red chile-guava glaze, and maple-ginger glazed salmon. The meringue Key lime pie is a dazzler. Full bar and prestigious wine list. Serving lunch and dinner daily. 404 Plaza Real, Boca Raton, FL 33432. (561) 368-0080. Go to: www.wtle.com/9480. ***Bistro, Contemporary. $$$.***

The River House ~ *Best Contemporary*

Nestled on the north bank of the New River in a century-old mansion, The River House affords one of the city's best views. This nostalgically romantic estate once housed the railroading family Bryan, who began boarding travelers in order to turn a small profit, thus establishing Fort Lauderdale's first hotel. This Riverwalk darling may look back in time for ambiance, but its menu faces forward, drawing on Caribbean, Asian, Mexican and Mediterranean cuisines to influence the New American menu of old favorites with a modern twist, such as crabmeat-encrusted halibut and The River House carrot cake. Live entertainment Thu–Sat evenings and the first Sun afternoon of each month. Full bar. Serving dinner Tue–Sun. Sun brunch 11 am–2:30 pm. Closed Mon. 301 S.W. 3rd Ave., Fort Lauderdale, FL 33312. (954) 525-7661. Go to: www.wtle.com/10096. ***Brunch, Contemporary. $$$.***

Sage French Café ~ *Best French*

Chef/owner Laurent Tasic continues his world-renowned career as a restaurateur and culinary consultant with his Sage French Café in the Oakland Park neighborhood. From learning to cook in his Italian grandmother's kitchen to owning celebrated restaurants in Paris, Monaco and the French Antilles, Tasic brings a wealth of experience to his latest Fort Lauderdale venture. In a country-bistro atmosphere, Sage French Café offers a reasonably priced menu of provincial French cuisine classics such as escargots and coq au vin. Sunday brunch (11 am–4 pm) features complimentary mimosas. Beer and wine available. Serving lunch and dinner daily. 2378 N. Federal Hwy., Fort Lauderdale, FL 33305. (954) 565-2299. Go to: www.wtle.com/10644. ***Brunch, French. $$.***

Southport Raw Bar ~ *Best Oysters*

Southport Raw Bar has remained a Fort Lauderdale staple for more than 30 years. This wildly popular watering hole and equally cheap seafood shack is the kind of place with many deep-rooted traditions held sacred by its loyal patronage. From ceiling tiles painted with neighborhood businesses' advertisements to friends splitting pitchers of beer and buckets of oysters on the waterfront patio, Southport's character is as much a star attraction as its classic seafood and drink specials. Beer and wine available. Serving lunch and dinner daily. 1536 Cordova Rd., Fort Lauderdale, FL 33316. (954) 525-2526. Go to: www.wtle.com/11322. ***Oysters, Seafood. $.***

Sushi Blues Cafe and Blue Monk Lounge ~ *Best Japanese/Sushi*

Restaurant proprietor and saxophone enthusiast Kenny Millions struck an eternal match (that of sushi and blues) with his original concept Sushi Blues Cafe, the oft-imitated Japanese eatery and music venue. Now considered a downtown Hollywood institution, Sushi Blues moved to Harrison Street in 2003 to accommodate the continually growing number of patrons who love the world-class cuisine and live music. When not jamming to blues Thursday through Saturday evenings, patrons enjoy a first-rate menu of nouveau Japanese dinners and artisanal sushi rolls such as the Dancing Eel and the Blues Roll. Drink choices include signature martinis and an extensive list of sakes and wines. Serving lunch Mon–Fri, dinner nightly. 2009 Harrison St., Hollywood, FL 33020. (954) 929-9560. Go to: www.wtle.com/10879. ***Japanese/Sushi. $$.***

FORT WORTH
TEXAS

10 LOCAL FAVORITES

Tantalizing Tex-Mex, big burgers and even bigger steaks dominate the Fort Worth dining scene, but even vegetarians won't leave the table unsatisfied.

Fort Worth Live Stock Exchange

Blue Mesa Grill ~ *Best Southwestern*

Spicy Southwestern fare, an award-winning happy hour with blue margaritas and free quesadillas, and Sunday brunch are a few of the attractions at Blue Mesa Grill. Meals begin with a complimentary basket of the restaurant's signature crunchy sweet potato chips, known for their delightfully addictive powers. When you order the "Chef Tacos for a Cause" entrée, $1 per taco goes to local charities. Otherwise, help yourself to Blue Mesa's other unique and fresh dishes, such as Texas Toothpicks (saucy meat and veggie skewers) or Adobe Pie (spicy chicken and peppers baked in a corn masa crust). The Sunday brunch buffet (10 am–2 pm), featuring unlimited champagne and mimosas, has been voted Best Brunch by both the *Fort Worth Star-Telegram* and *Fort Worth Weekly*. Full bar. Serving lunch and dinner daily. 1600 S. University Dr., Fort Worth, TX 76107. (817) 332-6372. Multiple locations. Go to: www.wtle.com/9273. ***Brunch, Southwestern. $$.***

Café Ashton

The six-story Italianate Ashton Hotel, which houses the resplendent Café Ashton, sits just a block away from downtown

Fort Worth's bustling Sundance Square shopping district. The restaurant's renovated interior offers a sophisticated ambiance for enjoying the award-winning bistro cuisine. The creative menu boasts a range of first-class dishes, such as pan-seared mozzarella, cold duck salad with goat cheese soufflé, and marinated pork tenderloin. The Oreo cheesecake is a favorite dessert. Afternoon tea is available Wednesday through Saturday, with reservations required one day in advance. Full bar. Serving breakfast, lunch and dinner daily. 610 Main St., Fort Worth, TX 76102. (817) 332-0100. Go to: www.wtle.com/8641. ***Breakfast, Contemporary, Hotel Restaurant. $$$.***

Cafe Aspen ~ *Best Contemporary*

When founder David Rotman opened Cafe Aspen more than 17 years ago, he knew little about food but plenty about customer service. His service savvy, coupled with his talented kitchen staff's ability to turn out fantastic American contemporary cuisine with a Mediterranean influence, has propelled this upscale but casual eatery to the top of local diners' lists. This Fort Worth fixture aims to please even the pickiest patrons, with the kitchen gladly accommodating personal tastes. At the tranquil bar in the back, low music and a full, ever-changing menu provide a haven for locals seeking a romantic evening. The year-round outdoor courtyard also provides a perfect setting to enjoy a leisurely meal. Chicken-fried lobster fingers and bourbon buttermilk fudge cake are two examples of the Cafe Aspen classics. Full bar. Serving lunch Mon–Fri, dinner Mon–Sat. Closed Sun. 6103 Camp Bowie Blvd., Fort Worth, TX 76116. (817) 738-0838. Go to: www.wtle.com/8591. ***Contemporary. $$$.***

Del Frisco's Double Eagle Steak House ~ *Best Steak House*

Situated in a turn-of-the-20th-century building said to have once been a brothel, Del Frisco's Double Eagle Steak House in Fort Worth today serves as an upscale steak house affiliated with the esteemed Lone Star Steakhouse chain. Traditional supper club décor paired with a quick staff — who can always adjust the pace if you'd rather linger — make for a first-class experience similar to that of the renowned national chains. But the restaurant's Texas roots make sure it sticks to Lone Star State values, such as monster-sized portions, generous sides and occasional Southwestern flavors dispersed among steak house staples (filet, rib eye, etc.). All desserts are made fresh daily. Full bar. Serving dinner nightly. 812 Main St., Fort Worth, TX 76102. (817) 877-3999. Go to: www.wtle.com/9316. ***Steak House. $$$.***

Joe T. Garcia's ~ *Best Mexican*

Opened in 1935 as a 16-seater, Fort Worth institution Joe T. Garcia's has expanded over the years into a labyrinth of outdoor dining areas that span an entire block. The restaurant's seven bars and fiesta gardens can seat up to 1,000. Enjoy the pool and cabana, or dine amidst greenery and Mexican pottery near the fountain on the patio. The surprisingly simple menu — a family sample platter, or beef or chicken fajitas for dinner, with a handful of additional à la carte favorites during lunch — lacks nothing when it comes to flavor. Weekend brunches (11 am–3 pm) feature tasty egg dishes served with Southwestern flair and perhaps the best red salsa in town. Reservations accepted for parties of 20 or more. Full bar. Cash only. Serving lunch and dinner daily. 2201 N. Commerce St., Fort Worth, TX 76106. (817) 626-4356. Go to: www.wtle.com/8871. ***Brunch, Mexican, Southwestern. $$.***

Kincaid's Hamburgers ~ *Best Burgers*

This favorite neighborhood hamburger joint built a loyal following in the mid-1960s when the Charles Kincaid Grocery and Market's butcher, O.R. Gentry, acquired the business and began grinding choice beef scraps and making hamburgers for hungry high schoolers. Today, with a few picnic tables up front and old grocery shelves cut down to make stand-up eating counters, this eatery is strictly self-service with no frills. Place your order at the counter for a half-pound, lean-but-juicy grilled chuck burger with all the traditional fixings, plus bacon or chili if you desire. Once your name is called, make sure you use two hands to eat your massive burger. (Hint: Use the white paper bag to catch any drippings.) Beer available. Cash only. Serving lunch and early dinner Mon–Sat. Closed Sun. 4901 Camp Bowie Blvd., Fort Worth, TX 76107. (817) 732-2881. Go to: www.wtle.com/8613. ***Burgers, Diner. $.***

Mi Cocina ~ *Best Tex-Mex*

Michael "Mico" Rodriguez, his wife Carolina and three business partners opened the first 12-table Mi Cocina restaurant in Dallas in 1991. By 1998, the partners had expanded what had become the popular local chain of eateries into the well-respected M Crowd Restaurant Group, made up of casual, fine-dining and other restaurant concepts. Flagship venture Mi Cocina offers nearly 20 locations with unique décor inspired by the surrounding neighborhoods, each specializing in Tex-Mex dishes as well as traditional Mexican fare. Several egg dishes are served all day as well, including huevos con chorizo (sautéed eggs with house-made Mexican sausage and fried potatoes). Full bar. Serving lunch and dinner daily. 509 Main St., Fort Worth, TX 76102. (817) 877-3600. Multiple locations. Go to: www.wtle.com/8820. ***Tex-Mex. $$.***

Saint-Emilion ~ *Best French*
This unassuming cottage is home to one of the most romantic restaurants in the area, where diners often linger for hours over country French food that has inspired a loyal following since 1985. This dinner-only restaurant offers a four-course, prix fixe meal; a regular menu of provincial seafood, beef and game dishes; and a list of daily specials highlighting Saint-Emilion's expertise with seafood. French classics such as roast duck, Dover sole, escargot, steak tartare and crème brûlée are featured. Reservations required. Full bar. Serving dinner Tue–Sat. Closed Sun–Mon. 3617 W. 7th St., Fort Worth, TX 76107. (817) 737-2781. Go to: www.wtle.com/8596. ***Continental, French. $$$.***

Sardines Ristorante Italiano ~ *Best Italian*
Three generations of the Matarese family have been serving traditional southern Italian fare at Sardines Ristorante Italiano since it opened in 1978. When the restaurant moved to University Boulevard in 2001, it brought along its trademark jazz bar ambiance. Whether you're popping the question or simply satisfying your craving for lasagna, prepare to be pampered. Start with an antipasto of assorted meats, cheeses and marinated vegetables, followed by one of the superb house-made pasta dishes with a tantalizing sauce for your main course. For dessert, try a slice of cappuccino pie or Italian ice cream. Live jazz begins at 7 pm nightly. Full bar. Serving lunch Mon–Fri, dinner Mon–Sat. Closed Sun. 509 University Dr., Fort Worth, TX 76107. (817) 332-9937. Go to: www.wtle.com/8773. ***Italian. $$.***

Spiral Diner & Bakery ~ *Best Vegetarian*
Despite being located in the heart of cattle country, the superlative Spiral Diner & Bakery is proudly all vegan, all the time. Proprietor and vegan Amy McNutt opened the eatery in 2002 when she was just 22 years old and moved to a much bigger site on the Southside's Magnolia Avenue in 2004. The extensive menu offers neither meat nor foods containing eggs, honey or dairy. But you won't miss them a bit. Highlights include an array of salads, wraps and entrées ranging from red coconut curry noodles to spaghetti with soy meatballs. For your sweet tooth, Spiral serves pies, cakes and cookies, along with sundaes and fruit shakes. A Dallas location opened in late February 2008. Beer and wine available, including organic varieties. Serving lunch and dinner Tue–Sun. Closed Mon. 1314 W. Magnolia Ave., Fort Worth, TX 76104. (817) 332-8834. Go to: www.wtle.com/6359. ***Bakery, Café, Vegetarian. $.***

HONOLULU
HAWAII

10 LOCAL FAVORITES

Hawaiian cuisine reaches its zenith *with local dining icon Alan Wong's nationally renowned restaurant, but you'll also delight in the grab-and-go style of French-Vietnamese sandwich shops, shrimp trucks and the Portuguese donuts called* malasadas.

12th Ave Grill ~ *Best Contemporary*

Responding to the Islands' lamentable lack of upscale-casual contemporary restaurants so commonplace on the mainland, veteran Honolulu caterer Kevin Hanney opened the quaint 12th Ave Grill on a Kaimuki back street in 2004. Merging European tradition with American modernity — or is it European modernity with American tradition? — the tiny neighborhood brasserie offers cuisine such as skate and New Zealand-farmed organic salmon in the form of down-home comfort food. Making good use of the kitchen's smoker, the small menu rarely misfires on such creations as apple chutney pork chops or the freshly prepared fish of the day. An in-house pastry chef turns out seasonal fruit crisps nightly. Full bar. Serving dinner Mon–Sat. Closed Sun. 1145 12th Ave., Honolulu, HI 96816. (808) 732-9469. Go to: www.wtle.com/11789. ***Contemporary, Dessert. $$.***

Alan Wong's Restaurant ~ *Best Hawaiian Regional*

Local dining icon Alan Wong has achieved an almost cult-like following among foodies across the Islands, and throughout the nation for that matter. A James Beard award-winning chef and leading pioneer of the Hawaiian cuisine movement in the 1990s, this mild-mannered culinary master has earned his reputation through zealous dedication to his four restaurants. His Honolulu flagship bears more than just his name: Alan Wong's is loaded with accolades, including being named No. 8 on *Gourmet* magazine's America's Top 50 Restaurants list. His Japanese- and American-influenced Hawaiian cuisine is laden with personality, from ginger onaga to coconut-crusted lamb chops. Try the nightly five- or seven-course tasting menus, complete with wine pairings, for a sampling of Wong's best. And who can't make room for five spoonfuls of crème brûlée in assorted flavors? Full bar. Serving dinner nightly. 1857 S. King St., Honolulu, HI 96826. (808) 949-2526. Go to: www.wtle.com/12069. ***Dessert, Hawaiian Regional. $$$.***

Ba-Le Sandwich Shop ~ *Best Vietnamese*

When Thanh Quoc Lam boarded a boat leaving Vietnam for a Malaysian refugee camp in 1979, he possessed little more than a small sum of money and a very limited knowledge of English. Now in his grasp is Ba-Le Sandwiches & Bakery, the largest purveyor of baked goods to airlines, hotels, supermarkets and restaurants in Hawaii. He also oversees more than two dozen neighborhood sandwich shops across the state, fusing the cuisines of France and Vietnam to produce a casual menu of sandwiches, appetizers, noodle dishes and other traditional Asian entrées. The standouts are the stellar sandwiches (crusty rolls stuffed with barbecued meats, tofus, pickled vegetables and flavorful sauces). No alcohol available. Serving lunch and dinner daily. 801 Alakea St., Honolulu, HI 96813. (808) 521-3973. Multiple locations. Go to: www.wtle.com/21211. ***Subs/Hoagies/Po-boys, Vietnamese. $.***

Giovanni's Original White Shrimp Truck ~ *Best Shrimp Truck*

Quite a ways from the white tablecloths of resort-saturated Waikiki, Oahu's North Shore upholds an equally important Hawaiian dining tradition: shrimp-themed plate lunches sold from various vans parked off of area beaches. Possibly the most famous among them, Giovanni's Original White Shrimp Truck appears as little more than a beat-up, graffiti-covered van off Kamehameha Highway. (You can find it settled near the sugar mill, more or less.) The half-dozen or dozen prawns dripping in sauce — garlic, lemon butter, or hot and spicy — are accompanied by two scoops of rice and a lemon, making it the ideal pre- or post-beach meal. No alcohol available. Serving lunch and early dinner daily. Kamehameha Hwy., Kahuku, HI 96731. (808) 293-1839. Go to: www.wtle.com/20134. ***Seafood, Shrimp Truck. $$.***

Hoku's

Consistently ranked as one of Hawaii's top restaurants, Hoku's brings glamorous dining to the highly acclaimed Kahala Hotel

& Resort. The elaborate design of this classy, contemporary eatery, with lush tropical lagoons of exotic fish and dolphins, fits its sophisticated menu. The delicate fusion of contemporary Hawaiian cuisine and Continental flavors pays particular homage to the Pacific Rim and Europe, but a glance into the open kitchen will show an eclectic mix of international cooking faculties. The kiawe-wood grill, tandoori oven and open-flame woks turn out creative entrées, from prime cuts of beef and lamb to crisp whole island fish. Full bar. Serving dinner nightly. Sun brunch 10:30 am–2 pm. 5000 Kahala Ave., Honolulu, HI 96816. (808) 739-8780. Go to: www.wtle.com/12485. ***Asian Fusion, Brunch, Contemporary, Hotel Restaurant. $$$.***

Hy's Steak House ~ *Best Steak House*

Originally a part of the Canadian-owned chain, Hy's Steak House of Honolulu maintains the excellent reputation of its former keeper through commitment to superior service, a sophisticated atmosphere and superlative fare. In addition to the live guitar Wednesday through Saturday nights, there's plenty to entertain you at Hy's: Tuxedo-clad waiters prepare traditional tableside dishes (Caesar salad, Châteaubriand and flambéed desserts), while a bustling team of chefs tends to the Broiler Room's centerpiece, a custom-made brass and copper cauldron of burning Hawaiian kiawe wood. Though each dish, from the lamb chops to the scallops, is broiled with the grill's flavor, the house-specialty, "The Only," a secret-sauced tender New York strip, is perhaps the paramount. Full bar. Serving dinner nightly. 2440 Kuhio Ave., Honolulu, HI 96815. (808) 922-5555. Go to: www.wtle.com/12680. ***Continental, Steak House. $$$.***

La Mer ~ *Best French*

Inspired by a refinement in classical French cuisine, yet paying homage to the mellow mindset of Hawaiian culture, La Mer restaurant in the elegant Halekulani hotel brings an unparalleled dining experience to the Honolulu community. AAA Five Diamond service and très haute cuisine — with an award-winning wine list, lavish cheese cart and a glass of complimentary champagne (the good stuff) to boot — come to a quintessentially Oahu setting, where the breeze from beautiful Waikiki Beach wafts through picturesque open-air vistas. The constantly evolving menu features the likes of escargot, caviar and skate, most often locally raised or caught directly off Hawaiian coasts but prepared in French style. Long-sleeved collared shirt or jacket required. Full bar. Serving dinner nightly. 2199 Kalia Rd., Honolulu, HI 96815. (808) 923-2311. Go to: www.wtle.com/12468. ***French, Hotel Restaurant. $$$.***

Leonard's Bakery ~ *Best Bakery*

You haven't done Hawaii if you haven't had a *malasada* (or several) from Leonard's Bakery. Fresh from the Kapahulu Avenue fryer come these light, fluffy and delicious burger-sized Portuguese donuts — now permanently ingrained in Island culture since being introduced by immigrant laborers in the late 1800s — covered in sugar and often filled with the likes of custard, chocolate, coconut and cinnamon. You'll find many a trademark white foam box open in the parking lot or on the way to nearby Waikiki beach, as Leonard's still-made-by-hand treats have become a morning, afternoon and evening tradition for tourists and locals alike, since 1952. No alcohol available. Serving from 6 am to late evening Mon–Sat. Closed Sun. 933 Kapahulu Ave., Honolulu, HI 96816. (808) 737-5591. Two locations. Go to: www.wtle.com/11843. ***Bakery, Breakfast, Dessert. $.***

Nick's Fishmarket ~ *Best Seafood*

Nestled in the lobby of the beautiful Waikiki Gateway Hotel is Honolulu institution Nick's Fishmarket. This serious seafood house invokes Chicago steak house romance with its dark and sophisticated setting, upscale fare and superior service. Salads are not to be missed, particularly the signature seafood salad with plump shrimp and a creamy spinach dressing. Fresh entrée catches hail from their specialty ports across the globe, from Alaskan king crab legs and Maine lobster to Norwegian salmon and Brazilian spiny lobster tail. Live entertainment in the cocktail lounge on the weekends draws an after-dinner crowd with its pseudo-nightclub scene. Weekly club event Sat. Full bar. Serving dinner Sun–Fri. 2070 Kalakaua Ave., Honolulu, HI 96815. (808) 955-6333. Go to: www.wtle.com/12669. ***Oysters, Seafood. $$$.***

Orchids ~ *Best Brunch*

When dining at the exquisite Halekulani hotel, request a table on the beachside patio of Orchids restaurant to enjoy the breathtaking panorama of Diamond Head along with your fantastic meal. Selections for one of Oahu's most acclaimed Sunday brunches (9:30 am–2:30 pm) change based on seasonal produce and the day's fresh catches, with almost 200 varieties of hot and cold entrées, sushi and sashimi, and island-inspired seafood. During the week, traditional American breakfasts come with an exceptional selection of teas and freshly squeezed juices. Salads, soups and sandwiches round out the lunch menu, while it's the seafood curries and steamed snapper dishes, in particular, that shine during dinner. Full bar. Serving breakfast and lunch Mon–Sat, dinner nightly. Sun brunch. 2199 Kalia Rd., Honolulu, HI 96815. (808) 923-2311. Go to: www.wtle.com/11906. ***Breakfast, Brunch, Contemporary, Hotel Restaurant, Seafood. $$$.***

HOUSTON TEXAS

10 LOCAL FAVORITES

***While justifiably proud — as only Texans can be —** of their stellar Mexican, Tex-Mex and beef (steak, burgers and barbecue), Houston boasts some of the nation's very best contemporary restaurants.*

Becks Prime ~ *Best Burgers*

For those who love the drive-through convenience of fast food but desire a nicer experience with better quality, Becks Prime is the answer. Each of the items on the diner-style menu is freshly prepared with choice ingredients; the service is friendly; and the restaurants are inviting. The juicy half-pound sirloin hamburgers are quite possibly the most popular in town. Try one of the hot plates, such as The Kitchen Sink (two beef patties with sautéed onions, bacon, etc.). The Parmesan crisps side — slices of Italian-style bread toasted with grated Parmesan cheese — makes a great accompaniment to any meal. Beer and wine available. Serving lunch and dinner daily. Memorial Park location also serving breakfast daily. 910 Travis St., Houston, TX 77002. (713) 659-6122. Multiple locations. Go to: www.wtle.com/14264. ***American Traditional, Burgers, Diner. $.***

Cafe Annie ~ *Best Contemporary*

Robert Del Grande, an originator and perpetual innovator of Southwestern cuisine, is the executive chef at one of Houston's — and Texas' — most highly regarded restaurants, Cafe Annie. Mexican flavors highlight many of the dishes, but the menu extends beyond locally popular food items and the bounty of the nearby Gulf for the best gourmet ingredients, including foie gras from Sonoma County and king salmon from the Pacific Northwest. The sweet plantain tamale with grilled pineapple is only one example of the creative desserts. The wine list and the service have long been considered some of the best in the area. A smaller, more casual menu is available at the full bar from 5:30 pm–11 pm Mon–Sat. Serving lunch Tue–Fri, dinner Mon–Sat. Closed Sun. 1728 Post Oak Blvd., Houston, TX 77056. (713) 840-1111. Go to: www.wtle.com/14514. ***Contemporary, Southwestern. $$$.***

Chez Nous ~ *Best French*

In 1984, chef/owner Gerard Brach opened his famed French restaurant in a former Pentecostal church in Humble, Texas, with every intention of moving it inside the loop once it became popular. Chez Nous soon gained such a devoted following (more so than the previous occupants) that relocating became unnecessary, as zealous Houstonians were more than happy to make the 20-minute trek to this suburb northeast of town. Decidedly romantic, yet cozy and rustic rather than overly formal, Chez Nous' décor is much like its menu: classic but not without charm and creative touches. Tried-and-true French favorites such as the charcuterie plate (duck mousse, pork rillettes and country pâté) and Châteaubriand Béarnaise for two are complemented by more adventurous daily specials that may include lamb moussaka or pan-seared grouper with mangoes, tomatoes, red onion, coconut and a black bean purée. Reservations suggested. Full bar. Serving dinner Mon–Sat. Closed Sun. 217 S. Avenue G, Humble, TX 77338. (281) 446-6717. Go to: www.wtle.com/22758. ***Continental, French. $$$.***

Churrascos ~ *Best Latin/South American*

The two boisterous but refined locations of this Latin American restaurant are among the most popular restaurants in Houston. Rooms have a chic, Latin ambiance with warm colors and earthy textures. The signature Churrasco steak, a tender and flavorful grilled tenderloin, is excellent. But other dishes, such as Key lime-sauced pork tenderloin and plantain-encrusted chicken, shine as well. The copious and complimentary plantain chips and the Argentine chimichurri sauce are hallmarks, as is Churrascos' luscious version of the *tres leches* cake, one of Houston's favorite desserts. Sunday brunch menus include eggs with chorizo and *torrejas* (the South American version of French toast), with specials on various cocktails and sangria. Full bar and South American-heavy wine list. Serving lunch and dinner daily. 9705

Westheimer Rd., Houston, TX 77042. (713) 952-1988. Two locations. Go to: www.wtle.com/14083. ***Brunch, Latin/South American. $$.***

Da Marco ~ *Best Italian*
Chef/owner Marco Wiles wanted to create a Houston restaurant that could be equally successful in Italy, and he succeeds with Da Marco, once named No. 29 on the America's Top 50 Restaurants list by *Gourmet* magazine. The cuisine is not just authentic, it's expertly prepared with the highest quality ingredients, both local and Italian. Very few concessions are made to the American palate, with dishes mostly inspired from the Friuli and Venezia regions of Italy. Try the fresh marinated anchovies or the Chianti-braised short ribs with risotto. The wine list is gloriously Italian with a great array of styles from a variety of regions. Beer also available. Serving lunch Tue–Fri, dinner Tue–Sat. Closed Sun–Mon. 1520 Westheimer Rd., Houston, TX 77006. (713) 807-8857. Go to: www.wtle.com/14623. ***Italian. $$$.***

Goode Co. Texas Bar-B-Q ~ *Best Barbecue*
The perfectly cooked meats and the excellent sides really separate this perennial award winner from the abundance of other quality local barbecue joints. The beef brisket is green mesquite-smoked for 18 hours, making it so moist, tender and delicious that knives and sauce are superfluous. Pair that with terrific Austin baked beans (cooked with apple pieces), excellent potato salad or flavorful jambalaya, and you've got a perfect Texas-barbecue meal. Freshly made buns and breads make for the best brisket sandwiches around. Don't miss the famous pecan pie. Beer and wine available. Serving lunch and dinner daily. 5109 Kirby Dr., Houston, TX 77098. (713) 522-2530. Two locations. Go to: www.wtle.com/14214. ***Barbecue. $.***

Hugo's ~ *Best Mexican*
Facing the bustle of lower Westheimer, Hugo's serves some of the very best Mexican food in Houston. The cuisine is regional Mexican, not Tex-Mex, so you'll find no chips and salsa here. But you can feast on the likes of lamb roasted in banana leaves and every kind of taco from pork to lobster. The plating is artful, and there is a lengthy wine list in addition to a wide array of tequilas. Hugo's also does Sunday brunch (11 am–3 pm) in fine fashion, with one of the best and more unique buffets, plus live music from the balcony above the dining room. Full bar. Serving lunch and dinner daily. 1600 Westheimer Rd., Houston, TX 77006. (713) 524-7744. Go to: www.wtle.com/14696. ***Brunch, Mexican. $$.***

Icon

Icon restaurant, formerly called BANK, one of downtown's favorite restaurants, still resides in its very attractive yet comfortable setting in the former lobby of a bank building, now the first floor of the Hotel Icon. The hotel itself might be one of the coolest (and getting cooler, as the hotel and restaurant revamp their looks) in the Houston area for visitors who want to take part in the Main Street club scene or just grab a drink at the hip upstairs Icon Bar. The restaurant maintains its focused and appealing menu featuring contemporary cuisine with French and Pan-Asian influences. Sweet-and-sour flavors are abundant, but several simply grilled meat and fish entrées for the less adventurous visitors round out the appealing choices. Past menus have included ribbons of tuna and seven-spice rack of lamb. Full bar. Serving breakfast and lunch daily, dinner Mon–Sat. 220 Main St., Houston, TX 77002. (832) 667-4470. Go to: www.wtle.com/15134. ***Breakfast, Contemporary, Hotel Restaurant. $$$.***

Mockingbird Bistro ~ *Best Bistro*

Veteran Houston restaurateur and chef John Sheely's Mockingbird Bistro is his most comfortable and satisfying venture yet, living up to all of its local and national press. Sheely first gained a reputation with seafood, which is prepared very well here, but about half of the menu is dedicated to meat — seared duck breast, steak frites and lamb, for example — to suit the tastes of his clientele. A well-chosen cheese plate and dessert wines provide an alternative or complement to rich desserts such as the luscious lemon tart. Full bar. Serving lunch Mon–Fri, dinner nightly. 1985 Welch St., Houston, TX 77019. (713) 533-0200. Go to: www.wtle.com/14078. ***Bistro, Contemporary, Wine Bar. $$.***

Pappas Bros. Steakhouse ~ *Best Steak House*

Pappas Bros. Steakhouse is the clear star and only DiRoNA winner among the multitude of Pappas-owned restaurants. The masculine and lively atmosphere is conducive to relaxing your inhibitions and truly enjoying the evening. Begin with bacon-wrapped scallops and move on to the signature turtle gumbo with sherry. The classics such as filet mignon, veal chop and lamb chops are all available. Service is chummy and Pappas-trademark efficient, while the wine list is one of the most extensive in the area. Jacket or tie suggested. Nightly piano music. Full bar. Serving dinner Mon–Sat. Closed Sun. 5839 Westheimer Rd., Houston, TX 77057. (713) 780-7352. Go to: www.wtle.com/15021. ***Steak House. $$$.***

INDIANAPOLIS
INDIANA

10 LOCAL FAVORITES

In keeping with its rib-sticking *Midwest heritage, Indianapolis' oldest restaurants remain some of its best, including The Rathskeller, Shapiro's Delicatessen and St. Elmo Steak House.*

Monument Circle

Café Patachou ~ *Best Breakfast*

Based on a nickname given during owner Martha Hoover's previous career as deputy prosecuting attorney, Café Patachou (cream puff, in French) offers some of Indy's favorite breakfasts. At each of these highly popular locations, French toast is made with flaky croissants; the cinnamon toast is thick and buttery; and the granola is full of plump cherries and almonds. The omelets are so good that *Bon Appétit* magazine mentioned them in its article, "Ten Favorite Places for Breakfast in the Nation." Breakfast is served all day, but there are light and healthy fresh sandwiches, soups and salads for lunch. The individual chocolate fondue is an especially indulgent dessert. No alcohol available. Serving breakfast and lunch daily. 8691 River Crossing Blvd., Indianapolis, IN 46240. (317) 815-0765. Multiple locations. Go to: www.wtle.com/2642. ***Breakfast, Brunch, Café. $.***

Elements ~ *Best Contemporary*

A bona fide smash hit since its fall 2003 opening in the trendy Massachusetts Avenue Arts District, Elements strips American contemporary gourmet dining down to its essence. The small, deftly lighted space features red walls and sparkling white linens, and during the warmer months, its intimate patio remains one of the most treasured dining spots in Indianapolis. Talented chef/owner and Indiana University grad Greg Hardesty apprenticed in renowned West Coast kitchens (including San Francisco's Rubicon) before returning to the Midwest. He melds Asian, French and Mediterranean influences, with each daily menu reflecting his obvious joy in creating a handful of simple, elegantly prepared dishes from the day's fresh market. When available, try the Indiana tomato salad. Bottled beer and attractively priced wine available. Serving dinner Tue–Sat. Closed Sun–Mon. 415 N. Alabama St., Indianapolis, IN 46204. (317) 634-8888. Go to: www.wtle.com/3403. ***Contemporary. $$$.***

India Garden ~ *Best Indian*

India Garden owner Darshan Mehra wants patrons to know that his Indianapolis restaurants are more than just places to eat: He believes that all people can share in the grace of God through the gift of food. The two India Garden locations offer tables of well-prepared northern Indian cuisine over which to share this harmony. From the widely varied lunch buffet to the rich, complexly spiced dinner entrées, the authentic curries, vindaloos and treats from the tandoori oven give diners plenty to rave about. Bottled beer at Broad Ripple. Serving lunch and dinner daily. N. Delaware St., Indianapolis, IN 46204. (317) 634-6060. Two Locations. Go to: www.wtle.com/3143. ***Indian. $$.***

Mama Carolla's Old Italian Restaurant ~ *Best Italian*

Occupying a 1920s Mediterranean-style home, Mama Carolla's Old Italian Restaurant is a little piece of the old country in the big city. Rambling, intimate rooms with stucco walls and soft lighting set a romantic mood that carries outside into the walled gardens and patio. Inspired by the ethnic neighborhood joints in their hometown of Omaha, owners Carole and Howard Leuer's menu doesn't veer far from the beaten path, but the basics are done well. Classic Italian fare, such as chicken rigatoni, can be spiced up or down according to preference. Try the cannoli for dessert. Full bar. Serving dinner Tue–Sat. Closed Sun–Mon. 1031 E. 54th St., Indianapolis, IN 46220. (317) 259-9412. Go to: www.wtle.com/3189. ***Italian. $$.***

Oakleys Bistro

Nationally respected chef/proprietor Steven J. Oakley began his culinary career at the age of 16 when he volunteered in kitchens near his hometown of Chicago just to learn the trade. He proceeded to work his way up the ranks at some of the country's most famous eateries, eventually earning a James Beard Foundation Rising Star Chef nomination. When he opened his Indianapolis venture in December 2002, Oakley hired talented people from some of the more prestigious restaurants across the United States, creating a staff that shares a sincere dedication to producing the best, most creative dishes for their appreciative clientele. Try the pork tenderloin, a favorite in these parts, or the duck breast with rock shrimp potato hash. Complimentary wine tastings Tuesday evenings. Full bar. Serving lunch and dinner Tue–Sat. Closed Sun–Mon. 1464 W. 86th St., Indianapolis, IN 46260. (317) 824-1231. Go to: www.wtle.com/3501. ***Contemporary. $$.***

The Rathskeller ~ *Best German*

Established in 1894, The Rathskeller is Indianapolis' oldest restaurant. Located in the basement of the historic Athenaeum Building, designed by author Kurt Vonnegut's grandfather as a German social club, it's still decidedly social, serving crowds of ale-and-brat lovers year-round. The restaurant takes up two floors, with a massive bar, banquet rooms and a biergarten, which features live music in warm months. Drinkers choose from an extensive selection of beers from Germany, Belgium and elsewhere, which pair nicely with flavorful jaegerschnitzel and other authentic German fare. Full bar. Serving lunch and dinner daily. 401 E. Michigan St., Indianapolis, IN 46204. (317) 636-0396. Go to: www.wtle.com/3062. ***German. $$.***

Sawasdee Thai Cuisine ~ *Best Thai*

Tiny and cozy Sawasdee Thai Cuisine welcomes all, from those with adventurous palates to those who are more hesitant when it comes to exotic food. Amiable owner Ty Chen greets patrons at the door and helps guide the unfamiliar through the menu, while his relatives oversee the preparation of the authentic Thai food in the kitchen. Their willingness to accommodate various tastes keeps Sawasdee consistently packed. (Most of the entrées can be made vegetarian and more, or less, spicy.) But if you're looking for the full Thai treatment, ask for your authentic entrée hot — with a side of ice water, just to be safe. Beer and wine available. Serving lunch Mon–Sat, dinner nightly. 1222 W. 86 St., Indianapolis, IN 46260. (317) 844-9451. Go to: www.wtle.com/3680. ***Thai. $.***

Shapiro's Delicatessen ~ *Best Deli*

In 1905, Russian immigrants Louis and Rebecca Shapiro

opened a tiny grocery in downtown Indy out of which they began to sell bottled beer when Prohibition ended in the early 1930s. Soon after, customers started asking for sandwiches to go with their drafts. As sandwich sales took off, tables were needed, and before long, the Shapiros had a full-fledged, somewhat-makeshift deli on their hands. Today, diners don't fuss about plastic tables and chairs — they come for the food. Each of the kosher kitchens serves some of the best corned beef sandwiches in the Midwest, and the latkes are equally famous. All food, from the matzo ball soup to the potato pancakes, is made daily on site. Beer available. Serving during breakfast, lunch and dinner hours daily. 808 S. Meridian St., Indianapolis, IN 46225. (317) 631-4041. Two locations. Go to: www.wtle.com/2376. ***Bagels, Breakfast, Deli. $.***

St. Elmo Steak House ~ *Best Steak House*
Operating from its street-corner location since 1902, Indianapolis landmark St. Elmo Steak House has stood the test of time by maintaining its classic menu and first-class service. The turn-of-the-century saloon décor has changed little, though veteran restaurateurs Stephen Huse and son Craig are now at the helm. Loyal patrons slice into top-notch standards, such as juicy prime rib and two-pound porterhouses. And with 20,000 bottles in the cellar, you should have no trouble finding the perfect wine to accompany your meal. Full bar. Serving dinner nightly. 127 S. Illinois St., Indianapolis, IN 46225. (317) 635-0636. Go to: www.wtle.com/3498. ***Steak House. $$$.***

Yats Restaurant ~ *Best Cajun/Creole*
With colorful beads, balls and lights draped everywhere, and mismatched furniture scattered inside and out, Yats provides a taste of Mardi Gras from its three Indianapolis locations. One of the most widely acclaimed restaurants in the city, Yats manages to feel homey and laid-back despite all the visual noise. A blackboard listing the day's offerings features all the N'awlins classics: Jambalayas, gumbos and étouffées are all available for the same fixed price, so the only tough decision is whether you want two entrées on your plate for a couple of extra bucks. Call ahead if you're looking for a particular dish, as Yats cooks up just a few selections each day. Luckily, the house favorite, chili-cheese étouffée, is always available. No alcohol available. Serving lunch and dinner daily. Massachusetts Avenue location closed Sun. 5363 N. College Ave., Indianapolis, IN 46220. (317) 253-8817. Multiple locations. Go to: www.wtle.com/2732. ***Cajun/Creole. $.***

JACKSONVILLE FLORIDA

10 LOCAL FAVORITES

***Besides its share of stellar contemporary restaurants**, a true Jacksonville dining experience is perhaps best exemplified by fried chicken from local treasure Beach Road Chicken Dinners or frog legs from Clark's Fish Camp.*

Main Street Bridge

bb's ~ *Best Contemporary*

A hit spin-off of the owners' flagship restaurant, bb's (as in Bistro Biscottis) is a loud and lively hot spot serving innovative American contemporary cooking in the San Marco neighborhood. The menus change daily, emphasizing fresh seafood and produce, and portions are substantial. Tempting entrées have included sea salt- and herb-crusted chicken and prosciutto-wrapped pork chop stuffed with mozzarella and spinach. Smaller plates and appetizers have included tuna tartare, Thai rock shrimp lollipops, crispy crab cake sandwiches and grilled flatbread stuffed with Brie and vegetables. Beer and wine available. Serving lunch and dinner Mon–Sat. Closed Sun. 1019 Hendricks Ave., Jacksonville, FL 32207. (904) 306-0100. Go to: www.wtle.com/10384. ***Bistro, Contemporary. $$.***

Beach Road Chicken Dinners ~ *Best Fried Chicken, Best Home-style*

En route to one of the very best fried chicken dinners in Jacksonville, if not the universe, keep in mind that what was once the only road to the area's beaches — aptly named Beach Road — is now known as Atlantic Boulevard. But the restaurant, a local treasure since 1939, has kept its name. Indeed, good luck prying the creamed peas recipe from one of the veteran waitresses. Even if they were so inclined, they're usually far too busy for much chit-chat, what with about 500 four-piece chicken dinners being sold each and every Sunday. Sides of mashed potatoes, fries or rice, gravy, coleslaw, and those aforementioned peas are served family-style in big bowls. No alcohol available. Serving lunch Sun, dinner Tue–Sun. Closed Mon. 4132 Atlantic Blvd., Jacksonville, FL 32207. (904) 398-7980. Go to: www.wtle.com/12107. ***Fried Chicken, Home-style. $$.***

Biscottis ~ *Best Brunch*
Jacksonville restaurateurs Barbara Sutton and Karin Tucker's first foray has been a smashing success. An inviting, richly decorated American contemporary restaurant amid Avondale's upscale boutiques and shops, Biscottis attracts crowds with its lighter fare, such as the signature mozzarella bruschetta, gourmet pizzas and sandwiches. Dinner specialties may include paprika-dusted flounder or beef tenderloin over wasabi potato purée. The restaurant especially shines during its popular Saturday and Sunday brunches (8 am–3 pm), featuring a variety of omelets and breakfast pizzas on Saturday, and vanilla waffles with fresh berries or the breakfast burrito with smoked cheddar grits on Sunday. Beer and wine available. Serving lunch and dinner daily. 3556 St. Johns Ave., Jacksonville, FL 32205. (904) 387-2060. Go to: www.wtle.com/10388. ***Brunch, Contemporary. $$.***

Bistro Aix ~ *Best French*
You'll be able to spot Bistro Aix (pronounced as the letter "x") executive chef and managing partner Tom Gray by his signature black beret, the perfect cranial accoutrement to wear in this expert rendition of a bustling bistro in the south of France. The Jacksonville native, a Culinary Institute of America grad, joined with partners in 1999 to open this attractive and hugely popular eatery in the historic San Marco district. The French and Mediterranean-dominated cuisine includes classic bistro options such as mussels, wood-fired pizzas and steak frites. The oak-fired fish "Aixoise," with artichokes and carrots, is a local favorite. Finish with Belgian chocolate cake and, *voilà*! Full bar. Serving lunch Mon–Fri, dinner nightly. 1440 San Marco Blvd., Jacksonville, FL 32207. (904) 398-1949. Go to: www.wtle.com/11035. ***Bistro, French. $$$.***

Blue Bamboo ~ *Best Asian Fusion*
From its blue and red neon-accented motif to its innovative menu, Asian Fusion relative-newcomer Blue Bamboo has wowed the public and local media since its 2005 opening. Chef/owner Dennis Chan is a grandson of the Eng family, notable purveyors

of Chinese fare in over 10 Jacksonville restaurants over the years, but Chan's cuisine redefines the classics with contemporary flair. The sizable sushi menu is divided into categories: earth sushi (avocado roll or garlic spinach roll), water sushi (sweet chile salmon roll or spicy tuna roll) and fire sushi (Peking duck roll or calamari roll). Entrées include coconut-lemongrass crab cakes, crispy orange duck and miso-glazed salmon. Beer, wine and sake available. Serving lunch Mon–Fri, dinner Mon–Sat. Closed Sun. 3820 Southside Blvd., Jacksonville, FL 32216. (904) 646-1478. Go to: www.wtle.com/10269. ***Asian Fusion, Japanese/Sushi. $$.***

Clark's Fish Camp ~ *Best Seafood*

A Jacksonville dining tradition for 30 years boasting one of the area's largest menus, Clark's Fish Camp in Mandarin overflows with rustic Americana ambiance and crowd-pleasing cuisine. An array of stuffed wild animals — bears, leopards and the like — crowds the lengthy bar almost as much as the actual patrons do. As you'd expect, seafood shines here: crab and shrimp of all sorts, oysters steamed in garlic butter, and frog legs, to name a few. For those on gastronomic safari, there are plenty of exotic choices, from mildly to definitely so: quail, rabbit, fried alligator and turtle, smoked eel, and fried or charred ostrich, kangaroo, venison, buffalo, antelope and rattlesnake. And yes, a number of them taste like chicken. Full bar. Serving lunch Sat–Sun, dinner nightly. 12903 Hood Landing Rd., Jacksonville, FL 32258. (904) 268-3474. Go to: www.wtle.com/12082. ***Seafood. $$.***

Havana-Jax Cafe ~ *Best Cuban*

Jacksonville's unsurpassed Cuban restaurant is actually owned and operated by a Nicaraguan named Silvia Pulido, a vivacious and seemingly tireless mother of four. Her Havana-Jax Cafe and adjoining Cuba Libre Bar have helped spark the local dining and drinking scene since the mid-1990s. Indulge in fried plantains and the Caribbean salad, Cuban sandwiches, and entrées such as marinated roast pork, grouper filet with mango salsa, and churrasco (a charbroiled steak with chimichurri sauce). Finish off your evening in the adjacent lounge with a refreshing mojito or some free salsa lessons — the Latin dance, not the beloved condiment — on weekends. Full bar. Serving lunch and dinner Mon–Sat. Closed Sun. 2578 Atlantic Blvd., Jacksonville, FL 32207. (904) 399-0609. Go to: www.wtle.com/10986. ***Caribbean/Tropical, Cuban. $$.***

Matthew's Restaurant

Since opening in 1997, Matthew's has been the standard-bearer for gourmet cuisine in Jacksonville. The dining room, a converted 1920s bank, creates a suave atmosphere with its earthy tones and inlaid bronze. Deposit yourself at the granite bar to witness the inner workings — or organized chaos — of the kitchen, or dine in style around the fountain on the outdoor patio. Matthew Medure, probably the most recognizable chef in Jacksonville, displays his adept fusion of Mediterranean, Middle Eastern, Asian and Southern traditions in such dishes as seared foie gras with Vidalia onion confit and marmalade, mushroom-dusted venison loin, and Maine lobster on angel hair pasta with lemon butter and asparagus. Beer and wine available. Serving lunch and dinner Mon–Sat. Closed Sun. 2107 Hendricks Ave. Jacksonville, FL 32207. (904) 396-9922. Go to: www.wtle.com/10229. ***Contemporary. $$$.***

The Tree Steak House ~ *Best Steak House*

Providing a sanctuary for diners with carnivorous appetites since 1969, The Tree Steak House has a distinct character and charm that won't be found at any chain. At this cozy supper club (complete with a piano bar in the lounge), the most popular steak is the legendary rib eye, which is brought whole to the table and cut to your specifications. The massive porterhouse and tender, slow-cooked prime rib are stand-out options as well. Seafood appears in creative ways, from the Creole fried shrimp appetizer to the cashew-crusted grouper. Each entrée includes a choice of baked potato, steak fries or rice pilaf, and unlimited trips to the signature salad bar. Try the candy bar crunch cheesecake if you have room. Full bar. Serving dinner nightly. 11362 San Jose Blvd., Jacksonville, FL 32223. (904) 262-0006. Go to: www.wtle.com/10261. ***Steak House. $$.***

Wine Cellar

Located on downtown's Southbank and founded in 1974, the Wine Cellar is one of Jacksonville's original fine-dining establishments. Exposed wooden ceiling beams and brick walls with arched windows create a relaxed and subtly elegant dining room, while a brick-paved garden allows for pleasant outdoor dining. Though the Wine Cellar earned its reputation because of its classic Continental cuisine, the menu now reflects more global influences and contemporary touches. Begin with bread crumb-encrusted asparagus, deep-fried and topped with Béarnaise sauce and lump crabmeat. Noted entrées include roasted New Zealand rack of lamb and broiled lobster tail on wild mushroom risotto. The extensive wine list features over 250 bottles (so it's not just a clever name). Full bar. Serving lunch Tue–Fri, dinner Mon–Sat. Closed Sun. 1314 Prudential Dr., Jacksonville, FL 32207. (904) 398-8989. Go to: www.wtle.com/10248. ***Contemporary. $$$.***

KANSAS CITY MISSOURI

10 LOCAL FAVORITES

One of the nation's centers for fine beef and barbecue, *Kansas City now boasts a growing number of nationally acclaimed gourmet chefs. Then there's the pan-fried chicken at Stroud's. . . .*

1924 Main

Housed in the wonderfully restored, circa-1915 Rieger Hotel in the Crossroads Arts District, 1924 Main has taken Kansas City's restaurant scene by storm since its 2004 opening. Talented chef/owner and Missouri native Rob Dalzell and his staff consult local farmers, ranchers and fishmongers to ensure that they receive only the freshest available ingredients for use in their contemporary cuisine. The "spontaneously seasonal" menu is limited, but offers no shortage of imaginative dishes. Dalzell tweaks the bargain-priced, two-to-three-course offerings each month. Past entrée choices have included pan-seared halibut, braised short ribs with white beans, or cod in parchment with black mussels. Wine pairings available. Full bar. Serving lunch Tue–Fri, dinner Tue–Sat. Closed Sun–Mon. 1924 Main St., Kansas City, MO 64108. (816) 472-1924. Go to: www.wtle.com/11375. ***Contemporary. $$.***

The American Restaurant ~ *Best Contemporary*

J.C. Hall's legacy lives on in the myriad of sentiments expressed within the greeting cards created by his first company, Hallmark. His passion for dining, though, led him to found another lasting

Kansas City institution. Now in its third decade, The American Restaurant is still the city's most celebrated eatery, boasting a collection of awards for its food, wine, chef and even its architecture. Celina Tio (*Chef Magazine*'s 2005 Chef of the Year and winner of the 2007 Best Chef: Midwest award from the James Beard Foundation) changes her menu regularly, and guests will delight in dishes such as the apple-brined pork tenderloin or her signature lobster shepherd's pie, when available. Jacket required. Full bar. Serving lunch Mon–Fri, dinner Mon–Sat. Closed Sun. 200 E. 25th St., Kansas City, MO 64108. (816) 545-8001. Go to: www.wtle.com/11402. ***American Traditional, Contemporary. $$$.***

Bluestem

If it's any indication of their culinary prowess, husband-and-wife chefs/owners Colby and Megan Garrelts met while working at renowned four-star restaurant Tru in Chicago. After acquiring additional restaurant savvy in Las Vegas and Los Angeles, the two decided to bring big-city dining to his hometown. With Colby, one of *Food & Wine* magazine's Best New Chefs 2005, directing the seasonal dinner menus and Megan preparing some of the best desserts in the state, such as lemon meringue bar with saffron rhubarb jam and strawberry sherbet, the Garrelts push the boundaries of culinary artistry night after night at Bluestem. The intimate little bistro offers an adjacent wine lounge with many boutique wine choices. Sunday brunch (10:30 am–2:30 pm) often showcases Colby's proficiency with Mediterranean flavors. Full bar. Serving dinner Mon–Sat. Closed Sun. 900 Westport Rd., Kansas City, MO 64111. (816) 561-1101. Go to: www.wtle.com/11590. ***Brunch, Contemporary, French. $$$.***

Fiorella's Jack Stack Barbecue ~ *Best Barbecue*

In a city where barbecue is king, the reigning royal family is the Fiorella clan of Fiorella's Jack Stack Barbecue. Since the restaurant's humble beginnings in a storefront south of Kansas City in the 1950s, the Fiorella family has built a barbecue dynasty, with a handful of eateries serving an extensive menu of smoked meats, steaks and sandwiches. The crowning jewel is the Freight House location, where patio diners look out at Union Station. The open-pit, wood-burning ovens fire up at 5 am and burn for 12 hours to create that night's smoky, tender ribs, chicken, pork and beef. Full bar. Serving lunch and dinner daily. 4747 Wyandotte St., Kansas City, MO 64110. (816) 531-7427. Multiple locations. Go to: www.wtle.com/11421. ***Barbecue, Steak House. $$.***

Hereford House ~ *Best Steak House*

If you're looking for subtlety, you'll have to disregard the cowboy décor and the larger-than-life steer head jutting from the exterior wall of the Hereford House in Kansas City's Crossroads District. But you'll find it where it matters: in the delicate flavor of the top-choice, aged-to-perfection beef that has made this steak house a Kansas City standout since it opened in 1957. The menu is a reminder that you are in the heart of cattle country, with favorites such as steak Oscar and the signature 16-ounce Kansas City strip. Full bar. Serving lunch and dinner daily. No lunch on weekends at the Crossroads or Leawood locations. 2 E. 20th St., Kansas City, MO 64108. (816) 842-1080. Multiple locations. Go to: www.wtle.com/11729. ***American Traditional, Steak House. $$$.***

Le Fou Frog ~ *Best French*

As a first-time visitor to Le Fou Frog, you might think that you're lost as you drive east through the River Market into a desolate-looking industrial zone, only to come upon a low-slung cinder block building. But press on, and you'll fall under the spell set by owners Barbara and Mano Rafael and their kitschy yet romantic dining room. By the time you bite into your first mouthful of one of chef Mano's inventive takes on traditional dishes, you'll be ready to join the chorus of Kansas Citians singing the restaurant's praises. The numerous entrées (written on chalkboards) change daily, but the selection always includes creative seafood, steaks and game, ranging from pheasant or rabbit to exotic ostrich. Full bar. Serving dinner Tue–Sun. Closed Mon. 400 E. 5th St., Kansas City, MO 64106. (816) 474-6060. Go to: www.wtle.com/11588. ***Bistro, Dessert, French. $$$.***

Lidia's Kansas City ~ *Best Italian*

On her nationally televised show, Lidia Bastianich can be seen digging for truffles or chatting with fishermen across Italy. But she made a significant contribution to the specific dining scene of the American Midwest when she opened her Kansas City restaurant in 1998. Situated in an abandoned freight house, the décor ranks among the city's most stylish, with its two-story red-brick walls, a 20-foot slate fireplace and hand-blown chandeliers. Locals love the Pasta Tasting Trio and its fresh, seasonal first-course selections. Entrée highlights include the gnocchi with duck and bistecca alla Kansas City, a local interpretation of steak Florentine featuring a rosemary- and anchovy-seasoned grilled rib eye. Full bar. Serving lunch Mon–Fri, dinner nightly. Sat–Sun brunch 11 am–2 pm. 101 W. 22nd St., Kansas City, MO 64108. (816) 221-3722. Go to: www.wtle.com/11620. ***Brunch, Italian. $$$.***

The Peppercorn Duck Club ~ *Best Dessert*
Since opening in the Hyatt Regency Crown Center in 1980, The Peppercorn Duck Club has been Kansas City's go-to place for intimate special-occasion dining. You'll see the night's ducks roasting on the floor-to-ceiling copper rotisserie. Order this signature meat over a bed of wild rice, or indulge in a veal chop stuffed with herbs and goat cheese, or the pan-seared striped bass, when available. Keep in mind, though, that dinner at The Peppercorn is not over until you've visited the gleaming Ultra Chocolatta Bar and its staggering assortment of desserts, free with any entrée. Full bar. Serving lunch Thu–Fri, dinner Mon–Sat. Closed Sun. 2345 McGee St., Kansas City, MO 64108. (816) 435-4199. Go to: www.wtle.com/11391. ***American Traditional, Dessert, Hotel Restaurant. $$$.***

Stroud's Restaurant ~ *Best Home-style*
Named a Regional Classic by the James Beard Foundation, Stroud's has been serving some of the best mashed potatoes and pan-fried chicken that Kansas City families have ever licked off their fingers, since 1933. You'll probably have to wait for a table at this converted 10-room farmhouse in the Northland, but strolling through the landscaped grounds or listening to the live, old-time piano music is part of the fun. The specialty fried chicken and other entrées, such as pork chops and chicken-fried steak, are accompanied by a salad or house-made chicken soup with wide egg noodles; baked, mashed or deep-fried potatoes; and cinnamon rolls. Full bar. Serving lunch Fri–Sun, dinner nightly. 5410 N.E. Oak Ridge Rd., Kansas City, MO 64119. (816) 454-9600. Go to: www.wtle.com/11591. ***American Traditional, Fried Chicken, Home-style. $$.***

Thai Place ~ *Best Thai*
Thai Place began serving its fresh and fiery food in 1991 in an Overland Park strip mall and has since added several locations, including downtown's Arun Thai Place Grill. Seafood pad thai (with shrimp, scallops, mussels and crab) is the signature dish, but the other noodle and rice dishes — the pineapple fried rice with shrimp, for example — are stellar. There are also plenty of curries, stir-fries and vegetarian options from which to choose. Full bar. Serving lunch and dinner daily. Downtown location closed Sun. 4130 Pennsylvania Ave., Kansas City, MO 64111. (816) 753-8424. Multiple locations. Go to: www.wtle.com/11751. ***Thai. $$.***

LAS VEGAS NEVADA

10 LOCAL FAVORITES

***Not surprisingly, many of the most rewarding experiences** in Las Vegas — outside of cashing in at the blackjack table, of course — can be had at the excellent casino-based restaurants.*

The Bootlegger Bistro ~ *Best Italian*

Often overshadowed by the Strip's neon lights, longtime family-run favorite Bootlegger Bistro reopened on the South Strip in 2001 to zealous local applause. The round-the-clock Italian eatery may be more likely to seat Gladys Knight than Paris Hilton, but the mellow adult crowd prefers the classic nightly lounge acts and home-style Mediterranean eats to Vegas' dime-a-dozen "ultra lounges." Where else could you split generous portions of shrimp scampi while owner (and Nevada's former lieutenant governor) Lorraine Hunt performs, or feast on late-night steak and eggs while Monday night karaoke regulars are accompanied by their own personal musicians? Full bar. Open 24 hours daily. 7700 Las Vegas Blvd. S., Las Vegas, NV 89123. (702) 736-4939. Go to: www.wtle.com/7984. ***Breakfast, Italian, Pizza. $$.***

Bradley Ogden

As Celine Deon or Bette Midler emphatically belt out hits at the nearby Colosseum, San Francisco-area transplant Bradley Ogden prepares a different — much less glass-shattering — kind of show at his namesake Caesars Palace restaurant. The renowned chef's first dining venture outside of California has remained white-hot since its 2003 opening, when he and his Culinary Institute-grad son, Bryan, brought into the spotlight the farm-fresh and wine-central approach of their native state's cuisine. An excellent selection of bottles from California, Oregon and Washington, with international choices as well, complements contemporary American heartland cooking to the tune of hot and cold foie gras with kumquats, seared dayboat scallops in spring onion soup, and oak-grilled lamb rack with fava bean and cumin spatzle. Full bar. Serving dinner nightly. 3570 Las Vegas Blvd. S. (Caesars Palace), Las Vegas, NV 89109. (702) 731-7413. Go to: www.wtle.com/7763. ***Contemporary, Hotel Restaurant. $$$.***

The Buffet at Bellagio ~ *Best Buffet/Cafeteria*

As its opulent host hotel set a new standard among Strip resorts, The Buffet at Bellagio debuted in 1998, supplanting the popular $3.99 steak buffets of yesteryear with celebrity chef cooking. Long lines of hungry patrons ribbon out from the various live-action cooking stations, where upscale selections from around the globe are made to order. From shark steak and beef Wellington to sushi and many different wood-fired pizzas, The Buffet's gourmet selection encourages diners to take piling one's plate to the extreme, particularly when it comes to the lavish dessert display. Full bar. Serving breakfast and lunch Mon–Fri, dinner nightly. Sat–Sun champagne brunch (7 am–4 pm). 3600 Las Vegas Blvd. S. (Bellagio), Las Vegas, NV 89109. (702) 693-7111. Go to: www.wtle.com/7859. ***American Traditional, Breakfast, Brunch, Buffet/Cafeteria, Hotel Restaurant. $$$.***

Lotus of Siam ~ *Best Thai*

Widely considered one of North America's most outstanding Thai restaurants, Lotus of Siam ignites (quite literally) the passion of its loyal clientele with its incendiary dishes hailing from the northern Issan region. Be forewarned: The owners' family recipes, along with Chinese and Burmese influence, form an extensive menu of highly authentic dishes spicy enough to set Wayne Newton's coif aflame. Deep-fried whole catfish, grilled sour pork sausage and crispy mussel omelets can be offset, however, with a refreshing choice from the *Wine Spectator* award-winning wine list. The small selection of excellent house-made desserts helps to further cool flaming palates. Beer and wine available. Serving lunch Mon–Fri, dinner nightly. 953 E. Sahara Ave., Las Vegas, NV 89104. (702) 735-3033. Go to: www.wtle.com/8145. ***Thai. $$.***

Mon Ami Gabi ~ *Best French*

With a quintessentially Vegas, cosmopolitan twist, Chicago-based Lettuce Entertain You Enterprises combines Paris' laid-back sidewalk cafés with classic bistros in the *magnifique* Mon Ami Gabi. The DiRoNA award-winning restaurant, aptly located in the Paris hotel and casino, proves decidedly less over-the-top than many of its thematic Strip counterparts. Begin with a baguette and a Bordeaux, followed by an exceptional version of hanger steak, filet mignon au poivre or steamed mussels. Massive desserts should be shared, but trying to split plates of the addictive pommes frites may lead your group to the center boxing ring at Caesars Palace. Full bar. Serving lunch Mon–Fri, dinner nightly. Late-night Fri–Sat. Sat–Sun brunch 11 am–3:30 pm. 3655 Las Vegas Blvd. S. (Paris), Las Vegas, NV 89109. (702) 944-4224. Go to: www.wtle.com/7945. ***Bistro, Brunch, French, Hotel Restaurant, Steak House. $$.***

Omelet House ~ *Best Breakfast*

Omelet House isn't quite as bright, shiny and spectacular as much of Las Vegas Boulevard, but loyal local diners have a certain fondness for the forgivingly dim lighting of the multiple quaint locations. Many an early morning (after a late night) wouldn't be complete without a stop at one of these mom-and-pop eateries, where country cookin' plays out in chicken-fried steak and eggs, six-egg omelets, and apple- and cream cheese-stuffed French toast. Whether swinging in for a bowl of house-made chili or a slice of some of the world's best pumpkin bread, diners leave stuffed in that classic American breakfast kind of way. No alcohol available. Serving breakfast and lunch daily. 2160 W. Charleston Blvd., Las Vegas, NV 89102. (702) 384-6868. Multiple locations. Go to: www.wtle.com/7828. ***Breakfast. $.***

Osaka Japanese Bistro ~ *Best Japanese/Sushi*

The only restaurant outside of Japan to be named one of the 50 Best Japanese Restaurants by Japan's largest weekly magazine, *Shukan Asahi*, family-owned Osaka Japanese Bistro offers three disparate ways to enjoy the authentic cuisine from both its West Sahara and Green Valley locations. A sleek sushi bar, a traditional tatami room and a boisterous *teppanyaki* grill area each serve the same selection of expertly prepared sushi, sashimi, and rice and noodle dishes that have made this restaurant a favorite local stop since 1967. From steamed clams to chicken sizzled on the hibachi grill, the careful execution of each dish has made Osaka a consistent winner of local best-of awards year after year. Full bar. Serving lunch, dinner and late-night daily. 4205 W. Sahara Ave., Las Vegas, NV 89102. (702) 876-4988. Two locations. Go to: www.wtle.com/7995. ***Japanese/Sushi. $$.***

Peppermill Fireside Lounge and Coffee Shop ~ *Best Diner*

Retro, family-friendly diner by day and cozy rendezvous for canoodling couples by night, the iconic Peppermill Coffee Shop and adjoining

Fireside Lounge have set the scene for several Hollywood hits, including *CSI: Crime Scene Investigation*. Order from the 24-hour breakfast menu or the exotic martini list: The seeming incongruence of this Vegas classic doesn't bother the carefree clientele — particularly those snuggling in the dark booths — who seem to live by the motto, "What happens in Vegas, stays in Vegas." The kids sit quietly for a moment and lovebirds come up for air when high stacks of pancakes, enormous omelets or decadent versions of French toast arrive. Burgers, pastas and steaks round out the dinner menu, but a banana split with two whole bananas is a winner any time. Full bar. Open 24 hours daily. 2985 Las Vegas Blvd. S., Las Vegas, NV 89109. (702) 735-4177. Go to: www.wtle.com/7929. ***Breakfast, Diner. $$.***

Rosemary's Restaurant ~ *Best Contemporary*

A 20-minute drive from the Strip's big-name celebrity chefs and decreasingly syllabled mega-restaurants, Rosemary's Restaurant offers all the sophistication of the center-city establishments with a generous helping of neighborhood charm on the side. Husband-and-wife team Michael and Wendy Jordan may boast Emeril training, but their Southern-slanting menu of progressive American cuisine reflects a lifetime of their own personal experiences. Both wine and beer pairings appear alongside creative entrées, from grilled pork chops in Creole mustard reduction to Texas barbecue shrimp with Maytag blue cheese cole slaw. With both DiRoNA and *Wine Spectator* awards under its belt, Rosemary's proves an all-around foodie-must experience. Reservations suggested. Full bar. Serving lunch Mon–Fri, dinner nightly. 8125 W. Sahara Ave., Las Vegas, NV 89117. (702) 869-2251. Go to: www.wtle.com/7766. ***Contemporary, Small Plates. $$$.***

The Steak House at Circus Circus ~ *Best Steak House*

Despite its location in the highly animated, often frenzied Circus Circus Hotel and Casino, The Steak House makes no fun and games when it comes to top-quality beef and chops. The roars from the indoor amusement park and raucous laughter from the year-round big top show seem miles away from the restaurant's serene atmosphere, where romance steps into center ring among cozy, intimate booths. Local media consistently name it Vegas' top steak house for a reason: The meat is dry-aged in a wood- and glass-enclosed case for 21 days, then mesquite-grilled and charred around the edges to create a bold, smoky flavor. Full bar. Serving dinner nightly. Sun champagne brunch 9:30 am, 11:30 am and 1:30 pm seating times. 2880 Las Vegas Blvd. S. (Circus Circus), Las Vegas, NV 89109. (702) 794-3767. Go to: www.wtle.com/8136. ***Brunch, Hotel Restaurant, Steak House. $$$.***

LOS ANGELES CALIFORNIA

10 LOCAL FAVORITES

While Wolfgang Puck's Spago and CUT steak house *continue on the cutting edge of American cuisine, some of Los Angeles' most beloved restaurants include the more plebian Langer's Delicatessen and Roscoe's House of Chicken 'n' Waffles.*

Campanile

When chefs/founders Mark Peel and Nancy Silverton converted silent film legend Charlie Chaplin's intended office space into the comfortable Campanile in 1989, they scored an immediate and lasting hit with Los Angeles' finicky restaurant-going crowd. The combination of Peel on the Cal-Mediterranean menu and Silverton on the beignets, soufflés and pot de crèmes has been enough to earn numerous local and national distinctions over the years, including three stars from the *Los Angeles Times*, a DiRoNA Award of Excellence and enough James Beard Foundation nominations to sink a ship. Everything, from the seasonally apt ingredients to the freshly baked bread (hailing from next door's legendary La Brea Bakery), illustrates Campanile's staunch commitment to remaining one of LA's top spots for tried-and-true foodies. Full bar. Serving lunch Mon–Fri, dinner Mon–Sat. Sat–Sun brunch 9:30 am–1:30 pm. 624 S. La Brea Ave., Los Angeles, CA 90036. (323) 938-1447. Go to: www.wtle.com/24095. ***Brunch, Contemporary, Dessert. $$$.***

CUT ~ *Best Steak House*

Esquire magazine's one-time Restaurant of the Year, James Beard Foundation Best New Restaurant nominee, and otherwise major media darling since its 2006 opening, CUT has reaped enough attention to banish this not-so-hidden gem to eternal non-hipness. But Wolfgang Puck's sleek Beverly Hills steak house remains a cut above the rest, consistently plating the world's most exclusive beef from its award-winning digs in the sophisticated Beverly Wilshire hotel. The bold and beautiful clientele sip Hemingway Daiquiris and Lost in Translation martinis while feasting upon the likes of aged, Nebraska corn-fed rib eye, American Wagyu sirloin and the exceedingly elite Kobe beef, imported from a single purveyor in Japan at about $20 per ounce. Full bar. Serving dinner Mon–Sat. Closed Sun. 9500 Wilshire Blvd., Beverly Hills, CA 90212. (310) 275-8500. Go to: www.wtle.com/24233. ***Contemporary, Hotel Restaurant, Steak House. $$$.***

La Cachette ~ *Best French*

Perhaps off the beaten path but certainly dead-on the national culinary map, La Cachette — French for "hideaway" — offers an exceptional retreat from the bedlam of city life in its hidden alley off Little Santa Monica Boulevard. Area foodies input the address of this charming Century City eatery into their SUVs' internal GPS systems and buckle up for the discerning dining experience to come. The traditional-French-with-an-L.A.-twist menu translates conventionally heavy country dishes into a delicate selection of daily vegan soups, lightly creamed crab and lobster bisque, simply roasted rack of lamb, and lightly sautéed squab. But, purists, fear not: Steering away from the French ritual of robustness only means more room for decadent chocolate soufflé. Full bar. Serving lunch Mon–Fri, dinner nightly. 10506 Little Santa Monica Blvd., Century City, CA 90025. (310) 470-4992. Go to: www.wtle.com/24118. ***Dessert, French. $$$.***

La Terza ~ *Best Italian*

Angelenos know Gino Angelini — who first cooked the area's most authentic Italian food behind the stoves of Rex and Vincenti and then scored his own hit with Angelini Osteria — as the man who brings the soul of Italy to Los Angeles. But it is his exquisite La Terza that seems to hold the chef/owner's heart. From his post in West Hollywood, Angelini channels his homeland through seasonal menus of brilliantly simple, inspired dishes incorporating the best products California has to offer. Add pumpkin *tortelli* and grilled *branzino* to an exceptional wine list and desserts from the recipe box of Campanile's Nancy Silverton, and dial the travel agent to cancel that now-superfluous year-end trip to Tuscany. Full bar. Serving breakfast, lunch and dinner daily. 8384 W. 3rd St., West Hollywood, CA 90048. (323) 782-8384. Go to: www.wtle.com/24251. ***Breakfast, Italian. $$.***

Langer's Delicatessen ~ *Best Deli*

Declaring a favorite Los Angeles deli may be as dangerous as proclaiming love for the Giants in Dodger Stadium. You can say with certainty, however, that since 1947, Angelenos have flocked to Langer's somewhat precarious neighborhood — just west of downtown, across from MacArthur Park — for what many claim is the world's best pastrami sandwich. Even a scattering of New York's corned beef connoisseurs cede to the superior tender layers of sugar-cured and seasoned meat, while curbside service and a recently added subway stop on the Metro Red Line have helped everyone from downtown heavyweights to Hollywood's most elite nosh alongside their kosher-style-loving brethren. Beer and wine available. Serving breakfast and lunch Mon–Sat. Closed Sun. 704 S. Alvarado St., Los Angeles, CA 90057. (213) 483-8050. Go to: www.wtle.com/24110. ***Breakfast, Deli. $.***

Matsuhisa ~ *Best Japanese/Sushi*

Revered by all, from the local fish markets to the finest sushi houses in Tokyo, Nobu Matsuhisa truly embodies the word "master." His cutting-edge cuisine sets the global standard by infusing South American spices with Japanese flavors, while his dozen-plus eponymous restaurants worldwide are among the best in every town they populate. His original Beverly Hills outpost is no exception: When Matsuhisa is not there himself (though he often is), his deft staff carries on his superior legacy with top-notch sushi, "new-style" sashimi and other inspired takes on Japanese-fusion cuisine. Full bar. Serving lunch Mon–Fri, dinner nightly. 129 N. La Cienega Blvd., Beverly Hills, CA 90211. (310) 659-9639. Go to: www.wtle.com/24171. ***Japanese/Sushi. $$$.***

Porto's Bakery ~ *Best Bakery*

Locals follow their noses — or their particularly perceptive sweet teeth — north to Glendale's family-owned and -operated Porto's, the community's first stop for specialty cakes, decadent pastries and down-home Cuban cooking for nearly four decades. This quintessential neighborhood bakery easily rivals its Miami counterparts, packing in a loyal patronage who can't get enough of the fresh potato balls, ham croquettes and sweet Latin treats. Warning: Unpublished scientific studies show a direct correlation between further bites of cappuccino mousse cake and increasing political approval of the Castros. No alcohol available. Serving breakfast and lunch daily, dinner Mon–Sat. 315 N. Brand Blvd., Glendale, CA 91203. (818) 956-5996. Go to: www.wtle.com/24062. ***Bakery, Café, Cuban, Dessert. $$.***

Providence ~ *Best Seafood*

To the old Patina space comes another epic eatery, the labor of love of former Water Grill chef Michael Cimarusti and, according to local restaurant critic Jonathan Gold, "among the best restaurants to ever hit Los Angeles." Once billed as one of America's Top 50 Restaurants by *Gourmet* magazine, Providence aims sky-high with its simultaneously ambitious and focused seafood list of velvety fish, perfectly chilled Kumamoto oysters and New England-worthy "chowda." Find salvation from hectic L.A. in the serene, food-central atmosphere, where Cimarusti's celestial experimentations transport faithful gourmands to another realm entirely. Full bar. Serving lunch Fri, dinner nightly. 5955 Melrose Ave., Los Angeles, CA 90038. (323) 460-4170. Go to: www.wtle.com/24230. ***Contemporary, Dessert, Seafood. $$$.***

Roscoe's House of Chicken 'n Waffles ~ *Best Soul Food*

Fried chicken. Waffles. Two foods, neither for which L.A. is particularly known. But put them together, serve them for breakfast, and — trust us — they will come. In a city of macrobiotic diets and Hollywood thin, there is something soulful and unifying about Roscoe's House of Chicken 'n Waffles. No matter who you may or may not be on the social scene, most everyone is happy to wait in line (as is usually the case) for a plate piled high with genuine Los Angeles tradition. No alcohol available. Serving breakfast, lunch and dinner daily. 1514 N. Gower St., Hollywood, CA 90028. (323) 466-7453. Multiple locations. Go to: www.wtle.com/24142. ***Breakfast, Fried Chicken, Home-style, Soul Food. $.***

Spago ~ *Best Contemporary*

A known training ground for the country's rising-star chefs, a regularly distinguished honoree of DiRoNA and *Wine Spectator*, and uniquely boasting stellar reviews from infamously tough *Los Angeles Times* critic S. Irene Virbila, this Beverly Hills flagship of the renowned Wolfgang Puck Fine Dining Group remains the kind of restaurant that continually surpasses its lofty reputation. Night after night, James Beard award-winning chef Lee Hefter pushes the envelope of American cuisine for the droves of enraptured patrons primed to be pampered by *Gourmet* magazine's once-No. 4 pick for America's Top 50 Restaurants. Hefter's menu refuses to sit still, scouring the globe for such intensely palatable dishes as seared rare bigeye tuna with salsa *verde*, caramelized organic veal chop and Hong Kong-style Florida grouper. Try the tasting menu with wine pairings to savor Spago's full potential. Full bar. Serving lunch Mon–Sat, dinner nightly. 176 N. Canon Dr., Beverly Hills, CA 90210. (310) 385-0880. Go to: www.wtle.com/24097. ***Contemporary. $$$.***

MEMPHIS TENNESSEE

10 LOCAL FAVORITES

***Do you prefer your pork shoulder** chopped or pulled, your ribs served wet or dry? In this musical mecca of W.C. Handy, Booker T. and Elvis Presley, different culinary tunes still sound sweet.*

Alcenia's Desserts & Preserves Shop ~ *Best Soul Food*

Most chefs simply serve food, but effervescent proprietress B.J. Chester-Tamayo also dispenses legendary full-body hugs to patrons of Alcenia's Desserts & Preserves Shop, named for her mother. She gives a whole new meaning to "soul food," treating her entire operation as a therapeutic exercise. (She started the business in 1996 after the sudden death of her son.) The menu, divided into classic meat-and-three combinations, replicates the flavorful cuisine of Meridian, Miss., her hometown. Save room for the hot water cornbread, followed by one of B.J.'s signature desserts — think bread pudding, buttermilk pie or sweet potato pie. No alcohol available. Serving lunch and early dinner Tue–Fri, breakfast and lunch Sat. Closed Sun–Mon. 317 N. Main St., Memphis, TN 38103. (901) 523-0200. Go to: www.wtle.com/10741. ***Breakfast, Dessert, Home-style, Soul Food. $.***

Central BBQ ~ *Best Barbecue Sandwich*

Here in Memphis, the only topic more inflammatory than politics, religion or the current whereabouts of Elvis is barbecue. Longstanding purveyors such as Payne's, Cozy Corner, The Bar-B-Q Shop and the Germantown Commissary are all worthy contenders on the local scene, but in Midtown (and with a location on Summer Avenue), relative newcomer Central BBQ is winning over barbecue enthusiasts. Customers rave about the generous helpings of tender, slow-cooked meat piled high on buns and topped with, yep, coleslaw, all for only a few dollars a plate. Follow your nose to the tiny building with the red-and-white checked tin roof that's nestled, incongruously, on one of Memphis' antique rows. No need to dress up — customers are more concerned with turning around their baseball caps as to avoid interference with the ability to shovel in mouthful after delicious mouthful. Beer available. Serving lunch and dinner daily. 2249 Central Ave., Memphis, TN 38104. (901) 272-9377. Two locations. Go to: www.wtle.com/9847. ***Barbecue. $.***

Chez Philippe ~ *Best French*

Culture, sophistication and refined French-Asian cuisine have made downtown institution Chez Philippe one of the most celebrated restaurants in the South. The famous Peabody Hotel lobby, with its fountain full of ducks, is home to the beautiful and elegant restaurant — one of the few in the Mid-South to receive a Mobil Four-Star rating — where Reinaldo Alfonso holds the reins. Take a global culinary tour with one of Alfonso's special World Dinners, or order specialties such as the crisp lobster cigar with Thai chili sauce or venison loin with juniper berry sauce, caramelized cipollini onions and Roquefort puffs. Fabulous desserts include house-made ice creams and sorbets. Jacket required. Full bar with extensive wine list. Serving dinner Tue–Sat. Closed Sun–Mon. 149 Union Ave., Memphis, TN 38103. (901) 529-4000. Go to: www.wtle.com/10648. ***Asian Fusion, Contemporary, French, Hotel Restaurant. $$$.***

Folk's Folly Prime Steak House ~ *Best Steak House*

For the past three decades, Memphians with a hankering for a steak have headed to Folk's Folly, one of the bastions of business dining in Memphis. Enjoy live piano music with drinks and complimentary fried dill pickles, a Southern favorite, in the Cellar lounge, one of the most celebrated rooms in town. You can't go wrong ordering any of the prime cuts, particularly the Maker's Mark Medallions (seasoned filets with whiskey-peppercorn sauce), or, if you're not a red meat devotee, try the ultra-fresh seafood. Uber-traditional sides and unique adults-only treats, including a crème de menthe parfait and bread pudding drizzled with Bushmills Irish Whiskey sauce, round out your exceptional dining experience. Full bar. Serving dinner nightly. 551 S. Mendenhall Rd., Memphis, TN 38117. (901) 762-8200. Go to: www.wtle.com/11309. ***Steak House. $$$.***

Grill 83

Located in the posh Madison Hotel, Grill 83 has established itself as an urban hot spot for serious foodies. Not only does Memphis-born chef Clay Lichterman design creative seasonal dishes such as roasted roasted salmon Napoleon with wilted spinach, he also maintains a traditional offering of prime steaks, salads and fresh vegetables. The Kobe Beef Blues Burger is a signature lunch item, and an extensive breakfast menu is available daily. Grill 83 offers live music, a full bar and tapas on the Madison Hotel rooftop from early spring until fall. Full bar with extensive wine and spirits list. Serving breakfast, lunch and dinner daily. Sun brunch. 83 Madison Ave., Memphis, TN 38103. (901) 333-1224. Go to: www.wtle.com/10653. ***Breakfast, Brunch, Contemporary, Hotel Restaurant, Small Plates. $$$.***

Jim's Place East

With menus boasting signature dishes such as pecan-crusted catfish, Dimitri's grilled shrimp and Jim's Special Filet Mignon, venerable Jim's Place East remains one of Memphis' most popular dining destinations. It's also one of the city's most romantic, called the "sweetheart of East Memphis" after its downtown days when many newlyweds would stop in for steaks. Whether you've got love on your mind or you're closing a business deal, celebrating a special occasion or just plain hungry for well-prepared cuisine, Memphians will point you to this suburban retreat for a truly satisfying meal. Full bar with extensive wine list. Serving lunch Mon–Fri, dinner Mon–Sat. Closed Sun. 5560 Shelby Oaks Dr., Memphis, TN 38134. (901) 388-7200. Go to: www.wtle.com/10656. ***Greek, Seafood, Steak House. $$$.***

McEwen's on Monroe ~ *Best Contemporary*

Tiny, slightly funky downtown bistro McEwen's on Monroe opened over a decade ago and has remained popular ever since. The kitchen's eclectic yet steady-handed approach to standard Southern ingredients reveals itself in dishes such as the watercress salad, sweet potato-crusted catfish and buttermilk fried oysters. No matter what you choose to eat — or how you choose to dress — you'll feel at home inside this red brick restaurant where laid-back attitudes and sophisticated cooking coexist with remarkable ease. Extensive wine and beer list. Full bar. Serving lunch Mon–Fri, dinner Mon–Sat. Closed Sun. 122 Monroe Ave., Memphis, TN 38103. (901) 527-7085. Go to: www.wtle.com/9843. ***Bistro, Contemporary, Small Plates. $$$.***

Rendezvous ~ *Best Barbecue Ribs*
Housed in a cellar off an alleyway near The Peabody Hotel in downtown Memphis, Charlie Vergos' iconic restaurant has been serving barbecued ribs to adoring locals and tourists — from Mick Jagger to Prince Albert of Monaco — since 1948. Thousands of black-and-white photographs dot the walls, while veteran white-coated and bowtied waiters provide stupendously unobtrusive service. But the atmosphere is just a small part of the Rendezvous' universal appeal. It's what's on the menu, a compendium of barbecued meats, that keeps 'em coming back for more. First-timers should order a full slab of the famous charcoal-broiled pork ribs, which are among the most lauded of their kind in the nation. Beer and wine available. Serving lunch Fri–Sat, dinner Tue–Sat. Closed Sun–Mon. 52 S. 2nd St., Memphis, TN 38103. (901) 523-2746. Go to: www.wtle.com/9866. ***Barbecue. $$.***

Ronnie Grisanti and Sons ~ *Best Italian*
The Grisanti name has been synonymous with Italian cuisine in Memphis since patriarch Rinaldo Grisanti opened his downtown café in 1903. Ronnie Grisanti and Sons, the family's outstanding bistro located in an upscale strip mall on busy Poplar Avenue, emphasizes high-end Tuscan fare served in elegant rococo-themed dining rooms. Wait until you hear the daily specials before ordering, though you can't go wrong with tried-and-true favorites such as the spaghetti (served with the Grisantis' signature meat gravy) and the Elfo Special (fresh pasta topped with butter-sautéed garlic, shrimp and mushrooms). The Grisantis' cooking really shines in fresh seafood offerings as well. Full bar. Serving dinner Mon–Sat. Closed Sun. 2855 Poplar Ave., Memphis, TN 38111. (901) 323-0007. Go to: www.wtle.com/10896. ***Italian. $$$.***

Tsunami ~ *Best Asian Fusion, Best Seafood*
A perennial winner on local media best-of lists, Tsunami consistently delivers fresh, innovative seafood dishes to hungry Midtowners. The décor amplifies the oceanic theme, effortlessly transporting the restaurant's typically young, hip clientele to a tranquil world beyond the busy Cooper-Young neighborhood. Chef/owner Ben Smith dives into Pacific Rim cuisine with notable aplomb. Savvy and discriminating diners take a tapas approach to the mouth-watering menu, which has included anything from molasses-glazed king salmon to goat cheese-crusted mahi mahi. Full bar with extensive wine list. Serving dinner Mon–Sat. Closed Sun. 928 S. Cooper St., Memphis, TN 38104. (901) 274-2556. Go to: www.wtle.com/10937. ***Asian Fusion, Seafood, Small Plates. $$.***

MIAMI FLORIDA

10 LOCAL FAVORITES

***Miami's exotic Caribbean, Cuban and French-inspired cuisines** make their distinctive marks, while Joe's Stone Crab has remained an undeniable local and national institution since 1913.*

Azul ~ *Best Contemporary*

A spectacular white marble kitchen, an outstanding raw bar and a splendid bay view through the floor-to-ceiling windows all compete for attention as you enter the elegant Azul in Miami's Mandarin Oriental hotel. As magnificent as it is, however, the atmosphere is surpassed by the outstanding food and exceptional service. Chef Clay Conley incorporates local produce into his diverse cuisine, blending Mediterranean flavors with Asian influences as in the grilled lamb with *harrisa* or the A Study in Tuna roll. The award-winning wine list offers both classic vintages and boutique wines, while a variety of domestic and imported cheeses along with pastry chef Patrick Lassaque's light soufflés and celestial tarts offer a fitting conclusion to the meal. Full bar. Serving lunch Mon–Fri, dinner Mon–Sat. Closed Sun. 500 Brickell Key Dr., Miami, FL 33131. (305) 913-8358. Go to: www.wtle.com/23146. ***Asian Fusion, Contemporary, Hotel Restaurant. $$$.***

Big Pink ~ *Best Diner*

Part late-night hangout, part mess hall and part nuclear fallout shelter (at least that's what it feels like), Big Pink delivers a post-modern approach to the American diner. School cafeteria-style tables, concrete floors and ever-present shades of pink define this truly atypical dining room. Whether you're seeking sustenance after a long evening out, having lunch with the family, or just fulfilling that craving for a bucket of deep-fried corndogs, Big Pink's colossal portions of classic comfort food (with an upscale twist) appeal to almost everyone. Breakfast is served all day, or you can indulge in a kitschy TV dinner in a six-compartment stainless steel tray. Pizzas and hefty burgers compete with entrées such as churrasco steak served with black beans and fried plantains. Delivery available. Full bar. Serving breakfast, lunch, dinner and late-night daily (until 5:30 am on weekends). 157 Collins Ave., Miami Beach, FL 33139. (305) 532-4700. Go to: www.wtle.com/23151. ***American Traditional, Breakfast, Diner, Pizza. $$.***

Caffe Abbracci ~ *Best Italian*

For almost 20 years, Caffe Abbracci in Coral Gables has offered Italian fine dining in a handsome and romantic Continental atmosphere. People watching is always fascinating, as many high-profile locals and celebrities frequent this elegant eatery, but owner Nino Pernetti and his attentive staff treat each and every guest like family. (Abbracci is Italian for "hug.") The authentic northern Italian menu includes hot and cold antipasti, grilled seafood dishes, creamy risottos, beef tenderloin, and fresh pastas such as black ravioli (made with squid ink) along with a lengthy wine list. Full bar. Serving lunch Mon–Fri, dinner nightly. 318 Aragon Ave., Coral Gables, FL 33134. (305) 441-0700. Go to: www.wtle.com/23160. ***Italian. $$$.***

Chef Allen's ~ *Best Dessert*

Still rooted in his classical French training, Chef Allen Susser joins flavors from diverse regions of the world — the Caribbean, the Mediterranean, Latin America and the Pacific Rim — in the style he now calls "Palm Tree Cuisine." His goal? "Fine, subtle combinations [and] daring new dishes." Many establishments now offer this fusion style of New World cuisine, but Chef Allen does it better than the hoards of imitators — from his collection of ceviches to his desserts, which are in a league of their own. (Order the signature chocolate truffle soufflé before dinner arrives, when available.) First-rate service and an extensive wine selection complete the journey. Jacket suggested. Full bar. Serving dinner nightly. 19088 N.E. 29th Ave., Miami, FL 33180. (305) 935-2900. Go to: www.wtle.com/23167. ***Contemporary, Dessert. $$$.***

Delicias de España ~ *Best Spanish*

Walls stocked with gourmet treasures — from paella pans and perfumes to seafood mousse and serrano hams — welcome

Delicias de España's constant clientele, who adore this neighborhood bakery, Spanish import store, fish market and café for bringing the best of the motherland to South Florida. Execs stop in before work to feast on pastries and cured ham and eggs, while the tapas and daily specials draw a continuous stream of locals longing for authentic dishes at lunch and dinner. Fish flown in twice a week from Spain is expertly prepared, while non-Spanish speakers can simply point to their selections in the glittering dessert cases when words can't express how tempting they look. Delicias is also the premier location for more than 200 Spanish wines, artisanal cheeses, olive oils, chocolates and collectables. Beer and wine available. Serving breakfast and lunch daily, dinner Mon–Sat. 4016 S.W. 57th Ave., Miami, FL 33155. (305) 669-4485. Go to: www.wtle.com/23172. ***Bakery, Café, Small Plates, Spanish, Takeout/Gourmet Takeout. $$.***

Joe's Stone Crab ~ *Best American Traditional, Best Seafood*

Established in 1913 and named one of America's Regional Classics by the James Beard Foundation, Joe's Stone Crab remains an undisputed Miami institution. Miamians have gathered for generations at Joe's for all manner of celebratory occasions despite the legendary wait to get a table — not to mention that the restaurant is only open when stone crab claws are in season, October through May. The elegant atmosphere and the impeccable service are big draws, but the real explanation for Joe's steady popularity lies in the consistently good food, from the superbly sweet stone crab claws to the renowned Key lime pie. Seafood, steaks, fried green tomatoes and Lyonnaise potatoes complete the menu. If you can't stand the wait, Joe's offers takeout and online ordering. Full bar. Serving (Oct–May only) lunch Tue–Sat, dinner nightly. Check for separate takeout hours. 11 Washington Ave., Miami, FL 33139. (305) 673-0365. Go to: www.wtle.com/23347. ***American Traditional, Seafood. $$$.***

Michy's

In a cozy, eclectic setting on Miami's up-and-coming Upper East Side, award-winning chef Michelle Bernstein has come into her own with Michy's. Drawing on her Latin heritage and classical French training, Bernstein weaves local ingredients into a truly cosmopolitan, fresh and comfortable menu, illustrating influence from the cuisines of Asia, Italy, Spain and the American South in dishes such as white gazpacho or the bouillabaisse with crispy rice. Half-orders are available so that you can take advantage of the menu's variety, complemented by the small wine list of high-quality boutique vintages. Make reservations in advance, or be prepared to eat very early or very late — Michy's stays crowded. Full bar. Serving lunch Tue–Fri, dinner Tue–Sat. Closed Sun–Mon. 6927 Biscayne Blvd., Miami Shores, FL 33138. (305) 759-2001. Go to: www.wtle.com/23357. ***Bistro, Contemporary, Small Plates. $$$.***

Ortanique on the Mile ~ *Best Caribbean/Tropical*
Chef Cindy Hutson's self-proclaimed "Cuisine of the Sun" focuses heavily on Caribbean flavors but displays Latin and Pan-Asian inspirations as well. The menu changes daily based on the freshest seafood available because Hutson simply won't settle for anything less. Her décor, much like the food, is full of tropical spice and color. Expect a lively atmosphere, but secluded dining areas are available. A friendly, well-informed staff can guide you through the wide-ranging wine list, and be sure to save room for creative island-themed desserts. Full bar. Serving lunch Mon–Fri, dinner nightly. 273 Miracle Mile., Coral Gables, FL 33134. (305) 446-7710. Go to: www.wtle.com/23367. ***Caribbean/Tropical, Contemporary. $$$.***

Pascal's on Ponce ~ *Best French*
French-born and -trained Pascal Oudin has paid his dues preparing Miami's signature New World cuisine, working under the influence of Latin and Caribbean flavors. But at his Pascal's on Ponce, he returns to his French heritage yet acknowledges still his Floridian culinary education, using local ingredients prepared in a contemporary French style. This intimate and comfortable neighborhood restaurant consistently delivers quality food that is elegant in its simplicity, such as lobster bisque with corn flan or local grouper with mushroom ragout. Full bar. Serving lunch Mon–Fri, dinner Mon–Sat. Closed Sun. 2611 Ponce de Leon Blvd., Coral Gables, FL 33134. (305) 444-2024. Go to: www.wtle.com/23370. ***French. $$$.***

Versailles ~ *Best Cuban*
For a taste of old Miami, don't miss Versailles, serving genuine Cuban fare to South Florida for nearly 50 years. Gilded mirrors and candelabra fill the large, old-fashioned dining room, while buttered tostadas and soups crowd the tables. Like the atmosphere, the portions are larger than life, and they rely heavily on superbly prepared meats. Prices are more than reasonable, and the sampler platters offer a good variety of Cuban specialties. Try the signature Moors and Christians (black beans and white rice). Full bar. Serving breakfast, lunch and dinner daily. 3555 S.W. 8th St., Miami, FL 33135. (305) 444-0240. Go to: www.wtle.com/23411. ***Breakfast, Cuban. $$.***

MILWAUKEE WISCONSIN

10 LOCAL FAVORITES

***Once home to numerous breweries**, Milwaukee's reputation for industrious food and drink continues with its restaurants, which include nationally renowned chef Sandy D'Amato's Sanford and Coquette Cafe, and the unparalleled Polish eatery Polonez.*

Bartolotta's Lake Park Bistro ~ *Best Bistro, Best Brunch, Best French*

It's not difficult to fall in love with beautiful Bartolotta's Lake Park Bistro, perched on a bluff overlooking Lake Michigan. So much of the food — mussels *marinière*, shrimp in garlic butter, filet mignon au poivre, steak frites — has now become a part of the classic fine-dining repertoire, you forget that these favorites began as French bistro standards, "bistro" being the forebear of "upscale casual." The attentive service, reliably excellent food and a superior view make Lake Park Bistro a great place to impress a date, earn valuable spousal points or just treat yourself to a deluxe meal. Full bar. Serving lunch Mon–Fri, dinner nightly. Sun brunch 10:30 am–2 pm. 3133 E. Newberry Blvd., Milwaukee, WI 53211. (414) 962-6300. Go to: www.wtle.com/20441. ***Bistro, Brunch, French. $$$.***

Coquette Cafe

Chef Sandy D'Amato creates globally influenced cuisine at his original restaurant, Sanford, and periodically contributes recipes to the *Milwaukee Journal Sentinel*. If you lack the funds or the proper dress for the former or the culinary proficiency and ingredients for the latter, Coquette Cafe provides an opportunity to sample the renowned fare of Milwaukee's most famous chef at bargain prices. Hearty sandwiches, Alsatian flatbread pizzas, and assorted pâtés and cheeses — served on bread freshly baked next door — are among local favorites. Entrées include the bacon-wrapped veal meat loaf and the hanger steak, served with pommes frites and garlic aioli (aka mayonnaise: the European ketchup). Full bar. Serving lunch Mon–Fri, dinner Mon–Sat. Closed Sun. 316 N. Milwaukee St., Milwaukee, WI 53202. (414) 291-2655. Go to: www.wtle.com/18297. ***Bistro, Contemporary, Dessert, French. $$.***

Cubanitas ~ *Best Cuban*

Cubanitas is the kind of authentically ethnic place you might not expect to find in the heartland, but there it is, surprising and thriving because of its great food. For lunch, delight in Latin America's heavyweight, the Cuban sandwich, loaded with two kinds of ham and thick slices of Swiss, then toasted. At dinner, begin with one of the city's best mojitos and the house-made empanadas. Proceed to entrées such as the *lechón asado* (roasted pork) and the *bistec* (steak) with a side of yuca con mojo, the tropical equivalent of garlic-mashed potatoes. Hot tip: When you-know-who topples from power in Cuba, the drink menu claims that Cuba libres, the classic rum and Coke, will be served free of charge! Full bar. Serving lunch and dinner Mon–Sat. Closed Sun. 728 N. Milwaukee St., Milwaukee, WI 53202. (414) 225-1760. Go to: www.wtle.com/18287. ***Cuban. $$.***

Eddie Martini's ~ *Best Steak House*

With a charming dining room resembling a 1940s supper club, Eddie Martini's fills up fast, so secure a reservation, and prepare for a beef eater's utopia. High-quality plates of protein are the order of the day here — even the lunch menu offers veal scaloppini, lamb chops and glazed pork. Dinner brings creative appetizers, such as sesame-seared tenderloin or griddled Brie with sweet onion compote. A must-try for seafood lovers is the Ocean Martini — shrimp, crab, lobster and oysters piled into a big martini glass. Strips, rib steaks and porterhouses are nicely aged, expertly chosen and beautifully cut. The tag-team service is as seamless as a well-choreographed dance. Full bar. Serving lunch Mon–Fri, dinner nightly. 8612 Watertown Plank Rd., Wauwatosa, WI 53226. (414) 771-6680. Go to: www.wtle.com/20442. ***Seafood, Steak House. $$$.***

Jake's ~ *Best American Traditional*

Old-school charm abounds at Jake's, a traditional steak and

seafood restaurant that has been family-run for more than 40 years. Its current Brookfield location is owned and operated by restaurant vets Jake Replogle Jr. and wife Karen, who remain true to the '50s and '60s dinner classics that Jake's father served to past generations, in addition to a more modern seasonal menu. Find a seat by the roaring fireplace, and indulge in their signature oversized onion rings, bubbling crab dip or bacon-wrapped water chestnuts. Featured entrées include crispy roast duck in an orange sauce and a variety of their famous steaks. Full bar. Serving dinner Mon–Sat. Closed Sun. 21445 W. Gumina Rd., Pewaukee, WI 53072. (262) 781-7995. Go to: www.wtle.com/21911. ***American Traditional, Steak House. $$$.***

Karl Ratzsch's ~ *Best German*

For more than 100 years, Karl Ratzsch's has been feeding homesick Germans, German-Americans and pretty much everyone residing in the Milwaukee area some of the best classic and contemporary German food. The leaded glass windows, heavy beams and the collection of steins, porcelain and European glassware will make you yearn for that little village on the Reine. If you think of German food as a feast of schnitzel, sausages and potatoes, you're going to be delighted: The menu features sauerbraten and stuffed pork chops with light, chewy house-made spatzle. If you think of German food as *only* the aforementioned delicacies, you'll be pleasantly surprised by the variety of options including *kase* spatzle (vegetables with sautéed German dumplings) and broiled salmon. Full bar. Serving lunch Wed–Sat, dinner Mon–Sat. Closed Sun. 320 E. Mason St., Milwaukee, WI 53202. (414) 276-2720. Go to: www.wtle.com/18316. ***Fish Fry, German. $$.***

Nanakusa ~ *Best Japanese/Sushi*

Spare, beautiful and chic, the interior of Nanakusa Japanese Restaurant sets the tone for an evening of fine Japanese and New Asian cooking. There's fresh sushi in bewildering abundance (including seven kinds of tuna). The ceviche roll is especially delicious, while the crab and mango Aloha Maki is admittedly addictive. If you prefer steak to sushi, Nankusa is a good place to try Kobe beef — the world-famous cattle are raised in Japan with specialized and somewhat-mysterious techniques. Order the shabu-shabu (seafood or beef) or the slow-cooked beef with daikon for a taste of Japanese home cooking. Full bar. Serving lunch and dinner Tue–Fri. Closed Sun–Mon. 408 E. Chicago St., Milwaukee, WI 53202. (414) 223-3200. Go to: www.wtle.com/18354. ***Asian Fusion, Japanese/Sushi. $$.***

Polonez Restaurant ~ *Best Polish*

Polka music, Old World décor and classic Polish food — you're in the Midwest now — characterize Milwaukee's Polonez Restaurant. That's right, *Matka* has tied on her apron and is stirring the soup, rolling out dough, and slicing cabbage and onion, all for you. Nourish yourself with the bigos (hunter's stew) or a plate of pierogies, pan-fried Polish dumplings filled with your choice of meat, cheese, sauerkraut or potato. Ordering the Polish Plate will ensure that you get a little bit of everything: a polish sausage, a stuffed cabbage roll, four pierogies and a potato pancake. The full bar features Polish vodkas, beers and slivovitz, a plum-based alcohol that's clear and scarily potent. Serving lunch Tue–Fri, dinner Tue–Sun. Sun brunch 11 am–2 pm. 4016 S. Packard Ave., St. Francis, WI 53235. (414) 482-0080. Go to: www.wtle.com/18401. ***Brunch, Fish Fry, Polish. $$.***

River Lane Inn ~ *Best Seafood*

The North Side building that houses River Lane Inn has served Milwaukee in one way or another for more than 100 years. It began as a hardware store, satiated the sweet-toothed as an ice cream parlor, and delivered frosty refreshment as a bar. But since 1980, it has been the town's favorite seafood restaurant, offering the freshest fish, imaginatively prepared and paired with good California wines. The menu changes every six weeks to accomodate seasonal harvests, but you will consistently find such dishes as the catch-of-the-day salad, sautéed sand dabs and the calamari steak. Full bar. Serving lunch Mon–Fri, dinner Mon–Sat. Closed Sun. 4313 W. River Ln., Milwaukee, WI 53223. (414) 354-1995. Go to: www.wtle.com/18408. ***Seafood. $$$.***

Sanford ~ *Best Contemporary*

Local media consistently name Sanford one of the best restaurants in Wisconsin, and it makes *Gourmet* magazine's list of the top 50 restaurants nearly every year. Four-course menus that change daily are famously inventive, but not unapproachable or pretentious. Spring may bring a chicken and pea dumpling in curry broth. In cool weather, you may be treated to roast duck with pomegranate glaze. Chef/owner Sanford "Sandy" D'Amato's genius is to take the familiar and make just a slight change or addition. The man makes his own pickles, smokes his own fish and turns horseradish mayonnaise into mousseline — you get the idea of the care that goes into the food. Full bar. Serving dinner Mon–Sat. Closed Sun. 1547 N. Jackson St., Milwaukee, WI 53202. (414) 276-9608. Go to: www.wtle.com/20440. ***Contemporary. $$$.***

MINNEAPOLIS-ST. PAUL
MINNESOTA

10 LOCAL FAVORITES

Befitting the sturdy Midwest sensibilities *of the area and its cuisine, the Twin Cities' most renowned chef, Lucia Watson, prefers the kitchen to any television studio.*

Black Forest Inn ~ *Best German*

In the spot-on words of its owners, "If you haven't been to the Black Forest Inn, you haven't been to Minneapolis." Renowned since its 1965 opening for its hearty German cuisine, extensive beer list and outdoor beer garden, this Minneapolis hot spot is not to be missed. The cozy tavern will warm you after a day in the Minnesota cold, and the enchanting vine-enclosed courtyard overflows with friendly beer lovers all summer long. Try the bratwurst, the potato pancakes with applesauce and sour cream, or recommended main dishes such as spatzle, wiener schnitzel and sauerbraten. Live music weekend nights. Full bar. Serving breakfast, lunch and dinner daily. 1 E. 26th St., Minneapolis, MN 55404. (612) 872-0812. Go to: www.wtle.com/4203. ***German. $$.***

Cafe Brenda ~ *Best Vegetarian*

Since 1986, Cafe Brenda has continuously proven that nutritional vegetarian cuisine — a frightening concept for some — can be both innovative and delicious. Its success might have something to do with the fact that chef/owner Brenda Langton is a wholehearted proponent of local growers and organic farming, or the fact that her menu changes seasonally to reflect farmers' harvests. Vegetarian dishes range from dips, pâtés, croquettes and salads to more avant-garde offerings such as mock duck tacos. For those in need of meat, seafood is a specialty here, with menu choices that may include shrimp quesadillas and an almond-encrusted walleye. There are also beef dishes sourced from Minnesota-based Thousand Hills Cattle Company. Beer and wine available. Serving lunch Mon–Fri, dinner Mon–Sat. Closed Sun. 300 1st Ave. N., Minneapolis, MN 55401. (612) 342-9230. Go to: www.wtle.com/4190. ***Contemporary, Seafood, Vegetarian. $$.***

Cecil's Delicatessen & Bakery ~ *Best Deli*

A restaurant that stocks two dozen kinds of mustards is bound to make delicious sandwiches. Cecil's Delicatessen & Bakery has been doing just that since 1949. Though breakfast favorites include sumptuous omelets and a tasty array of pastries baked in-house, Cecil's is best known for its sandwiches, served in two sizes: the regular and the bursting-at-the-seams, half-pound New York option. The Reuben is a classic, as is the turkey club and the famed fried salami. Tucked away in the Highland Park neighborhood of St. Paul, Cecil's unassuming exterior might fool you into thinking there's nothing to be found inside. This would be a mistake of gastronomical proportions. No alcohol available. Serving breakfast, lunch and dinner daily. 651 Cleveland Ave. S., St. Paul, MN 55116. (651) 698-6276. Go to: www.wtle.com/2851. ***Breakfast, Deli, Subs/Hoagies/Po-boys. $.***

Convention Grill ~ *Best Burgers, Best Diner*

In the burger business, some fight passionately for the right to embellish between the buns. And then there are those who choose not to mess with a good thing, those who believe in the standard architecture of one of America's proudest foodstuffs. If your ideal burger fits the latter description, look no further than suburban Edina's classic throwback diner, Convention Grill, which dates back to 1934. No frills. No monkey business. Aided only by a colossal stack of skin-on fries that, alone, are worth a visit. And what are a cheeseburger and fries without a thick, delicious malt or a cherry and vanilla Coke? The retro décor, complete with a jukebox in the corner and yellow-and-red plastic squeeze bottles on each table, will remind you of a simpler time, or of Nick at Nite at the very least. No alcohol available. Serving lunch and dinner daily. 3912 Sunnyside Rd., Edina, MN 55424. (952) 920-6881. Go to: www.wtle.com/2250. ***Burgers, Diner. $.***

Lucia's Restaurant and Wine Bar ~ *Best Contemporary*

Centrally located near Lake Calhoun and Lake of the Isles, this wildly popular spot has been a meeting ground for the casually chic for more than 20 years. Chef/proprietor Lucia Watson, a James Beard award winner, does not have the demeanor you might expect from a high-profile chef, preferring to labor in the kitchen of her down-to-earth restaurant rather than seek the spotlight. Her weekly changing menu that emphasizes locally grown ingredients and reflects culinary traditions of the Midwest has included entrées such as baked lemon sole with beurre meunière sauce and pan-roasted chicken breast with braised white beans. Full bar. Serving lunch and dinner Tue–Sun. Sat–Sun brunch 10 am–2 pm. Closed Mon. 1432 W. 31st St., Minneapolis, MN 55408. (612) 825-1572. Go to: www.wtle.com/2049. ***Bistro, Brunch, Contemporary, Wine Bar. $$.***

Manny's ~ *Best Steak House*

If a restaurant does steak right, it doesn't matter if the bread is burnt. No, they don't burn the bread at Manny's, but there are no candles, floral arrangements or other atmospheric enhancements. Nonetheless, the restaurant, located in downtown Minneapolis' Hyatt Regency, is frequently packed with locals as well as traveling business executives. The rolling meat cart is impressively laden with one perfect dry-aged cut after another. Whether you want a filet mignon so tender that a knife becomes unnecessary or one of the most flavorful 22-ounce porterhouses you've ever encountered, Manny's has it. Full bar. Serving dinner nightly. 1300 Nicollet Ave., Minneapolis, MN 55403. (612) 339-9900. Go to: www.wtle.com/4165. ***Hotel Restaurant, Steak House. $$$.***

The Oceanaire Seafood Room ~ *Best Seafood*

Topping Minneapolis' list of seafood eateries is The Oceanaire Seafood Room, a faux art deco palace in the downtown Hyatt Regency. Designed to resemble a 1930s ocean liner, The Oceanaire creates a luxe atmosphere with dark wood walls, high-backed leather furniture and plush booths. Relax in the silver-and-blue lounge with an old-fashioned cocktail, or belly up to the oyster bar while waiting for a table. For starters, try the crab cakes, which are breaded just enough to hold together. Though the menu varies depending on what is fresh, fish entrées may include the much-recommended Arctic char, fried whole and served with citrus soy dipping sauce, or the "Black and Bleu" blue marlin steak. Full bar. Serving dinner nightly. 1300 Nicollet Ave., Minneapolis, MN 55403. (612) 333-2277. Go to: www.wtle.com/2909. ***Hotel Restaurant, Oysters, Seafood. $$$.***

Origami Restaurant ~ *Best Japanese/Sushi*
Housed in a former 19th-century meat market, the original Origami has been packing in hordes of sushi lovers since 1991. The lucky ones snag a spot at the sushi bar for a front-row view of talented chefs slicing, dicing, rolling and arranging their way through icy piles of the freshest seafood. The *unagi* maki (freshwater eel roll) is both sweet and savory. The *toro* (fatty part of tuna) is so rich it may leave you with no appetite for dessert. If the sushi menu overwhelms with choice, try a sashimi platter, and let the chef choose for you. Full bar. Serving lunch Mon–Fri, dinner nightly. West location serving lunch and dinner daily. 30 N. 1st St., Minneapolis, MN 55401. (612) 333-8430. Two locations. Go to: www.wtle.com/2985. ***Japanese/Sushi. $$.***

Solera ~ *Best Spanish*
Tim McKee and Josh Thoma fell in love with the quality-over-quantity cuisine concept and brought their tapas ideas to Minneapolis in 2003, when they opened the immediately hot Solera restaurant. The portions may be small, but the building is big, with three floors, a sidewalk patio and rooftop dining space, art nouveau-ish booths, and mosaic-tiled walls. On any given night, there are 40 small dishes from which to choose. How about mini balls of fried goat cheese or perhaps just one perfect scallop, grilled, with a touch of saffron? Maybe just one more — the tender roast duck with figs. And you are perfectly within your rights as a small-portion diner to order dessert, even those sinful churros, Spain's answer to Krispy Kreme. Full bar. Serving dinner nightly. 900 Hennepin Ave., Minneapolis, MN 55403. (612) 338-0062. Go to: www.wtle.com/2858. ***Small Plates, Spanish. $$.***

Vincent - A Restaurant ~ *Best French*
Vincent - A Restaurant blends the elegance of French dining and the accessibility of American contemporary fare, celebrating both. Chef/owner Vincent Francoual, trained in France, is widely acknowledged to be one of Minneapolis' finest treasures in the kitchen, and his ever-changing menu consistently reaffirms the city's faith in his artistry. To start, consider the popular carpaccio of red beets with whipped goat cheese and frisée greens, when available. Francoual is also famed for his fish, so don't hesitate to order entrées that may include pan-seared skate wing or serrano and olive-encrusted monkfish. Full bar. Serving lunch Mon–Fri, dinner nightly. 1100 Nicollet Ave., Minneapolis, MN 55403. (612) 630-1189. Go to: www.wtle.com/2301. ***Contemporary, French. $$$.***

NASHVILLE TENNESSEE

10 LOCAL FAVORITES

***With a growing number of top-flight** contemporary restaurants, Music City remains a standard-bearer for home-style meat-and-three plates, as well as cayenne pepper-spiced, skillet-fried hot chicken.*

Ryman Auditorium

Caffe Nonna ~ *Best Italian*

Caffe Nonna, the invitingly raucous home-style Italian restaurant in Sylvan Park, gets hopping in a hurry, especially on weekends. Given the noise level on a Saturday night, the 45 or so diners that can be jammed into this cozy place must all be talking at the same time — inevitably about the wonderful food. Chef and co-owner Daniel Maggipinto has created a number of winning dishes based on his childhood and inspired by his own *nonna* (Italian grandmother). Signature entrées include butternut squash lasagna and the sublime seafood Angelina (mussels, shrimp, scallops and baby clams over fettuccini). Full bar. Serving lunch Mon–Fri, dinner Mon–Sat. Closed Sun. 4427 Murphy Rd., Nashville, TN 37209. (615) 463-0133. Go to: www.wtle.com/2263. ***Italian. $$.***

Jimmy Kelly's ~ *Best Steak House*

Dapper proprietor Mike Kelly usually greets the famous and the not-so-famous at the door of this quintessential Nashville steak house that his grandfather first opened in 1934. The supper club-like atmosphere of this restored Victorian mansion attracts local politicians and other city leaders. Rock star Neil Young once made it his home away from home while working on an album. With bars downstairs and upstairs, and several cigars available for purchase and smoking, this place is old-school with a capital O. Signature dishes include a shrimp remoulade appetizer, Châteaubriand for two and pecan pie à la mode. Just don't fill up on the habit-forming corn cakes before dinner arrives. Full bar. Serving dinner Mon–Sat. Closed Sun. 217 Louise Ave., Nashville, TN 37203. (615) 329-4349. Go to: www.wtle.com/2345. ***Steak House. $$$.***

La Hacienda Taqueria ~ *Best Mexican*

What started out as a little tortilla shop and Mexican grocery on internationally diverse Nolensville Pike has expanded into a spacious sit-down Mexican restaurant that rates as Nashville's most authentic, busiest and best. It has also expanded to add another slightly more upscale eatery down the street called La Hacienda Marisqueria and Supermercado, specializing in seafood dishes. Breakfast specials are available all day: Viva eggs and Mexican sausage served any time! The margaritas and specialty drinks from the well-stocked bar are reasonably priced and quite good, as is the real sangria, either original or peach. There is an ample selection of Mexican and domestic beers, too. Serving lunch and dinner daily. 2615 Nolensville Rd., Nashville, TN 37211. (615) 256-6142. Go to: www.wtle.com/2318. ***Mexican. $.***

Loveless Cafe ~ *Best Home-style*

Despite many years of well-deserved publicity, the half-century-old Loveless Cafe fell on some hard times, until an investment group led by local restaurateur Tom Morales took over ownership of the diner in late 2003 and financed the restoration of the building, bringing it back to its former homey charm. Many locals will swear Loveless's signature fried chicken, country ham, biscuits, preserves and house-made pies are just as good as ever. Few would argue otherwise. In fact, many would venture that the sides and new dinner additions (pan-fried trout, barbecued shrimp and grits, smoked pork chops) make Loveless even better than before. Breakfast is offered all day, with the country ham, eggs and red-eye gravy the standard-setters. No alcohol available. Serving breakfast, lunch and dinner daily. 8400 Hwy. 100, Nashville, TN 37221. (615) 646-9700. Go to: www.wtle.com/2192. ***Breakfast, Home-style. $$.***

Margot Café & Bar

Chef/owner Margot McCormack is easy to spot behind the counter of the open-air kitchen in her self-named and critically acclaimed restaurant in East Nashville's funky Five Points neighborhood. A veteran in the kitchens of first Nashville, then New York, McCormack returned to open Margot's in what was once a filling station in June 2001. The short menu, which changes daily, reflects her passion for peasant and rustic bistro cooking from France and Italy. It's stellar stuff, notably the entrées, including braised lamb shank, linguine with littleneck clams and steak au poivre. Save room for dessert, particularly the outstanding ice creams, sorbets and tarts. The Sunday brunch (11 am–2 pm) is one of Nashville's most popular. McCormack has also opened a European-style café and marketplace close-by called Marché Artisan Foods. Full bar. Serving dinner Tue–Sat. Closed Mon. 1017 Woodland St., Nashville, TN 37206. (615) 227-4668. Go to: www.wtle.com/19527. ***Brunch, Contemporary, Dessert. $$.***

Prince's Hot Chicken Shack ~ *Best Hot Chicken*

The meat-and-three and cayenne pepper-spiced skillet-fried chicken are Music City's truly indigenous foodstuffs, and North Nashville's appropriately named Prince's has long reigned as the crown royalty for the latter. Located in a nondescript strip mall, Prince's is owned by Andre Prince, whose heritage in the kitchen dates back to her great-uncle Thornton Prince, whose girlfriend invented this style of hot chicken as revenge when Thornton came home a little "too late" after a night of carousing. But he loved it. The restaurant has only five booths, and you'll wait from 20 to 45 minutes for your chicken (either a quarter dark or quarter white meat) to arrive, not long after it leaves its oversized cast iron skillet. Trust us — order the medium if you think you want the hot; mild if you think you want the medium. No alcohol available. Serving lunch and dinner Tue–Sat. Closed Sun–Mon. 123 Ewing Dr., Nashville, TN 37207. (615) 226-9442. Go to: www.wtle.com/17489. ***Hot Chicken, Soul Food. $.***

Restaurant Zola

Award-winning chef and co-owner Deb Paquette is considered one of Nashville's most creative and consistent in the kitchen, and her Restaurant Zola has proven worthy of her many skills. Co-owned by husband/wine director Ernie Paquette, the intimate hideaway seems worlds away from nearby, busy West End Avenue. The cozy collection of dining rooms feels more like a home than a business establishment, and the menu, too, is light-hearted in its fusion of Mediterranean and Old South. A hint of Moroccan and a dash of Greek peek into signature dishes such as pecan fried beet salad and the paella, so dining here is a world-tour of fun and flavor. The desserts are among the city's best. Full bar. Serving dinner Mon–Sat. Closed Sun. 3001 West End Ave., Nashville, TN 37203. (615) 320-7778. Go to: www.wtle.com/2287. ***Contemporary, Dessert. $$.***

Sunset Grill ~ *Best Contemporary*

Veteran hardcore Nashville foodies followed influential

restaurateur Randy Rayburn through several different eateries until he finally opened his own place, Sunset Grill, in 1990 in the Hillsboro Village neighborhood. With its affordable and consistent fine dining, outstanding service and casual atmosphere — it's *the* place for a jeans-and-jacket Music Row power lunch or dinner — there is no better restaurant in Nashville. Talented, longtime-executive chef Brian Uhl, with his adept feel for Southern touches, oversees the extremely creative seasonal menus that generally feature several seafood dishes and interesting meat choices. The late-night menu is as extensive and as expertly prepared as any in town, as is the dessert list. Full bar. Serving lunch Tue–Fri, dinner nightly. 2001 Belcourt Ave., Nashville, TN 37212. (615) 386-3663. Go to: www.wtle.com/2175. ***Contemporary, Dessert. $$.***

Swett's ~ *Best Soul Food*

North Nashville meat-and-three mainstay Swett's has been owned and operated by members of the Swett family since 1954, and there has been absolutely no reason to fool with the family-tested recipes. Service is cafeteria-style, and lunch in particular draws perhaps Nashville's most diverse crowd of city officials, business leaders, blue-collar workers, and students and staffers from nearby Tennessee State University, Fisk University and Meharry Medical College. Soul food and Southern cooking staples such as fried chicken, barbecued pork ribs and meat loaf are among the best in town. Ditto for the various pies and cobblers for dessert. No alcohol available. Serving lunch and dinner daily. 2725 Clifton Ave., Nashville, TN 37209. (615) 329-4418. Two locations. Go to: www.wtle.com/17493. ***Home-style, Soul Food. $.***

Watermark

Watermark has made quite a splash since its November 2005 opening in the white-hot Gulch district, just south of downtown. Part-owner and Nashville native Jerry Brown recruited top chefs and other staff from renowned Birmingham, Ala., chef Frank Stitt's Bottega restaurant, helping to facilitate Music City's continually rising rank among culinary epicenters in the Southeast. The upscale, regionally inspired contemporary menu caters to an urbanly sophisticated clientele with such inspired dishes as ricotta-stuffed squash blossoms, braised lamb osso buco and sautéed Hawaiian *walu*. And there may be no better way to spend a Nashville night than on the gorgeous outdoor terrace atop Watermark's edifice. Full bar and well-chosen wine list. Serving dinner Mon–Sat. Closed Sun. 507 12th Ave. S., Nashville, TN 37203. (615) 254-2000. Go to: www.wtle.com/19648. ***Contemporary. $$$.***

NEW ORLEANS
LOUISIANA

***New Orleans' well-deserved reputation for culinary excellence** has remained intact post-Hurricane Katrina, with the likes of newer star restaurants joining cherished stalwarts such as Commander's Palace, Galatoire's and Mother's.*

Bayona ~ *Best Contemporary*

Care most certainly did not forget this New Orleans treasure, where James Beard award-winning chef/co-owner Susan Spicer specializes in all things fresh. Three charming dining rooms await diners, and there's also the patio, which maintains some of its original Creole cottage feel. Spicer's menu is difficult to classify, with unique starters such as oyster gratin or smoked quail salad, and the entrée list always includes a variety of dishes such as Gulf Coast bouillabaisse and cider-glazed pork shank. For dessert, you may find frozen lemon bombe with gingersnap crumble and blueberries. Extensive and rare wine list. Full bar. Serving lunch Wed–Sat, dinner Mon–Sat. Closed Sun. 430 Dauphine St., New Orleans, LA 70112. (504) 525-4455. Go to: www.wtle.com/24017. ***Contemporary. $$$.***

Camellia Grill ~ *Best Diner*

Purchased by local restaurateur Hicham Khodr after Hurricane Katrina, Camellia Grill is back up and running. Aside from an exterior paint job and some kitchen remodeling, Khodr has kept this iconic diner just as it was. The look — white columns and a neon sign out front — hasn't changed in decades. Locals, students and visitors alike can again enjoy those juicy burgers, freshly made omelets and rich milkshakes at this Uptown landmark. From the famous chili omelet and pecan pie à la mode to the charismatic cooks and bowtied servers, this is a real New Orleans legend. No alcohol available. Serving breakfast, lunch and dinner daily. 626 S. Carrolton., New Orleans, LA 70118. (504) 309-2679. Go to: www.wtle.com/24277. ***Breakfast, Brunch, Burgers, Diner. $.***

Casamento's Restaurant ~ *Best Oysters*
For the best oyster loaf in the Crescent City, head to Casamento's. Co-owner and founder Joe Casamento really knew what he was doing when he created the now signature "pan bread" rather than using the traditional French loaf. White-tiled inside and out, this Dixie tradition since 1919 serves a delicious blend of Italian traditional cooking and Louisiana seafood. Classics such as gumbo and soft-shell crab are excellent, and you can watch the pros shuck oysters right in front of you at the bar. Just take note: Casamento's is so dedicated to serving quality oysters, they are closed when oysters are out of season, as custom dictates, during those "r"-less summer months. Beer available. Serving lunch Tue–Sat, dinner Thu–Sat. Closed Sun–Mon, and June, July and Aug. 4330 Magazine St., New Orleans, LA 70115. (504) 895-9761. Go to: www.wtle.com/24277. ***Oysters, Seafood. $.***

Central Grocery Co. ~ *Best Deli, Best Muffuletta*
The originator of the now world-famous muffuletta sandwich, Central Grocery has been serving hungry New Orleanians since 1906. It appears at first glance to be just an old Italian grocery store, but the line of customers inside snaking up and down the tiny aisles should tell you that this place is not your average anything. And if a giant loaf of foccacia-like bread with salami and ham, mozzarella and provolone cheeses, and a scrumptious smothering of olive salad spread thick throughout doesn't fill you up, well … it will. And since Central Grocery provides only very limited stool seating, you can bring your sandwich (with a giant stack of napkins) across the street to a bench along the Mississippi River or to Jackson Square for some people watching. Beer available. Serving during breakfast, lunch and early dinner hours Tue–Sat. Closed Sun–Mon. 923 Decatur St., New Orleans, LA 70116. (504) 523-1620. Go to: www.wtle.com/24039. ***Deli, Muffuletta, Takeout/Gourmet Takeout. $.***

Cochon ~ *Best Cajun*
Locals have been big on the pig since Cochon debuted. Chef/co-owner Donald Link, winner of the 2007 James Beard Foundation's Best Chef: South award, has been serving his authentic version

of the Cajun food of his childhood to rave reviews. An in-house boucherie, wooden tables and artisan-designed chairs set the stage for mint juleps, crawfish pie, and spoon bread with okra and tomatoes. With its rustic and inviting ambiance, this "swine"-dining establishment is a great example of the city's true Southern appeal. (They even have real moonshine.) Try Link's signature roasted Gulf fish "fishermen" style, as well as his superb andouille. Full bar. Serving lunch Mon–Fri, dinner Mon–Sat. Closed Sun. 930 Tchoupitoulas St., New Orleans, LA 70130. (504) 588-2123. Go to: www.wtle.com/24301. ***Cajun, Contemporary. $$.***

Commander's Palace ~ *Best Brunch*

As definitively New Orleans as Mardi Gras, upscale and wonderfully classic Commander's Palace has commanded the New Orleans restaurant scene for over two centuries. Since 1974, the Brennan family has made Commander's one of the most famous and award-winning restaurants in the world. This James Beard and DiRoNA award-winning Creole/American (not Cajun) mecca, situated in the beautiful Garden District, remains today "a well-run party given by old friends," as the restaurant itself claims. The Jazz Brunch in the courtyard (Sat 11:30 am–1 pm, Sun 10:30 am–1:30 pm) with live Dixieland and jazz music is a New Orleans experience like none other. Traditionally, the brunch includes Gulf seafood gumbo, crawfish boudin and eggs, and, of course, the Creole bread pudding soufflé. Jacket suggested for dinner. Full bar. Serving lunch Mon–Fri, dinner nightly. Sat–Sun brunch. 1403 Washington Ave., New Orleans, LA 70130. (504) 899-8221. Go to: www.wtle.com/24041. ***Brunch, Creole, Dessert. $$$.***

Galatoire's ~ *Best Creole*

At Galatoire's, the grand dame of New Orleans cuisine, the word is tradition. This DiRoNa award-winning restaurant continues to serve outstanding French Creole food under the direction of the restaurant's fourth-generation family/owners. Presented in opulent dining rooms with beautiful table settings, the food itself is simple and elegant, authentic New Orleans fare. Patrons will be happy to know that the restaurant's previously unwavering policy of "no reservations" (not even for presidents) has been slightly altered. They now allow reservations for the second-floor dining room. To sit in the original main dining room downstairs, though, you'll have to wait in line like everyone else, but it's well-worth your while for the shrimp remoulade and *poisson* meunière amandine. Jacket required for dinner and all day Sun. Full bar. Serving lunch and dinner Tue–Sun. Closed Mon. 209 Bourbon St., New Orleans, LA 70130. (504) 525-2021. Go to: www.wtle.com/24070. ***Creole, French. $$$.***

Jacques-Imo's

After waiting at the crowded bar and following the hostess through the hot kitchen to your table (with its mismatched plates and flatware), you may wonder what you've gotten yourself into. But just relax and enjoy as you *laissez les bon temps rouler* at this unbelievable Uptown hot spot. Every meal at Jacques-Imo's begins with corn bread drizzled with melted butter. Then the spinach salad — simple enough, with a vinaigrette dressing and topped with two fried oysters. That alligator cheesecake as an appetizer? Rich and delightful. And the blackened red fish and fried chicken have both developed cult-like followings. Don't be surprised if Jacques himself (in his signature Bermuda shorts and white chef's jacket) hops over to your table to see how you're doing. Full bar. Serving dinner Mon–Sat. Closed Sun., 8324 Oak St., New Orleans, LA 70118. (504) 861-0886. Go to: www.wtle.com/24101. ***Cajun, Contemporary, Creole. $$.***

Mother's Restaurant ~ *Best Home-style*

If you plan on eating at Mother's, which you must, you'll have to familiarize yourself with their dictionary first. (Yes, they literally provide one for you on the menu.) The scraps of roast beef that fall into the gravy while it's baking in the oven? Well, that's "debris" (pronounced day-bris). When they serve it on fresh French bread, you've got yourself a debris po-boy. Get it "dressed," and they'll add shredded cabbage, pickles, mayo, and Creole and yellow mustard. A N'awlins institution, this is the place to go for some of the best Cajun and Southern soul food you'll ever have, for breakfast, lunch and dinner. Mother's has been serving its famous po-boys since 1938, so it has an extensive history to boot. Don't leave without trying the bread pudding. Full bar. Serving breakfast, lunch and dinner daily. 401 Poydras St., New Orleans, 70130. (504) 523-9656. Go to: www.wtle.com/24147. ***Breakfast, Cajun, Creole, Home-style, Subs/Hoagies/Po-boys. $.***

Restaurant August

James Beard award-winning chef/owner John Besh really did it right with this lavishly refined restaurant, where guests are pampered from start to finish. Upscale, sumptuous décor, complete with elegant wood paneling and Parisian-style chairs, provides a refined ambiance, though the service exhibits a more comfortable, laid-back, quintessentially New Orleans feel. And the food? Choices may include sugar-and-spice duckling with grits, or lemonfish with tomato comfit. Besh also offers a superlative five-course, prix fixe tasting menu. Full bar. Serving lunch Fri, dinner Mon–Sat. Closed Sun. 301 Tchoupitoulas St., New Orleans, LA 70130. (504) 299-9777. Go to: www.wtle.com/24180. ***Contemporary, Creole. $$$.***

NEW YORK NEW YORK

10 LOCAL FAVORITES

Celebrity chefs and gourmet restaurants *abound in the Big Apple, but New York-style hot dogs and pizza will never go out of style, nor will the steaks from timeless Brooklyn-institution Peter Luger.*

Babbo ~ *Best Italian*

Babbo Ristorante e Enoteca possesses 90 of the most foodie-coveted seats in the city. That is, at least in part, due to chef/co-owner Mario Batali's national reputation as emperor of the restaurateuring world. Though he owns interest in ventures from New York's Esca, Lupa and Del Posto to Los Angeles'—and perhaps the country's — toughest reservation, Osteria Mozza, Batali sets his throne inside the kitchen of his Greenwich Village pet most evenings, jamming to his iPod (which plays throughout the dining room) and preparing his most intensely flavored menu of all. From goose liver ravioli to lamb's tongue salad, His Highness brings new meaning to haute cuisine, preparing flawless pastas and succulent meat dishes as he imagines an Italian in the Hudson Valley would. Full bar. Serving dinner nightly. 110 Waverly Pl., New York, NY 10011. (212) 777-0303. Go to: www.wtle.com/21697. ***Italian. $$$.***

Bouley ~ *Best French*

The rather trying evolution of august chef David Bouley's namesake TriBeCa restaurant aptly illustrates why most simply can't cut it in the major leagues — and that the ones who survive make Manhattan the top dining destination in the country. From a 9/11 closure to a significant staff turnover, Bouley's envisioned culinary empire seemed doomed when *The New York Times* stripped away that coveted fourth star in 2004. But the controversial, reserved Connecticut native took a deep breath, fell back on his French grandmother's teachings, and kept cooking his progressive French dishes with his signature moxie for tropical flavors. Bouley has since emerged from the ashes, reborn and perhaps better than ever, proudly baring unparalleled clarity of flavor and concept. Full bar. Serving lunch and dinner daily. 120 W. Broadway., New York, NY 10013. (212) 964-2525. Go to: www.wtle.com/21764. ***Contemporary, French. $$$.***

Craft

Head judge of Bravo's *Top Chef* series and James Beard award-winning chef status aside, Tom Colicchio is known locally as a culinary god. The refined simplicity of his contemporary menus and his almost obsessive commitment to the world's purest ingredients come to the second of his ventures (the first being Union Square's fair-haired Gramercy Tavern). Craft's debut left many diners stunned by the true à la carte dining approach. But Colicchio's kitchen makes build-your-own plate a build-your-own adventure, each bite of preferred protein and sides revealing an exciting burst of sublime flavor. From black bass to beef tongue, braised is best, but it's hard to go wrong with such expert execution. This integrity follows through to dessert, dubbed by some to be the best in town. Full bar. Serving lunch Mon–Fri, dinner nightly. 43 E. 19th St., New York, NY 10003. (212) 780-0880. Go to: www.wtle.com/21718. ***Contemporary, Oysters. $$$.***

Estiatorio Milos ~ *Best Greek*

If New York were Mount Olympus, Estiatorio Milos would be the Zeus of divine Mediterranean seafood restaurants, reigning proudly over lesser deities. Greek expatriate Costas Spiliadis launched his massive, elegant Midtown Manhattan space in 1997 to the fervent "oopahs" of New York foodies eager to benefit from Spiliadis' intimate relationships with boutique fisheries across the globe. Priced-by-the-pound fish and tentacled delicacies shine like the Golden Fleece from iced display cases, tempting diners with choices from Icelandic Arctic char to Floridian swordfish. Each catch's pure preparation using only lemon, olive oil and herbs — granted any garnish from honey to caper is specially imported from the world's most reputed distributors — transports diners to a small, nameless village in the Cyclades, where life hangs on the enjoyment of each celestial bite. Full bar. Serving lunch Mon–Fri, dinner nightly. 125 W. 55th St., New York, NY 10019. (212) 245-7400. Go to: www.wtle.com/21690. ***Greek, Seafood. $$$.***

The Four Seasons ~ *Best Continental*

If ever a single space were to live and breathe Manhattan, The Four Seasons is it. Dine in Trump or Bloomberg's shoes at one of America's most iconic eateries. GPS coordinates for New York's anointed power-lunch posse lie somewhere inside the walls of the Grill Room — the location of JFK's 45th birthday party — while the elegant Pool Room hosts many a polished pair seeking the indubitably magical experience of dining in Manhattan's only restaurant designated an official landmark. Though perhaps not on the forefront of progressive Continental cuisine, the kitchen shines with the classics: Châteaubriand, rack of lamb and Dover sole. Jacket required. Full bar. Serving lunch Mon–Fri, dinner Mon–Sat. Closed Sun. 99 E. 52nd St., New York, NY 10022. (212) 754-9494. Go to: www.wtle.com/21684. ***Contemporary, Continental. $$$.***

Gray's Papaya ~ *Best Hot Dogs*

Sometimes, amid all the delicate veal sweetbreads, fall-off-the-bone braised short ribs and pan-seared sea scallops that Manhattan's fine-dining establishments have to offer, a New Yorker just needs a hot dog. For those times, there's Gray's Papaya, with three locations on the West Side. One perfectly grilled dog on a toasted bun: a buck and some change. A second frank and a non-alcoholic papaya drink: $3.50. Sinking your teeth into the all-beef, slightly crunchy casing: priceless. No alcohol available. Cash only. Open 24 hours daily. 402 6th Ave., New York, NY 10011. (212) 260-3532. Multiple locations. Go to: www.wtle.com/23209. ***Hot Dogs. $.***

Le Bernardin ~ *Best Seafood*

The only restaurant to maintain all four of *The New York Times*' stars for its two-decade lifespan, Le Bernardin was born from the dreams of French-born/Michelin-starred/brother-sister duo Maguy and Gilbert Le Coze. The principles of purity acquired in the Le Coze's small Brittany fishing village have never faltered, even after Gilbert's unexpected death brought Eric Ripert to the team. The conscientious Ripert consistently shuns a celebrity-chef media circuit in favor of Le Bernardin's kitchen, from which his impeccably prepared French seafood dishes with Asian accents — from fluke ceviche to wild striped bass — continually win over the food world's toughest critics with depth and subtlety of flavor. Full bar. Serving lunch Mon–Fri, dinner Mon–Sat. Closed Sun. 155 W. 51st St., New York, NY 10019. (212) 554-1515. Go to: www.wtle.com/21708. ***French, Seafood. $$$.***

Lombardi's ~ *Best Pizza*

Presiding over New York's illustrious pizza pedigree,

Lombardi's has more than just its famed clam pizza to recommend it. Pies come with a slice of history as well as sweet Italian sausage, imported anchovies and house-made meatballs. Undisputed godfather of NY-style pizza Gennaro Lombardi founded this NoLIta mainstay over a century ago, just a few doors down from the current digs, making it the first licensed pizzeria in Manhattan. Loyalists would duel anyone denying the heavenly powers of the smoky, slightly charred crust, sumptuous beefsteak tomatoes and freshly sliced mozzarella. And the full bar doesn't hurt. Serving lunch and dinner daily. 32 Spring St., New York, NY 10012. (212) 941-7994. Go to: www.wtle.com/21747. ***Pizza. $$.***

Momofuku Noodle Bar ~ *Best Noodle Shop*

Cooking whatever the *@#$ he wants, young David Chang isn't your average James Beard Rising Star Chef. This noodle shop cowboy has an affinity for fast food and foul language. He's a French Culinary Institute grad, but he cooks some of New York's cheapest eats. When customers complained about the lack of meatless menu options, he chucked pig tails and pork belly in all but one vegetarian dish. Regardless of whatever standards he doesn't follow, David Chang can be counted on for one thing: giant, shockingly good bowls of succulent noodles filled with Berkshire pork, braised tripe and Long Island razor clams. He maintains such a cult following among New York foodies, groupies have already begun designing Momofuku T-shirts. A move down the street to updated, enlarged digs only adds to his growing appeal. Beer and sake available. Serving lunch and dinner daily. 171 1st Ave., New York, NY 10003. (212) 777-7773. Go to: www.wtle.com/23244. ***Asian Fusion. $$.***

Peter Luger Steak House

Peter Luger shines as the Vatican City of all things red and beefy. Twice-a-week customer Sol Forman purchased America's steak house sovereign in 1950, and the Forman women have since been the only ones trusted with the exacting task of purchasing the 10 tons of beef consumed under their roof per week. A dining party's only decision here — aside from, perhaps, choosing between divine creamed spinach or signature German fried potatoes — is how many servings of prime porterhouse to split. After dry-aging the finest cuts in-house for a highly secretive amount of time, the Luger team butchers, barely sizzles and even slices steaks for their guests. Pretty much the only thing Peter Luger will allow diners is to enjoy each precious bite. Full bar. Cash only. Serving lunch and dinner daily. 178 Broadway, Brooklyn, NY 11211. (718) 387-7400. Go to: www.wtle.com/21711. ***Steak House. $$$.***

OAKLAND CALIFORNIA

10 LOCAL FAVORITES

***East Bay foodies have long been blessed** with an abundance of imaginative and influential restaurants, including Bay Wolf, Lalime's, Oliveto and Alice Waters' California cuisine forerunner, Chez Panisse.*

The San Francisco - Oakland Bay Bridge

À Côté ~ *Best French*

Ultra-trendy À Côté restaurant in Oakland's Rockridge district packs in diners seeking Mediterranean-inspired French cuisine served tapas-style. There's nearly always a crowd buzzing outside the restaurant due to its no-reservations policy. But inside, the tables are widely spaced; the lighting is flattering; and the meals are quiet. The term "small plate" is used rather loosely, with substantial portions for each dish on the ever-changing one-page menu. Excellent desserts can range from brown butter waffles with roasted pears, ricotta and honey syrup, to a collection of cheeses. The restaurant's extensive wine bar is open late. Full bar. Serving dinner nightly. 5478 College Ave., Oakland, CA 94618. (510) 655-6469. Go to: www.wtle.com/9782. ***Contemporary, French, Small Plates, Wine Bar. $$.***

Bay Wolf Restaurant ~ *Best Contemporary*

Bay Wolf has served as an unshakable pillar of East Bay dining for more than 30 years, with founding owner Michael Wild acting as a role model for many area restaurateurs and the restaurant's menu helping to shape the California cuisine movement. Patrons can expect consistently sophisticated dishes from the monthly changing menu, plus great service from the veteran waitstaff. The restaurant's specialty is duck, which is listed in nearly every corner of the menu. For one, duck liver flan — rich and buttery, served with pickled onions, gherkins and olives — is almost always on the menu. Beer and wine available. Serving lunch Mon–Fri, dinner nightly. 3853 Piedmont Ave., Oakland, CA 94611. (510) 655-6004. Go to: www.wtle.com/9025. ***Contemporary. $$.***

César ~ *Best Spanish*

Dining at either of the two César locations proves a decisively fun experience. Whether packed in Berkeley's brightly colored dining room or enjoying the open-café setup of the Oakland branch, Bay Area residents can't get enough of the spectacular small-plate menu. And how could they? With such a range of creative choices — from marinated olives and Spanish cheeses to clams with house-made sausage and smoked trout salad.The length of the drink list includes wines, beer and cider, plus specialty cocktails and martinis. Fine sherries, rare bourbons and a little black book of drinks also make the bar special. Reservations are only accepted for Shattuck Avenue's communal table, which seats 12–15 guests. Serving lunch and dinner daily. 1515 Shattuck Ave., Berkeley, CA 94709. (510) 883-0222. Two locations. Go to: www.wtle.com/21426. ***Contemporary, Small Plates, Spanish. $$.***

Chez Panisse Restaurant and Café

Using ingredients produced in an ecologically sound manner, culinary goddess Alice Waters has been setting an international standard for top-notch cuisine since her milestone restaurant opened in north Berkeley in 1971. A recipient of numerous awards — from the James Beard Foundation's Best Chef in America to being named one of the world's 10 best chefs by renowned French culinary organization Cuisine et Vins de France — Waters continues to lead the gastronomic revolution toward the use of local, seasonal and organic ingredients. Chez Panisse's nightly changing menus of Californian cuisine have earned the casually elegant eatery a consistent place on *Gourmet* magazine's America's Best Restaurants list. The wine list is edited daily. The more formal downstairs restaurant (reservations required) offers two nightly seatings Mon–Sat with a fixed-price menu, while the more casual upstairs café serves lunch and dinner à la carte. Closed Sun. 1517 Shattuck Ave., Berkeley, CA 94709. (510) 548-5525. Go to: www.wtle.com/9030. ***Contemporary. $$$.***

Chow Lafayette ~ *Best American Traditional*

Chow Lafayette recognizes the cultural melting pot's effect on American cuisine by including Asian, French, Italian and Mexican flavors alongside menu classics such as burgers and seafood. Like any modern and socially dutiful California restaurant, produce and meats come from local suppliers, but classic diner Americana is revered with such touches as silverware contained in empty Hershey's cans at every table. Several inexpensive wines and beers are available along with interesting non-alcoholic drinks such as tangerine-lime cooler and raspberry lemonade. There are two San Francisco Chow locations, but only Chow Lafayette has a retail section offering menu items to go plus local vegetables, meats, gourmet cheeses and wine. Serving breakfast Mon–Fri, lunch and dinner daily. Sat–Sun brunch 8 am–1 pm. 53 Lafayette Cir., Lafayette, CA 94549. (925) 962-2469. Go to: www.wtle.com/9039. ***American Traditional, Breakfast, Brunch, Contemporary. $$.***

Genova Delicatessen ~ *Best Deli*

Busy from the moment the doors open in the morning until the last customer is ushered out in the early evening, Genova Delicatessen, serving deli sandwiches, hot Italian favorites and gourmet groceries, has thrived in the Bay Area since 1926. Take a number, and wait your turn to order one of the house-specialty sandwiches, such as the pancetta with mortadella, fresh mozzarella and sun-dried tomatoes, though many customers choose to create their own, inspired by the salamis and cheeses dangling from the ceiling. The pasta salads, antipasto and house-made ravioli are also sure to please. In the grocery section, there is a vast selection of Italian seasonings, meats and cheeses, desserts, wines, pastas, and other dry goods available for purchase. Beer and wine available. Serving during breakfast, lunch and early dinner hours daily. 5095 Telegraph Ave, Bldg A, Oakland, CA 94609. (510) 652-7401. Go to: www.wtle.com/9738. ***Deli, Italian, Subs/Hoagies/Po-boys. $.***

Kirala ~ *Best Japanese/Sushi*

Although nearly 20 years old, Berkeley's Kirala Sushi Bar & Robata Grill still brings in diners as if it's the latest, hippest restaurant in the Bay Area. Due to the no-reservations policy, there is often a substantial wait, but loyal patrons still pack the sleek dining room nightly for classic and specialty sushi and nigiri as well as for cooked Japanese entrées. A real treat is the robata grill, which turns out delicious skewers of various meats and vegetables. Kirala also has a takeout-only location on Shattuck Avenue. Full bar, including sake. Serving lunch Tue–Fri, dinner nightly. 2100 Ward St., Berkeley, CA 94705. (510) 549-3486. Go to: www.wtle.com/9902. ***Japanese/Sushi. $$.***

Lalime's

In a warm and unassuming space in Berkeley's Westbrae neighborhood, Lalime's simple settings make an appropriate stage for this Bay Area standby's true focus: the food. And we mean foodie's food, the menu extending far beyond the traditional boundaries of Mediterranean cuisine to include other sun-loving ingredients from California and Mexico. The three-course menu changes bi-monthly according to what's available locally, as Lalime's strives to use organic and sustainably farmed ingredients whenever possible in dishes such as California white sea bass with a Marseilles-style seafood stew. Though the nightly menu remains à la carte, Lalime's offers occasional elaborate, prix fixe dinners, which are celebrations in themselves. Full bar. Serving dinner nightly. 1329 Gilman St., Berkeley, CA 94706. (510) 527-9838. Go to: www.wtle.com/9794. ***Contemporary, Dessert. $$.***

Le Cheval ~ *Best Vietnamese*

One of the most beloved Oakland restaurants, Le Cheval is truly like no place else in the Bay Area. Businesspeople, large families and couples alike gather in the lively warehouse-like structure, spinning family-style dishes on lazy Susans. Authentic Vietnamese, sometimes beyond the limits of less adventurous American tastes, is the menu's subject. (Don't be alarmed at the sight of fermented snakes in the aptly named snake wine, for instance.) Multiple pages of soups, stews and noodle dishes featuring various meats, poultry, seafood and vegetables may be a bit daunting at first glance, but the descriptions in English help. When in doubt: The famed Bo 7 Mon, beef prepared seven ways, steals the show. Full bar. Serving lunch Mon–Sat, dinner nightly. 1007 Clay St., Oakland, CA 94607. (510) 763-8495. Go to: www.wtle.com/10044. ***Asian Fusion, Vietnamese. $.***

Oliveto Cafe & Restaurant ~ *Best Italian*

Oliveto brings formal dining and casual eating together in a single building. Upstairs, former Pacific Bell-executive-turned-chef Paul Canales serves up nationally recognized Italian dishes in a formal setting, while the *East Bay Express* describes the downstairs café as the most affordable way to enjoy the least affordable Italian restaurant. The café is open all day, with a menu that changes daily according to the availability of local ingredients. The more formal upstairs restaurant offers pasta dishes, grilled fish and other rotisserie favorites, while the occasional themed special dinners are a real treat. Full bar. The café serves breakfast, lunch and dinner daily. The restaurant serves lunch Mon–Fri, dinner nightly. 5655 College Ave., Oakland, CA 94618. (510) 547-5356. Go to: www.wtle.com/9835. ***Breakfast, Café, Italian. $$.***

OKLAHOMA CITY
OKLAHOMA

10 LOCAL FAVORITES

***Get your culinary kicks off old Route 66** at some of Oklahoma City's colorful and flavorful diners and restaurants, such as circa-1946 Johnnie's Grill and its legendary onion-fried burgers.*

Cattlemen's Steakhouse ~ *Best Steak House*

Located in Stockyards City since 1910, Cattlemen's is the oldest continuously running restaurant in Oklahoma City. Like many great restaurants across the country — well ... maybe not — Cattlemen's was won in a dice game when the late Gene Wade rolled a "hard six" to acquire the restaurant in 1945. Signature dishes such as the juicy T-bone steak or lamb fries, i.e., lamb testicles (impress your friends with your ruggedness), have attracted not only locals through the years but celebrities such as Gene Autry, John Wayne and country star Reba McEntire. Other recommended menu items include the rib eye or filet mignon, fried catfish, and ham steak with red-eye gravy. Full bar. Serving breakfast, lunch and dinner daily. 1309 S. Agnew Ave., Oklahoma City, OK 73108. (405) 236-0416. Go to: www.wtle.com/1258. ***Breakfast, Steak House. $$.***

The Coach House ~ *Best Contemporary*

The Coach House looks slightly out of place alongside a paved parking lot, the restaurant's white exterior and wooden trim more suited for a cottage in the English countryside. Inside the intimate 50-seat dining room, low light and linen-covered tables create a welcoming elegance for business lunches and romantic dinners alike. Chef/owner Kurt Fleischfresser utilizes Oklahoma-grown foodstuffs to fashion his inventive, seasonally changing menus. For starters, if available, try crab empanadas or grilled jumbo shrimp with cheddar grits cake. Dinner entrées such as rack of lamb, pecan cornbread-crusted salmon with tomato butter and sautéed Dover sole are accompanied by an award-winning wine list. Full bar. Serving lunch Mon–Fri, dinner Mon–Sat. Closed Sun. 6437 Avondale Dr., Nichols Hills, OK 73116. (405) 842-1000. Go to: www.wtle.com/1222. ***Contemporary. $$$.***

Deep Fork Grill

Originally an Italian restaurant called Portobello, this upscale Nichols Hills dining room was transformed in 1995, becoming one of the finest purveyors of fresh seafood in the area. Deep Fork emphasizes sustainable agricultural practices, using locally raised beef and regional produce to create its extensive American contemporary menu. The house specialty is the cedar-plank salmon with a sweet mustard glaze and ginger risotto, but other offerings from the sea are the coriander-crusted ahi and the grilled Chilean sea bass served with sweet potato fries. Entrées include gourmet pizzas such as the Frutti Di Mare (shrimp and scallops with basil pesto), steaks such as the rib eye with house-made worcestershire sauce, and multiple vegetarian entrées. Enjoy live classical guitar during Sunday brunch (10:30 am–4 pm). Full bar. Serving lunch Mon–Fri, dinner nightly. 5418 N. Western Ave., Oklahoma City, OK 73118. (405) 848-7678. Go to: www.wtle.com/1674. ***American Traditional, Brunch. $$.***

Jamil's Steakhouse ~ *Best Middle Eastern*

Established in the 1960s, Jamil's Steakhouse entices patrons with aromatic smoke drifting from the two-story dwelling's smokehouse out back. The combination of Middle Eastern and North African cuisine with traditional American steak house offerings provides cross-cultural dining far more daring and delicious than most contemporary restaurants that advertise "fusion." Kabobs and Lebanese hors d'oeuvres (hummus, cabbage rolls and tabouli salad) complement rib eye, smoked prime rib, T-bone and filet mignon on the menu. Other entrées include smoked bologna, cold water lobster tails, ribs and crab legs. Full bar. Serving lunch Mon–Fri, dinner Mon–Sat. Closed Sun. 4910 N. Lincoln Blvd., Oklahoma City, OK 73105. (405) 525-8352. Go to: www.wtle.com/1637. ***Middle Eastern, Steak House. $$.***

Johnnie's Grill ~ *Best Diner*
At the intersection of Route 66 and the Chisholm Trail lies the historic town of El Reno, host to the annual Onion-Fried Burger Day Festival, during which the world's largest onion burger is created, all 750 pounds of it. A much more manageable rendition of this local specialty, however, can be found at Johnnie's Grill. This roadside restaurant has been serving these caramelized onion-laden burgers since opening in 1946, and they are titanic in taste. On a daily basis, the diner specializes in such hearty fare as chili and Fritos pie, the Arkansas sandwich (two eggs between pancakes), and a sublimely sloppy Coney dog topped with chili and sweet coleslaw. The pies and cakes are heavenly. No alcohol available. Serving breakfast, lunch and dinner daily. 301 S. Rock Island Ave., El Reno, OK 73036. (405) 262-4721. Go to: www.wtle.com/19787. ***Breakfast, Burgers, Diner. $.***

La Baguette Bistro ~ *Best Bakery, Best Bistro*
Co-owned by brothers Michel and Alain Buthion, this French favorite opened in 1988 as a bakery and evolved into a bistro with an innovative menu. Red walls lined with art and wine racks help set the stage for the popular breakfast, which can include lamb chops with scrambled eggs, silver dollar pancakes, or crêpes with a range of fillings. Featured dinner entrées can include seared duck breast with a cherry port sauce and twin lobster cakes. The bistro offers a variety of cakes and tarts along with imported items such as caviar, smoked salmon or pâté. Full bar. Serving breakfast and lunch Mon–Sat, dinner nightly. Sun brunch. 7408 N. May Ave., Oklahoma City, OK 73116. (405) 840-3047. Go to: www.wtle.com/1573. ***Bakery, Bistro, Breakfast, Brunch, French. $$.***

Pearl's Lakeside Seafood Grill ~ *Best Seafood*
A sister restaurant to Pearl's Oyster Bar, Pearl's Lakeside Seafood Grill specializes in fried seafood and boasts a gorgeous view of Lake Hefner. The faux-New Orleans atmosphere is thematically consistent with the Cajun-inspired menu of fried alligator and oysters on the half shell among the starters, while entrées include red beans and rice, and crawfish étouffée. Recommended entrées of the breaded nature include fried pecan-crusted trout, fried crawfish and coconut shrimp. Sunday brunch (10:30 am–2 pm) features such items as andouille omelets and eggs Monique (poached eggs over crab cakes). Full bar. Serving lunch and dinner daily. 9201 E. Lake Hefner Pkwy., Oklahoma City, OK 73210. (405) 748-6113. Go to: www.wtle.com/1270. ***Brunch, Cajun/Creole, Seafood. $$.***

Redrock Canyon Grill

Cactus-themed décor, stone-cut walls and mahogany beams adorn the interior of Redrock Canyon Grill, but when the weather is nice, it's difficult to pass up a chance to sit on the outdoor patio and watch the sunset or the sailboats navigate Lake Hefner. The menu specializes in Southwestern and American Traditional favorites including starters such as the deep-fried stuffed poblano pepper, or tortilla soup. The signature dish is the spit-roasted rotisserie chicken, but the meat loaf, the chicken enchilada platter, mustard-crusted pork chops and barbecued ribs are also recommended entrées. The iron skillet cornbread is a necessity with any meal. Serving dinner nightly. Sun brunch begins 10 am. 9221 Lake Hefner Pkwy., Oklahoma City, OK 73120. (405) 749-1995. Go to: www.wtle.com/1700. ***American Traditional, Southwestern. $$.***

Sushi Neko ~ *Best Japanese/Sushi*

Upon entering Sushi Neko, don't be alarmed if a knife-wielding sushi chef yells, "irashai," as this is merely Japanese for "Come in and make yourself at home." The tatami room offers traditional Japanese dining with seating on the floor, and patrons are asked to take off their shoes. If you accidentally wore your rainbow-colored, individual-toe socks, keep your shoes on, and find a seat at the sushi bar, on the outdoor terrace or in the main dining room. Those less comfortable with raw fish can try the Sushi Virgin Sampler, which includes freshwater eel, shrimp, *tamago* (sushi omelet) and California rolls. A vast array of specialty rolls and sashimi slices are available, as are entrées such as Five Spices Duck Breast and crispy salmon with a honey-miso soy glaze. Full bar. Serving lunch and dinner Mon–Sat. Closed Sun. 4318 N. Western Ave., Oklahoma City, OK 73118. (405) 528-8862. Go to: www.wtle.com/1606. ***Japanese/Sushi. $$.***

Ted's Café Escondido ~ *Best Mexican*

Ted Curtis opened his first Ted's Café Escondido location in 1991 and immediately encountered a great problem to have: hungry patrons waiting outside in a long line. Since expanding to accomodate them with additional restaurants, each location boasts the promise, "If it's not the best, it's on the house." The meat for their famous fajitas marinates overnight and is grilled with fresh peppers and onions, then speedily delivered to the table in a sizzling skillet with accompanying soft tortillas (some 10,000 of which reportedly are made daily). Generous portions and the complimentary chips, salsas — hotheads will enjoy the "atomic" green salsa — and sopaipillas keep Ted's constantly busy, but the wait is worth your while. Full bar. Serving lunch and dinner daily. 2836 N.W. 68th St., Oklahoma City, OK 73116. (405) 848-8337. Multiple locations. Go to: www.wtle.com/1633. ***Mexican. $.***

ORLANDO FLORIDA

10 LOCAL FAVORITES

***Far from being a Mickey Mouse dining scene**, Orlando boasts fine restaurants that run the gamut of culinary styles, from African and soul food to sushi bars and steak houses.*

Swan paddle boats on Lake Eola

Amura Japanese Restaurant ~ *Best Japanese/ Sushi*

With three locations in the Orlando metro area, Amura Japanese Restaurant's "hi-definition" sushi and sashimi menu has drawn quite the crowd since the original restaurant opened on Church Street in 1998. Modest décor doesn't deter downtown's trendiest clientele from enjoying the reasonably priced lunch specials that have placed this hot spot on many local best-of lists. Both traditional and creative sushi rolls from the extensive menu are presented with artistic flair, while a full list of fresh seafood, steaks and traditional dishes is also available. Full bar. Serving lunch Sun–Fri, dinner nightly. 55 W. Church St., Orlando, FL 32801. (407) 316-8500. Multiple locations. Go to: www.wtle.com/17304. ***Japanese/Sushi. $$.***

Boma - Flavors of Africa ~ *Best African/Ethiopian*

Boma - Flavors of Africa brings the feel of an open-air marketplace to the Animal Kingdom Lodge in true Disney fashion, complete with jungle décor and thatch-roof cabanas. Despite the heavy tourist traffic associated with any Disney resort, the family-style buffet and half-dozen live cooking stations draw a significant local crowd that loves the extensive selection of approachable African fare. Breakfast boasts American standards alongside more traditional African specialties such as *pap* (a cornmeal dish closely resembling grits) and South African sausage. Dinner ventures even closer to African authenticity with entrées such as curried coconut seafood stew and banana leaf-wrapped sea bass. Full bar. Serving breakfast and dinner daily. 2901 Osceola Pkwy., Orlando, FL 32830. (407) 939-3463. Go to: www.wtle.com/16602. ***African/Ethiopian, Breakfast, Buffet/Cafeteria. $$.***

Charley's Steak House ~ *Best Steak House*

Consistently ranked among the nation's top steak houses, Charley's Steak House remains the cornerstone venture of local, family-owned Talk of the Town Restaurant Group. The four Central Florida locations boast individual ambiances, but each uses the same painstaking preparation of beef — derived from an old Seminole Indian method — aging cuts for up to six weeks, then hand-seasoning and cooking them over the open flame of a custom wood-burning grill. The result? Some of the finest two- to three-inch thick filets, porterhouses and New York strips in the state. The signature Ultimate Surf and Turf, a whopping 20-ounce filet with a two-pound Australian lobster tail to boot, may be one of the largest dishes anywhere. Full bar. Serving dinner nightly. 6107 S. Orange Blossom Trail. Orlando, FL 32806. (407) 851-7130. Multiple locations. Go to: www.wtle.com/17410. ***Steak House. $$$.***

HUE

Claiming nearly every local media best-of award — from best atmosphere to best signature dish — since its 2002 opening in Orlando's ultra-hip Thornton Park Central retail center, HUE adds another jewel to the crown of locally based Urban Life Management Restaurant Group. Orlando's voguish sip green apple martinis and munch on goat cheese flatbread at the exceedingly fashionable bar or on the popular outdoor patio. An urban loft interior proves the perfect space for indulging in progressive American entrées to the tune of wood-grilled filet mignon, tamari roasted duck breast and Southwestern crusted mahimahi. Sunday brunch (11:30 am–3 pm) offers a contemporary twist on cinnamon toast, egg scrambles and chocolate chip pancakes. Full bar. Serving lunch and dinner daily. 629 E. Central Blvd., Orlando, FL 32801. (407) 849-1800. Go to: www.wtle.com/16641. ***Brunch, Contemporary. $$.***

Johnson's Diner ~ *Best Soul Food*

Downtown icon Johnson's Diner has been a regular stop for soul food-seeking locals — including area politicians and NBA basketball players — since 1955. Its June 2006 move to Church

Street's City View apartment building expanded seating from the cramped 21 to 120. But matriarch Lillie Johnson's "soul food to please the taste" is the same ole rotating selection of Southern soul food standards, including fried catfish, meat loaf and smothered pork chops, all served with a basket of cornbread or rolls. Mix and match with veggies such as fried okra and green beans, but a slice of the sweet potato pie is almost requisite. No alcohol available. Serving breakfast Mon–Sat, lunch and dinner daily. 595 W. Church St., Orlando, FL 32805. (407) 841-0717. Go to: www.wtle.com/17398. ***Breakfast, Home-style, Soul Food. $.***

Julie's Waterfront ~ *Best American Traditional*

From the shores of Lake Jennie Jewel shines one of Orlando's quintessential dining gems, Julie's Waterfront. A longstanding favorite for both family outings and romantic nights for two, this American seafood eatery serves a diverse menu of old standbys with large helpings of charm on the side. The somewhat rustic outdoor setting, complete with a grassy shore and honking geese, evokes a comfortable, Old Florida feel. Choose from the heart-healthy menu, or sit back with a pitcher of beer and some conch fritters. Although the cheeseburger is one of the best in town, assorted grilled and fried seafood platters prove quite popular, as well. Beer and wine available. Serving breakfast Sat–Sun, lunch daily, dinner Tue–Sun. 4201 S. Orange Ave., Orlando, FL 32806. (407) 240-2557. Go to: www.wtle.com/16778. ***American Traditional, Breakfast, Brunch, Seafood, Vegetarian. $$.***

La Coquina ~ *Best Brunch*

Of all The Villas of Grand Cypress resort's restaurants, it is La Coquina's Sunday brunch that remains one of Orlando's most coveted dining experiences. A seat in the bright and airy room overlooking Lake Windsong requires months-in-advance reservations for the highly popular Sunday brunch (10:30 am–2 pm). And that's not just because the resort's exclusive-label champagne is complimentary (and unlimited). The impressively extensive selection of New World cuisine in addition to classic brunch items prove the perfect combination of French inspiration and Asian influence, offering the season's freshest fruits, meats and seafood from Florida's coasts. Dinner has been retooled into a communal chef's table concept featuring five courses that vary daily. Full bar. Serving dinner Thu–Sat. Sun brunch. Closed Mon–Wed. 1 Grand Cypress Blvd., Orlando, FL 32836. (407) 239-1234. Go to: www.wtle.com/21248. ***Brunch, Contemporary, Hotel Restaurant. $$$.***

Le Coq Au Vin ~ *Best French*

Amid the convenience stores populating Orange Avenue sits one of Orlando's most acclaimed yet delightfully humble eateries, Le Coq Au Vin. The husband-wife proprietorship of chefs Louis and Magdalena Perrotte focuses more on the consistent quality of authentic French cuisine than the hoards of praise they've achieved over the years. Locals know Le Coq Au Vin as the place frequented by chefs on their nights off to enjoy regularly changing, seasonal menus, which particularly shine with dishes containing the chef's specialty sweetbreads. The coq au vin, perfectly braised in burgundy wine, is always available due to popular demand. Order a Grand Marnier soufflé for something extra special. Beer and wine available. Serving dinner Tue–Sun. Closed Mon. 4800 S. Orange Ave., Orlando, FL 32806. (407) 851-6980. Go to: www.wtle.com/17210. ***Bistro, French. $$.***

Seasons 52 ~ *Best Contemporary, Best Dessert*
Another smash hit from Orlando-based Darden Restaurants, Seasons 52 successfully responds to America's call for healthy dining options. The 2003 flagship operation in Orlando has grown to a small but wildly popular chain, prompting *Nation's Restaurant News* to name Seasons 52's you'd-never-know-it's-healthy model one of the hottest concepts of 2006. In a sophisticated contemporary setting, customers indulge in a seasonal menu of calorie-conscious fare, with each grilled halibut, pork tenderloin and roasted rack of lamb containing fewer than 475 calories. Three-ounce mini-desserts offer bite-sized indulgences decadent enough to satisfy the sweet tooth but small enough to keep the carbs under control. Full bar. Serving lunch and dinner daily. 7700 W. Sand Lake Rd., Orlando, FL 32836. (407) 354-5212. Two locations. Go to: www.wtle.com/21242. ***Contemporary, Dessert. $$.***

White Wolf Cafe ~ *Best Café*
Offbeat and off the beaten path, White Wolf Cafe provides a rather charming break from dime-a-dozen tourist spots. This is precisely what husband-and-wife founders Michael and Anne Marie Hennessey aimed for when they established their unassuming gem — named for their snow-colored German shepherd — in Orlando's bohemian district in 1991. Today they serve a loyal following that adores the eclectic menu of funky, gourmet fare. From brown sugar-and-pear salmon to a classic peanut butter and jelly sandwich with banana slices, dishes are as fun as they are interesting. Really, any place that serves ice cream floats and fine wine under one roof must be a winner. Beer and wine available. Serving lunch and dinner Mon–Sat. Closed Sun. 1829 N. Orange Ave., Orlando, FL 32804. (407) 895-9911. Go to: www.wtle.com/17207. ***Café, Contemporary, Vegetarian. $$.***

PHILADELPHIA PENNSYLVANIA

10 LOCAL FAVORITES

***It's all about the cheese steaks**, to be certain, but Philly's prominent dining scene has also helped kick-start the Asian Fusion and gastropub movements, to name just two.*

Independence Hall

Buddakan ~ *Best Asian Fusion*

Restaurateur extraordinaire Stephen Starr opened Buddakan in 1998 to critical praise and overwhelming popularity. The sleek décor — including a waterfall and a 10-foot golden statue of the Buddha — makes Buddakan, like all Starr restaurants, a theatrical dining experience and a place to be seen. Under the direction of executive chef Scott Swiderski, the Asian Fusion cuisine does not take second billing to the glamorous atmosphere and bar scene, though. Artfully designed entrées such as the Japanese black cod or the roasted duck breast with five-spice jus are meant to be shared, as portions are colossal. Full bar. Serving lunch Mon–Fri, dinner nightly. 325 Chestnut St., Philadelphia, PA 19106. (215) 574-9440. Go to: www.wtle.com/24146. ***Asian Fusion. $$$.***

Fountain Restaurant ~ *Best Contemporary*

If frustrated by the short tempers of cheese steak vendors or weary of the do-it-yourself approach of the trendy BYOBs popping up all over town, find your way to nationally recognized Fountain Restaurant in the Four Seasons Hotel in Center City. Here, you'll find attentive, world-class service in an extravagantly elegant setting. With wood-paneled walls, liberally spaced tables and a view of the gorgeous Swann Fountain for which the restaurant is named, the furnishings are among the city's most luxurious. The six-course tasting menu allows guests to sample a variety of chef Martin Hamann's French-inspired contemporary fare. Fountain Restaurant also features an extensive Sunday brunch (11 am–2:15 pm). Jacket suggested for dinner. Full bar. Serving breakfast, lunch and dinner daily. 1 Logan Sq., Philadelphia, PA 19103. (215) 963-1500. Go to: www.wtle.com/24316. ***Breakfast, Brunch, Contemporary, Hotel Restaurant. $$$.***

L'Angolo

A quintessential South Philly trattoria, L'Angolo has been serving delectable yet affordable Italian cuisine since 2000. The charming 35-seat BYOB is owned and operated by Italian-born David Faenza and his wife, Kathryn. Though somewhat hidden, this local favorite is far from being a secret, as the consistently packed dining room can attest. The tender calamari highlights the appetizers list, while fresh seafood specials, pastas and a couple of well-crafted veal dishes round out the entrées. Cleanse your palate with the house-made, complimentary limoncello (a sweet lemon liqueur available by request only) or the espresso chocolate torte, when available. BYOB. Serving dinner Tue–Sun. Closed Mon. 1415 W. Porter St., Philadelphia, PA 19145. (215) 389-4252. Go to: www.wtle.com/24421. ***Italian. $$.***

Le Bec-Fin ~ *Best French*

Georges Perrier garnered national attention for Philadelphia's dining scene when he founded the dazzling Le Bec-Fin in 1970. Following a ratings fiasco in 2002, Perrier revamped and remodeled his restaurant, solidifying its position as the epitome of decadent dining in Philadelphia. The jaw-dropping white and gold décor, complete with chandeliers from the first incarnation of the restaurant, mimic the late 19th-century elegance of a Parisian salon. The six-course, prix fixe menu of classic French cuisine is the best way to sample a variety of delicacies and makes dining here a truly special experience. Save room for the legendary desserts. Full bar. Serving lunch Mon–Fri, dinner Mon–Sat. Closed Sun. 1523 Walnut St., Philadelphia, PA 19102. (215) 567-1000. Go to: www.wtle.com/24284. ***French. $$$.***

Marigold Kitchen

A Victorian boardinghouse-turned-restaurant, open since 2004, the quaint Marigold Kitchen has created enough buzz that it can no longer be called Philadelphia's best-kept secret. Steven Cook's University City restaurant proves that a cutting-edge culinary experience does not necessitate white linen.

New executive chef Erin O'Shea incorporates her "modern takes on Southern cooking" into the creative and imaginative but not inaccessible cuisine. Appetizers are not to be missed here: Try the sweetbread nuggets with lentil and root vegetable stew, when available. Bring your own wine, but make sure it is worthy of the elegant stemware provided by Marigold Kitchen. BYOB. Serving dinner Tue–Sun. Closed Mon. 501 S. 45th St., Philadelphia, PA 19104. (215) 222-3699. Go to: www.wtle.com/24417. ***Contemporary. $$$.***

Shank's and Evelyn's Luncheonette

Most Philadelphia sandwich debates revolve around the three largest cheese steak purveyors, but locals who are in-the-know will direct you to Shank's and Evelyn's Luncheonette for a truly satisfying sandwich. What this hole in the wall, open since 1960, lacks in space and décor, it more than makes up for in South Philly's Italian character. Evelyn and the women behind the counter provide friendly service with an edgy attitude that is indigenous to the neighborhood. Politicians are often spotted having breakfast here or feasting on the signature roast beef sandwich smothered with gravy. Pickled hot peppers remain an irresistible side. BYOB. Serving breakfast and lunch Mon–Sat, dinner Thu–Sat. Closed Sun. 932 S. 10th St., Philadelphia, PA 19147. (215) 629-1093. Go to: www.wtle.com/24398. ***Breakfast, Italian, Subs/Hoagies/Po-boys. $$.***

Standard Tap ~ *Best American Traditional, Best Burgers*

This Northern Liberties establishment helped start the local momentum of the gastropub concept and continues to be the benchmark. The blaring jukebox, dartboards, dim lighting and emphasis on local beers may suggest that this two-story renovated building is merely a comfortable neighborhood watering hole. The menu — listed on blackboards with matter-of-fact descriptions simply saying "Pork Sandwich" and "Smelts" — may not do justice to the culinary prowess of the kitchen either, but the food remains some of the most creative and popular in town. The Standard Burger, known for its sautéed-mushroom topping, is a standout, and for the adventurous, there are options such as the duck salad or grilled octopus. Full bar. Serving dinner nightly. Sun brunch 11 am–3 pm. 901 N. 2nd St., Philadelphia, PA 19123. (215) 238-0630. Go to: www.wtle.com/23800. ***American Traditional, Brunch, Burgers, Gastropub. $$.***

Susanna Foo Chinese Cuisine

Since opening in 1987, Susanna Foo's restaurant on Walnut

Street has perpetually astounded critics and locals alike with its inspired French-influenced Chinese cuisine. Celebrity chef/ owner Susanna Foo set the standard for the now ever-present concept of Asian Fusion years ago, and she continues to redefine seemingly ordinary Chinese staples, such as won ton soup and crispy duck, by utilizing European technique. The space, filled with silk lanterns and mirrors, provides a tranquil backdrop for a memorable meal facilitated by an efficient waitstaff uniformed in tuxedos. Full bar. Serving lunch Mon–Fri, dinner Mon–Sat. Closed Sun. 1512 Walnut St., Philadelphia, PA 19102. (215) 545-2666. Go to: www.wtle.com/24425. ***Asian Fusion, Chinese, French. $$$.***

Tony Luke's Old Philly Style Sandwiches ~

Best Cheese Steaks

Much like Benjamin Franklin, the Liberty Bell and Rocky Balboa, the Philly cheese steak is integral to the identity of Philadelphia. Cultural significance aside, it's an especially delicious creation at Tony Luke's Old Philly Style Sandwiches. Located near the Eagles' Lincoln Financial Field and featuring a view of an I-95 overpass, the best scenery at Tony Luke's is the eclectic crowd that gathers. The cheese steaks may be the main food attraction, but Tony Luke's has drawn critical acclaim for its hot pork sandwiches — garlicky roast pork, broccoli rabe and provolone — as well. Ask the cheese steak enthusiast in line next to you about the ordering procedure, unless of course you feel that absorbing some Philadelphia attitude from the employees will give you the full experience. No alcohol available. Cash only. Serving breakfast, lunch and dinner Mon–Sat. Closed Sun. 39 E. Oregon Ave., Philadelphia, PA 19148. (215) 551-5725. Go to: www.wtle.com/24344. ***Cheese Steaks. $.***

Vetri ~ *Best Italian*

With the accolades piling up, including being named the James Beard Foundation's 2005 Best Chef: Mid-Atlantic, Marc Vetri could capitalize on his success. As of yet, he does not have his own TV show or a line of pasta sauces bearing his likeness on the label, and he still has not expanded his 35-seat townhouse-turned-restaurant in Center City (though he has opened a new venture, Osteria, on Broad Street). Vetri oversees the kitchen, while business partner and maitre d' Jeff Benjamin handles the wine pairings for Vetri's creations, which have many clamoring that this could be the best Italian restaurant in the country. Though menus change seasonally, and Saturday nights feature customized tasting menus for each table, Vetri is best known for its fresh pastas made with ingredients that are hand-selected by the chef and for the succulent pit-roasted goat. Full bar. Serving dinner Mon–Sat. Closed Sun. 1312 Spruce St., Philadelphia, PA 19107. (215) 732-3478. Go to: www.wtle.com/24299. ***Italian. $$$.***

PHOENIX ARIZONA

10 LOCAL FAVORITES

***Beyond superlative Southwestern and Mexican eateries**, Phoenix is home to Deseo and its chef Douglas Rodriguez, an originator of upscale classic Nuevo Latino cuisine.*

Chelsea's Kitchen ~ *Best Home-style*

A 2005 addition to the highly touted LGO Hospitality pedigree, Chelsea's Kitchen adds a touch of unusual to the dining monopoly. Downtown meets down-home in the relaxed, upscale atmosphere of this chicly urban eatery, where a made-to-order menu — down to the last tortilla shell — seldom inhibits super-quick service. The decidedly Southwestern burgers, tacos, steaks and chicken (all with a twist) transport the every-day to extraordinary. From the spicy ahi tuna burger to beef short ribs with an over-easy egg, bold flavor is the Chelsea's standard. Full bar. Serving lunch and dinner daily. Sun brunch 10 am–3 pm. 5040 N. 40th St., Phoenix, AZ 85018. (602) 957-2555. Go to: www.wtle.com/10265. ***Brunch, Contemporary, Dessert, Home-style, Southwestern. $$$.***

Deseo ~ *Best Latin/South American*

It doesn't get much trendier than The Westin Kierland Resort & Spa's Deseo in Scottsdale. Named after the Spanish word for "desire," this super-sexy establishment excels in service, atmosphere and cuisine. Country club-gone-hip décor sets the stage for locals seeking a cool cocktail or a spicy New Latin meal.

The menu — developed by James Beard award-winner, Cuban native and recognized originator of the Nuevo Latino genre Douglas Rodriguez — steers away from Phoenix's Southwestern roots in favor of flavors from the tropical neighbors to the south. Drink and ceviche specials draw a hip crowd early in the evening, but locals begin packing in at dinnertime for the outstanding and inventive small plates and entrées. Don't miss dessert. Full bar. Serving dinner nightly. 6902 E. Greenway Pkwy., Scottsdale, AZ 85254. (480) 624-1030. Go to: www.wtle.com/10176. ***Contemporary, Latin/South American, Seafood. $$$.***

El Chorro Lodge

Located on 14 desert acres in Paradise Valley, El Chorro Lodge — *chorro* being the Spanish word for "a sudden gush of liquid" — has been a refreshing oasis for its steady crowd of regulars parched for first-class cuisine. The romantic, old Arizona adobe was originally designed as a schoolhouse for girls, though today it serves as a favorite place for locals to enjoy a cool cocktail on the spectacular outdoor patio. The timeless European menu favors classic dishes. Châteaubriand and rack of lamb are prepared tableside, per custom, but the equally famed sticky buns characterize this landmark eatery's familiar, neighborhood appeal. Full bar. Serving lunch Mon–Fri, dinner nightly. Sun brunch (Oct–May) 9 am–2 pm. 5550 E. Lincoln Dr., Paradise Valley, AZ 85253. (480) 948-5170. Go to: www.wtle.com/9551. ***American Traditional, Brunch, Contemporary. $$$.***

Los Dos Molinos ~ *Best Mexican*

Known for its party-like atmosphere and very hot salsas, Los Dos Molinos doesn't know how to make it mild. So says owner/chef Victoria Chavez, the 70-something wizard behind the curtain who still wakes up at 2 am to begin her workday. Patrons can clearly stand the heat she's bringing, however, as this Springerville, Ariz., original has grown from its Navajo County roots to a small chain, including a New York City location. Giant portions of incendiary New Mexican cuisine are served with copious glasses of water, but be warned: Any entrée containing the word "chili" will require an entire pitcher. Recommendations include red chili-smothered *adobada* ribs or shrimp Veracruz (prawns and chili over rice). Full bar. Serving lunch and dinner Tue–Sat. Closed Sun–Mon. 8646 S. Central Ave., Phoenix, AZ 85042. (602) 243-9113. Go to: www.wtle.com/21108. ***Mexican. $$.***

Mastro's Steakhouse ~ *Best Steak House*

Recently acquired by two New York-based private equity firms forming Rare Restaurant Group, the soon-to-be-expanded

Mastro's Steakhouse chain boasts local roots, founded by Scottsdale's Mastro Group, LLC. The swanky original is where the Valley's well-heeled clientele flock to enjoy top-notch ambiance, service and cuisine. In a white-tablecloth atmosphere complete with live pianist, diners find massive top cuts of well-flavored chops, lobsters and steaks with accompanying à la carte hors d'oeuvres and sides. Seasoned bartenders serve up some of the best cocktails in the area or a choice from the outstanding wine list that consistently receives *Wine Spectator*'s Award of Excellence. Full bar. Serving dinner nightly. 8852 E. Pinnacle Peak Rd., Scottsdale, AZ 85255. (480) 585-9500. Go to: www.wtle.com/10489. ***Steak House. $$$.***

Roaring Fork ~ *Best Contemporary*

James Beard award-winning chef/former-owner Robert McGrath brought to Scottsdale what might be considered the Southwest's most quintessential restaurant with his much-lauded Roaring Fork. The Texas native prefers his Stetson to a toque, and a playful yet decidedly gourmet menu to a fancy list of frills. In a cowboy-casual atmosphere, Roaring Fork serves classic American Western cuisine (a genre McGrath helped popularize) with his own upscale twist. Dine finely on braised short ribs in Dr. Pepper barbecue sauce, or anchor both hands around the oft-hailed and aptly named "Big Ass" Burger (12 ounces of beef, piled high with chiles, grilled onions and bacon, served only in the Saloon). Whichever you choose, a side of green chile macaroni completes each dish. Full bar. Serving dinner nightly. 4800 N. Scottsdale Rd., Scottsdale, AZ 85251. (480) 947-0795. Go to: www.wtle.com/9560. ***Contemporary. $$$.***

Sea Saw ~ *Best Japanese/Sushi*

Named one of the country's top new chefs of 2003 by *Food & Wine* magazine, and the 2007 James Beard Foundation winner for Best Chef: Southwest, Sea Saw's Nobuo Fukuda is one of the superstars of Phoenix's restaurant scene. His simple yet innovative Japanese small plates and sashimi presentations, from miso-marinated foie gras to steamed sea bass with green tea soba noodles, come to the tiny, 28-seat Sea Saw situated on Scottsdale's restaurant row. Co-owner and wine steward Peter Kasperski keeps an award-winning cellar of 225-plus grape varietals, which pair nicely with Fukuda's cuisine. Full bar. Serving dinner nightly. 7133 E. Stetson Dr., Scottsdale, AZ 85251. (480) 481-9463. Go to: www.wtle.com/24005. ***Asian Fusion, Japanese/Sushi. $$.***

Sugar Bowl Ice Cream Parlor ~ *Best Ice Cream*

Many old-fashioned soda shops appear as if they're straight out of a storybook. With the Sugar Bowl in Old Town Scottsdale, that's actually quite accurate. *The Family Circus* creator Bil Keane drew on his experiences from this 1950s original as inspiration for his phenomenally successful daily comic strip depicting American family life. Not much at the Sugar Bowl has changed since that time. The full-service menu offers soups, salads and sandwiches, but the real reason to go is the sweet selection of sugary goodness. Sherbets, sodas, shakes, scoops, floats and more than 14 flavors of malts are largely portioned and hugely delicious. Much recommended is the banana split, complete with raspberry sorbet and Turkish coffee ice cream, but it's hard to beat a good old-fashioned sundae. No alcohol available. Serving lunch and dinner daily. 4005 N. Scottsdale Rd., Scottsdale, AZ 85251. (480) 946-0051. Go to: www.wtle.com/10314. ***Ice Cream. $.***

T. Cook's ~ *Best Continental*

Housed in the luxurious Royal Palms Resort and Spa, T. Cook's remains one of Phoenix's top spots for proposals, anniversary dinners and all endeavors of L-O-V-E. (Just call the resort's resident "romance planner" for ideas.) Couples stroll the beautiful grounds arm-in-arm or gaze into each other's eyes over the chef's nightly five-course tasting menu, offered in the dining room's gorgeous Mediterranean-oasis setting. The highly upscale, seasonal menu captures the best of Spanish and Tuscan cuisines, from Mediterranean paella and truffle-glazed quail to grilled veal shank and roasted pork belly. Breakfast, lunch and Sunday brunch (10 am–2 pm) are more casual without compromising quality. Full bar. Serving breakfast, lunch and dinner daily. 5200 E. Camelback Rd., Phoenix, AZ 85018. (866) 579-3636. Go to: www.wtle.com/10185. ***Breakfast, Brunch, Continental, Hotel Restaurant. $$$.***

Vincent on Camelback ~ *Best Southwestern*

Chef Vincent Guerithault's international reputation registers nothing short of exemplary, as he has earned some of the most distinguished culinary honors in both America and his native France. His Camelback eatery has similarly achieved much distinction with its unique menu that encompasses French cooking techniques and Southwestern ingredients, and vice versa. The distinctive combination of cuisines is most fully realized in dishes such as blue cornmeal-crusted sweetbreads, Anaheim chile and raisin duck tamales, and rosemary-thyme rack of lamb with spicy pepper jelly. Dessert is an absolute must, truly: If you don't order one, Chef Vincent may well send one over anyway. Extensive, award-winning wine list and full bar. Serving lunch Mon–Fri, dinner Mon–Sat. Closed Sun. 3930 E. Camelback Rd., Phoenix, AZ 85018. (602) 224-0225. Go to: www.wtle.com/10471. ***Contemporary, Dessert, French, Southwestern. $$$.***

PITTSBURGH PENNSYLVANIA

10 LOCAL FAVORITES

***No food best represents the sturdy** inventiveness of Pittsburgh cuisine quite like the storied Primanti Brothers sandwich: a half-pound of towering meat, cheese, tomatoes, crispy fries and coleslaw piled on crusty Italian bread.*

Cafe Zinho ~ *Best Continental*

Relaxed, funky Cafe Zinho attracts young trendsters and senior foodies alike to its converted-garage setting in the Shadyside neighborhood. What brings them here is not the flea-market-esque décor — though that certainly has appeal of its own — but the casual, eclectic gourmet cuisine, designed to show off the chef's creativity, attention to detail and commitment to fine ingredients. Seasonal soups, meal-sized salads, sandwiches, well-crafted entrées and excellent house-made desserts are prepared with a Continental flair. Try the restaurant's most popular entrée, oven-roasted shrimp cake with Dijon mustard and pistachio lime sauce. Reservations not accepted. BYOB. Cash or check only. Serving dinner nightly. 238 Spahr St., Pittsburgh, PA 15232. (412) 363-1500. Go to: www.wtle.com/1395. ***Contemporary, Continental. $$.***

The Carlton ~ *Best Contemporary*

Tucked into the heart of Pittsburgh's downtown business district at One Mellon Center, proprietor Kevin Joyce's The Carlton has the look and feel of the quintessential power-lunch or business-dinner spot. Since its 1984 opening, it has earned numerous honors, including the city's only DiRoNA award. Dark wood paneling, caricatures of city celebrities on the walls, and creative hardwood-grilled meats and seafood compare favorably with national steak house leaders. The daily changing menu allows for the talented kitchen staff to add a certain local panache that makes The Carlton's contemporary fare some of the most exciting in the city, with dishes such as lamb osso buco and lobster ravioli. Full bar and extensive wine list. Serving lunch Mon–Fri, dinner Mon–Sat. Closed Sun. 500 Grant St., Pittsburgh, PA 15219. (412) 391-4099. Go to: www.wtle.com/1127. ***Contemporary, Seafood. $$$.***

The Church Brew Works ~ *Best Brewpub*
Church and beer unite — yes, church and beer — at Lawrenceville's The Church Brew Works. Originally constructed in 1902 as St. John the Baptist Church, changing neighborhood demographics forced it to shut down in 1993. Three years later, however, it was resurrected as a brewpub, maintaining its original character with pews for seating, the altar for the brew house, and the original organ pipes proudly on display against the front walls. The Church Brew Works serves a variety of colorfully named house brews in addition to its extensive menu of upscale pub food, including wood-fired pizzas, sandwiches, pastas and top steaks such as the Kobe flank. Full bar. Serving lunch and dinner daily. 3525 Liberty Ave., Pittsburgh, PA 15201. (412) 688-8200. Go to: www.wtle.com/1316. ***American Traditional, Brewpub. $$.***

Grand Concourse ~ *Best Brunch*
Owned since 2002 by Houston-based Landry's restaurant chain, the Grand Concourse opened in 1978 in the renovated former-Pittsburgh & Lake Erie railroad terminal. The circa-1901 building, now on the National Register of Historic Places, features an unparalleled dining atmosphere that transports diners back to a time when steel barons ruled the city and spearheaded the country's industrial growth. The seasonally changing menu offers excellent selections such as coconut shrimp and Maryland crab cakes, while the Sunday all-you-can-eat brunch buffet (10 am–3 pm) is so popular that reservations are a must. Full bar. Serving lunch Mon–Fri, dinner nightly. 100 W. Station Sq. Dr., Pittsburgh, PA 15219. (414) 261-1717. Go to: www.wtle.com/1121. ***Brunch, Contemporary, Seafood. $$.***

Le Pommier ~ *Best French*
Housed in a restored 1869-era building, South Side's Le Pommier has the look and casual feel of a French country cottage. Founded more than 20 years ago, former employees Mark Collins (executive

chef) and Jeremy Carlisle (house manager) now run the show. Together, the pair has continued Le Pommier's tradition of serving seasonal, rustic French cooking and employing the freshest local produce. On any given menu, you might find dishes ranging from classic grilled hanger steak and pommes frites to escargots. Don't miss the sweet endings prepared by the in-house pastry chef — including house-made sorbets and indulgent chocolate crêpes. Full bar and expansive wine list. Serving dinner Mon–Sat. Closed Sun. 2104 E. Carson St., Pittsburgh, PA 15203. (412) 431-1901. Go to: www.wtle.com/1430. ***French. $$$.***

Lidia's Italy Pittsburgh ~ *Best Italian*

Lidia Bastianich, two-time James Beard award-winning chef, author and TV personality, has opened several successful Italian restaurants across the country, including Lidia's Italy Pittsburgh in 2001. Bastianich visits her comfortable Strip District spot, with its white-clothed tables surrounding a large fireplace, several times annually to help train chefs in preparing the Italian-American specialties first popularized in her New York City restaurants. Along with the daily pasta tastings, you'll find real Italian classics such as lemon chicken with capers and olives. Brunch is offered on Saturdays and Sundays 11 am–2:30 pm. Full bar. Serving lunch and dinner Tue–Sun. Closed Mon. 1400 Smallman St., Pittsburgh, PA 15222. (412) 552-0150. Go to: www.wtle.com/1319. ***Brunch, Italian. $$.***

The Pines Tavern ~ *Best American Traditional*

This country inn-style restaurant on the outskirts of Pittsburgh, in Pines, has more than two acres of gardens and a greenhouse that produces many of the herbs, vegetables, fruits and greens that go into the cooking. The extensive, eclectic menu changes several times a year according to the season and the whims of partner and executive chef Jason Culp. Whether indulging in turtle soup and grilled vegetable ravioli, soft-shell crab or a tavern sirloin, rest assured that most ingredients are organic and from sustainable, local farms, if not the restaurant's own garden. An extensive and much-celebrated wine selection includes a wine flight option, which pairs a different wine with each course of your dinner. Full bar. Serving lunch and dinner Tue–Sat. Closed Sun–Mon (except open Mon during Dec). 5018 Bakerstown Rd., Gibsonia, PA 15044. (724) 625-3252. Go to: www.wtle.com/1173. ***American Traditional. $$.***

Primanti Brothers ~ *Best Deli*

A true Pittsburgh institution that has inspired a nationwide chain, Primanti Brothers restaurants specialize in towering sandwiches made up of a half-pound of meat, cheese, tomatoes, crispy fries, and sweet-and-sour coleslaw, all piled on crusty Italian bread and served on wax paper. Lore has it that the original Primanti's (in the Strip District at 18th Street) invented the sandwich as a one-handed meal for on-the-go truckers hauling produce to nearby markets. But then again, the owners simply may have run out of flatware and improvised by cramming a plateful of food between two pieces of bread. Either way, there's no denying the gut-level appeal of these gargantuan sandwiches. Try the double egg pastrami and cheese, the Pittsburger cheese steak, or the hot sausage and cheese. Full bar. Open 24 hours at the original 18th Street location; hours vary at the other locations. 46 18th St., Pittsburgh, PA 15222. (412) 263-2142. Multiple locations. Go to: www.wtle.com/1300. ***Breakfast, Deli. $.***

Tessaro's ~ *Best Burgers, Best Steak House*

Regarded for years as the best burger joint in the 'Burgh, casual Little Italy neighborhood bar and restaurant Tessaro's earned its reputation serving perfectly charred gourmet burgers and steaks grilled over hardwood. When their preferred butcher shop closed several years ago, the Harrington family hired an in-house butcher, who was tasked to incorporate steak and filet scraps into the custom-ground chuck that goes into Tessaro's hand-patted, half-pound wonders. The fabulous grilled home fries, instead of traditional potato wedges, and a hearty helping of coleslaw complete the trinity. The flavorful steaks are best enjoyed "Pittsburgh-style" — charred on the outside, rare to medium-rare on the inside. Full bar. Serving lunch and dinner Mon–Sat. Closed Sun. 4601 Liberty Ave., Pittsburgh, PA 15224. (412) 682-6809. Go to: www.wtle.com/1195. ***American Traditional, Burgers, Steak House. $$.***

Umi ~ *Best Japanese/Sushi*

Located up two long flights of stairs, just above Shadyside's Soba Lounge, sits the sumptuously decorated Umi. The local standard-bearer for all things sushi and sashimi since its 1999 debut, the restaurant has award-winning executive chef Shyh-Dyi Shu to thank for its continued success. Mr. Shu, as most patrons know him, holds court behind a small but dramatic-looking sushi bar that stays jam-packed most evenings. The handful of teriyakis and cooked noodle dishes round out a menu of maki, sushi and sashimi made from the freshest fish flown in from around the world. Night after night, willing patrons place the fate of their dinners in the hands of Mr. Shu, as his *omakase* — chef's choice, literally translated as "trust the chef" — remains undoubtedly one of the best in the city. Full bar. Serving dinner Tue–Sat. Closed Sun–Mon. 5849 Ellsworth Ave., Pittsburgh, PA 15232. (412) 362-6198. Go to: www.wtle.com/1782. ***Japanese/Sushi. $$.***

PORTLAND OREGON

10 LOCAL FAVORITES

Long known for its cutting-edge contemporary cuisine at such restaurants as Wildwood and Caprial's Bistro, Portland was home to American culinary icon James Beard.

Andina ~ *Best Latin/South American*

As with many Pearl District restaurants, much-lauded and family-owned Andina is located upstairs in a renovated warehouse featuring wooden beams, theatrical lighting and original Peruvian artwork. Patrons love the upscale tapas and entrées that are featured on the menu, created by a native Peruvian chef and consisting of a mix of pre-colonial and contemporary ingredients. Start with a Spanish-style potato frittata, fried seafood won tons or even a grilled octopus kabob. Entrées include lamb shank simmered in cilantro and black beer, and a vegetarian stew of squash, Andean grains and cheese. Live music at Bar Mestizo. Full bar. Serving lunch Mon–Sat, dinner nightly. 1314 N.W. Glisan St., Portland, OR 97209. (503) 228-9535. Go to: www.wtle.com/17846. ***Contemporary, Latin/South American. $$.***

Caprial's Bistro ~ *Best Bistro*

Celebrity chefs and husband-and-wife team Caprial and John Pence have built the boisterous Caprial's Bistro into a local treasure since its 1992 opening, and they consequently have helped put Portland on the national food map. Dedicated fans — when not watching the Pences on TV as they scavenge the Pacific Northwest for elusive and fresh ingredients, or argue among themselves in front of a national audience — sit at the bistro's tables, view the open kitchen, or rush to the Pence's cooking classes held in the back room. The monthly changing menu showcases flavorful Northwest cuisine with global accents. When available at lunch, try the Hot-As-Hell Chicken, a sweet chili- and cilantro-seasoned breast served on Chinese noodles with a fiery peanut sauce. The gourmet hushpuppies and the specialty seasonal fish are local favorites. Full bar. Serving lunch and dinner Tue–Sat. Closed Sun–Mon. 7015 S.E. Milwaukie Ave., Portland, OR 97202. (503) 236-6457. Go to: www.wtle.com/17905. ***Bistro, Contemporary. $$$.***

The Heathman Restaurant & Bar ~ *Best Brunch*

Located in Portland's Theater District at the historic art deco Heathman Hotel, The Heathman Restaurant offers French-inspired Continental bistro food highlighted by one of the area's best weekend brunches. Contemporary and classic pieces of art hang on beige walls in the dimly lighted dining room, which has high-backed chairs and the look and feel of old-school hotel dining. The ever-changing menu of Northwestern fare molded by French technique has previously included roasted pheasant, duck à l'orange, and rainbow trout sautéed with hazelnuts, cranberries, mushrooms and zucchini. Recommended brunch items include brioche French toast, eggs Benedict with kitchen-smoked salmon, and corned beef hash with poached eggs. Full bar. Serving breakfast and dinner daily, lunch Mon–Fri. Sat–Sun brunch 9 am–3 pm. 1001 S.W. Broadway. Portland, OR 97205. (503) 790-7752. Go to: www.wtle.com/17794. ***Breakfast, Brunch, Contemporary, Hotel Restaurant. $$$.***

Higgins Restaurant and Bar

The much-lauded tri-level restaurant Higgins, named after co-owner Greg Higgins, specializes in upscale Northwestern fare with French influences. Focused mainly on local, sustainable and organic ingredients, the innovative and oft-changing menu attracts crowds of locals to the classy but unpretentious dining room. Windows allow passersby to check out the open kitchen as well as the pressed-tin ceiling. From the bistro menu, try the ground sirloin burger (a high-end interpretation of the American classic) or the signature charcuterie appetizer with house-cured meats and Higgins pickles. For dinner, entrées may include cider-glazed pork loin with chili-onion relish, duck confit with brandied blood-orange conserve, and a plethora of delicious vegetarian options. Beer connoisseurs and the after-work crowd take comfort in the full bar, which features a staggering array of Belgian, German and English beers. Serving lunch Mon–Fri, dinner nightly. 1239 S.W. Broadway., Portland, OR 97205. (503) 222-9070. Go to: www.wtle.com/17795. ***Contemporary. $$.***

Jake's Famous Crawfish ~ *Best Seafood*

The inviting dark-wood interior at Jake's Famous Crawfish possesses old-school ambiance for good reason: It has been providing fresh seafood to Portland since 1892. The menu changes each day to reflect fresh fish and crustacean arrivals, with more than 30 varieties from which to choose. When available, start with oysters on the half shell, crab cakes, jumbo prawn cocktail, or creamy seafood and corn chowder. Recommendations for dinner include seared ahi, steamed Maine lobster, and salmon stuffed with Dungeness crab, shrimp and Brie. Full bar. Serving lunch Mon–Sat, dinner nightly. Closed Sun. 401 S.W. 12th Ave., Portland, OR 97205. (503) 226-1419. Go to: www.wtle.com/18065. ***American Traditional, Seafood. $$.***

Mio Sushi ~ *Best Japanese/Sushi*

Mio Sushi's flagship location in a Victorian house in northwest Portland invariably attracts long lines of diners at prime eating times. In contrast to the minimalist décor, the sushi and other Japanese dishes (for the sashimi-phobic) are inspired and ambitious. Try the crowd-pleasing sushi pizza, which is seaweed topped with creamy sauce, sticky rice, fish or shrimp, and green onions. Sample specialty rolls include the Dragon Roll — eel, spicy tuna, avocado, and sesame seed with unagi sauce — or the Sunset Roll — tuna, salmon, crab, cream cheese, avocado, green onion and *masago* (smelt roe). Beer, wine and sake available. Serving lunch and dinner Mon–Sat. Closed Sun. 2271 N.W. Johnson St., Portland, OR 97210. (503) 221-1469. Multiple locations. Go to: www.wtle.com/21665. ***Japanese/Sushi. $$.***

Mother's Bistro & Bar ~ *Best Home-style*

Downtown Portland's Mother's Bistro & Bar features an abundance of ambitious comfort food served in an upbeat, window-ensconced dining room that is jam-packed with tables. Chef/owner Lisa Schroeder takes pride in preparing slow-cooked dishes made from scratch, such as chicken and dumplings, beef pot roast and meat loaf with gravy. For those who find no comfort in home-style comfort food, the specialty "Mother of the Month" menu represents a collaboration between moms from around the world and features dishes influenced by each of their cultures. Bistro favorites include steak frites and vegetarian Thai green curry. For breakfast, choices include a wild salmon hash or the grilled portobello mushroom and asiago cheese scramble. Full bar. Serving breakfast Tue–Fri, lunch Tue–Sun, dinner Tue–Sat. Sat–Sun brunch 9 am–2:30 pm. Closed Mon. 212 S.W. Stark St., Portland, OR 97204. (503) 464-1122. Go to: www.wtle.com/17927. ***Bistro, Breakfast, Brunch, Home-style, Vegetarian. $$.***

Park Kitchen

Securing an immediate table at this tiny Pearl District restaurant may be difficult, but the wait may prove to be more enjoyable than some dining experiences elsewhere. Test your mettle on the bocce ball courts directly outside, or partake of the award-winning signature cocktails, such as the Park Martini or the Battle of the Bourbons (two miniature Manhattans) before sitting down to chef Scott Dolich's imaginative cuisine. The menu emphasizes food that is fresh from the farmers' market, so it changes frequently. A four-course tasting menu of small plates is a bargain and the best way to avoid regret for only trying one entrée. When in season, the fried green beans served in a cone are legendary, while past large plates have included sliced duck breast with hominy or salt cod fritters served with malt vinegar. Full bar. Serving lunch Mon–Fri, dinner Mon–Sat. Closed Sun. 422 N.W. 8th St., Portland, OR 97209. (503) 223-7275. Go to: www.wtle.com/17801. ***Brunch, Contemporary. $$.***

RingSide Steakhouse ~ *Best Steak House*

Family-owned RingSide Steakhouse, a Portland institution since 1944 that ranks among the nation's best steak houses, serves nostalgia alongside its thick and juicy steaks. With dim lighting, fireside dining and formally attired servers (many of whom have been there for decades), RingSide epitomizes class and comfort. Start by ordering the thick-cut RingSide onion rings. Chops include filet mignon and a bone-in 14-ounce New York strip steak. Or try the locally admired house specialty: exquisitely marbled prime rib. At the Glendoveer location, the wine cellar takes up the center of the dining room with a list of more than 600 labels, earning the restaurant multiple accolades. Full bar. Serving dinner nightly downtown. Glendoveer location serving lunch Mon–Fri, dinner nightly. 2165 W. Burnside St., Portland, OR 97210. (503) 223-1513. Two locations. Go to: www.wtle.com/18084. ***Steak House. $$$.***

Wildwood ~ *Best Contemporary*

Since 1994, this acclaimed restaurant near Forest Park's Wildwood Trail has won over local diners with its creative Northwest contemporary fare. The interior features many works of art by local artists, including a glass and ceramic mural that is a tribute to renowned food author and Portland native James Beard. Executive chef Dustin Clark and chef/owner Cory Schreiber, a James Beard award winner, change the menu weekly and use local and seasonal ingredients. Begin with a pizza baked in the clay oven or the classic skillet-roasted mussels. Entrées may include pan-seared Alaskan halibut or lamb served with summer squash and feta. Secure a seat at the Chef's Counter to observe the care and artistry that go into each dish. Full bar. Serving lunch and dinner Mon–Sat. Closed Sun. 1221 N.W. 21st Ave., Portland, OR 97209. (503) 248-9663. Go to: www.wtle.com/17807. ***Contemporary. $$.***

RALEIGH-DURHAM NORTH CAROLINA

10 LOCAL FAVORITES

***The Triangle region of North Carolina** has become the epicenter of what national food magazines have dubbed the New Southern movement, perhaps best exemplified by the shrimp and grits popularized at Crook's Corner.*

Angus Barn ~ *Best Steak House*

Since restaurant novices Thad Eure Jr. and Charles Winston opened the Angus Barn in 1960, it has amassed more than 200 local and national distinctions, including induction into the *Nation's Restaurant News* Fine Dining Hall of Fame. The classically red, curiously unceremonious, honest-to-goodness converted barn seems a highly unlikely contender for housing one of the nation's top steak houses. But this local dining icon has earned its reputation and its success in the same way as many other famous establishments: Shortcuts are simply unacceptable. Beef is aged to perfection on site; the staff cooks filets until exactly as ordered; and the crab cakes are to die for. Every detail — from the basket of complimentary apples at the entrance to the walk-in humidor — focuses on indulging the customer. The world-class, 30,000-bottle wine cellar complements a full bar. Serving dinner nightly. 9401 Glenwood Ave., Raleigh, NC 27617. (919) 781-2444. Go to: www.wtle.com/7274. ***Steak House. $$$.***

Bloomsbury Bistro ~ *Best Bistro*

A standout in a town known for its foodie appeal, chef/owner John Toler's culinary resume rivals any in the state. Polished is the word for everything at his Bloomsbury Bistro at Five Points: From well-executed dishes to gracious, informed service, this tribute to French gastronomy impeccably reflects the refinement of Parisian culture. Regulars return to indulge in the novelty of his frequently changing contemporary menus. From sautéed oxtail gnocchi to beef short ribs over black pepper spatzle, his inspirations for flavor know no global bounds. Dessert is equally far-reaching. A well-rounded wine list and sizable martinis complete the night. Full bar. Serving dinner Mon–Sat. Closed Sun. 509 W. Whitaker Mill Rd., Raleigh, NC 27608. (919) 834-9011. Go to: www.wtle.com/5138. ***Bistro, Contemporary, Dessert. $$.***

Clyde Cooper's Barbeque ~ *Best Barbecue*

Clyde Cooper's Barbeque, founded in 1938, is as much a historic landmark as a casual joint for quality 'cue. One step through the door verifies the appeal and popularity of this downtown Raleigh darling. Sit among old-timey photographs, the buzzing service counter and the sweet aroma of down-home cooking while enjoying your complimentary basket of crunchy cracklings. Barbecue comes chopped, sliced or spare-ribbed, and chicken barbecued, fried or chopped. Not up for such a power-punch of meat? The Brunswick stew, though still a hearty, meat-based meal, is a favorite alternative to the barbecue. Sweet tea and super-sugary lemonade are a given. No alcohol available. Serving lunch Mon–Sat. Closed Sun. 109 E. Davie St., Raleigh, NC 27601. (919) 832-7614. Go to: www.wtle.com/6662. ***Barbecue. $.***

Crook's Corner

Landmark eatery Crook's Corner, dubbed "sacred ground for Southern foodies" by *The New York Times*, serves a helping of Chapel Hill history along with its famed shrimp and grits. In the same spot on the busy West End of Franklin Street where local fish market owner Rachel Crook was mysteriously murdered three decades earlier, Southern culinary legend Bill Neal and partner Gene Hamer opened a narrow, diner-like haven for country cooking in 1982. Crook's has been a leader in New Southern cuisine ever since. Inventive menu items, such as the tomato and watermelon salad or the green Tabasco chicken, receive consistent recognition for their creativity. Some dishes have inspired entire movements. (Many consider Crook's to be the birthplace of those spectacular shrimp and grits.) Full bar. Serving dinner Tue–Sun. Sun brunch 10:30 am–2 pm. Closed Mon. 610 W. Franklin St., Chapel Hill, NC 27516. (919) 929-7643. Go to: www.wtle.com/7269. ***Brunch, Contemporary, Home-style. $$.***

Fins Restaurant ~ *Best Seafood*

There's now even more to admire at Fins Restaurant's new home in downtown's Two Progress Plaza building. Local foodies have flocked to North Raleigh to partake in this critically acclaimed, seafood-intensive, Asian and Pacific Rim cuisine — the expert cooking of chef/proprietor William D'Auvray, whose influences stem from a childhood in the Philippines, a relocation to Southern California and a stint at The Ritz-Carlton in Washington, D.C. A complimentary, locally lauded vegetarian spring roll kicks off the constantly changing menu, which, in the past, has included crispy Thai snapper, peekytoe crab soufflé and citrus-grilled squid. Lamb, duck and pork tenderloin are among the regular non-seafood choices. Full bar. Serving dinner Tue–Sat. Closed Sun–Mon. 110 E. Davie St., Raleigh, NC 27601. (919) 834-6963. Go to: www.wtle.com/7241. ***Asian Fusion, Contemporary, Seafood. $$$.***

Lucky 32 ~ *Best American Traditional, Best Brunch*

Though Dennis Quaintance and Mike Weaver recently closed their beloved Lucky 32 in Raleigh to concentrate on the "Kitchen & Wine Bar" concept of the Cary branch, much about the original model remains the same. This Triangle favorite is upscale enough for romantic wining and dining, yet sufficiently casual for the whole family to enjoy some juicy burgers and sweet tea. The classic fare offers Southern staples, such as fried green tomatoes, along with all-American favorites and an award-winning wine list. In addition, a supplementary menu highlights a seasonal, ethnic or regional theme, ranging from the tropical cuisine of Hawaii to the Cajun delights of New Orleans. Full bar. Serving lunch and dinner Mon–Sat. Sunday brunch 10 am–3 pm. 7307 Tryon Rd. Cary, NC 27511. (919) 233-1632. Go to: www.wtle.com/9133. ***American Traditional, Brunch. $$.***

Magnolia Grill ~ *Best Contemporary*

"Not Afraid of Flavor" is the mantra by which Magnolia Grill's chefs/owners Ben and Karen Barker eat, sleep and cook. Tucked away in Old West Durham, their charmingly understated neighborhood eatery remains on par with the nation's leading restaurants, evident by its recent superior ranking of No. 11 on *Gourmet* magazine's America's Top 50 Restaurants list and a 2007 nomination for the Outstanding Restaurant Award nationally by the James Beard Foundation. Ben drives the progressive, New Southern menu with creative impulses and firm North Carolina fundamentals. For example, an early summer menu offered a meat-and-three of pan-crisped pork shoulder confit with Creole red beans, Southern greens and creamy cole slaw. Karen's superb desserts — from frozen limeade to goat cheese waffles — provide perfectly sweet endings. Full bar. Serving dinner Tue–Sat. Closed Sun–Mon. 1002 9th St., Durham, NC 27705. (919) 286-3609. Go to: www.wtle.com/6829. ***Contemporary, Dessert. $$.***

Mama Dip's Kitchen ~ *Best Soul Food*
Mama Dip, aka Mildred Council, opened her Kitchen with just $64 on a November 1976 Sunday morning. Since then, vegetables have been served soft, lemonade sipped slowly, and collard greens have reigned supreme. Today, images of the large brown house on Chapel Hill's Rosemary Street can be spotted on the likes of *Oprah* and the Food Network, as this Triangle institution has become nationally renowned for its ability to put the "soul" into soul food. Taste the Southern goodness with every chitterling, salmon cake, or bowl of chicken and dumplings. After supper, the pecan pie and banana pudding are "mmm, mmm good." Beer and wine available. Serving breakfast, lunch and dinner daily. 408 W. Rosemary St., Chapel Hill, NC 27514. (919) 942-5837. Go to: www.wtle.com/7271. ***Breakfast, Home-style, Soul Food. $.***

Vin Rouge ~ *Best French*
Another dining gem by wildly successful local restaurateur Giorgios Bakatsias, Vin Rouge effectively recreates the white-tablecloth atmosphere and classic menu of an authentic French bistro. Some diners share bottles of Bordeaux over escargots and beet salads on the romantic outdoor patio, while others canoodle between bites of bouillabaisse, hanger steak and sautéed calves liver. And when in Rome — er, Paris — one must indulge in a delectable crème brûlée. Sunday brunch (10:30 am–2 pm) does eggs the français way, with sterling renditions of various omelets and eggs Benedict. Full bar. Serving dinner Tue–Sun. Closed Mon. 2010 Hillsborough Rd., Durham, NC 27705. (919) 416-0466. Go to: www.wtle.com/6937. ***Bistro, Brunch, French. $$$.***

Waraji Japanese Restaurant ~ *Best Japanese/Sushi*
Removed from the heart of Raleigh activity in an inconspicuous strip mall near RDU airport lies some of the most sought-after sushi in the state. When chefs Masa and Kazu combined their collective 35 years of experience to open Waraji in 1997, Triangle sushi and sashimi lovers began driving from all corners to enjoy the expertly crafted, flavorsome rolls. Grab a spot at the sushi bar, where many a customer interact with the friendly chefs for suggestions, or just a little Nigiri 101. An assortment of classic Japanese entrées — including tempura, teriyakis and the fondue-like shabu-shabu — are also available. Full bar. Serving lunch Mon–Fri, dinner Mon–Sat. Closed Sun. 5910 Duraleigh Rd. Raleigh, NC 27612. (919) 783-1883. Go to: www.wtle.com/13202. ***Japanese/Sushi. $$.***

ROCHESTER NEW YORK

10 LOCAL FAVORITES

***Boasting a number of fine-dining spots**, Rochester's culinary scene is best known for its diners, fish frys, "white hot" dogs, and the unique and iconic, three-tiered Garbage Plate at Nick Tahou Hots.*

High Falls on the Genesee River

Bill Gray's ~ *Best Burgers, Best Fish Fry*

Bill Gray passed away in 1994, but his legend lives on at his regional restaurant chain, beloved by upstate New Yorkers. Bill Gray's began as a weekend-only hot dog stand in 1938, so it's no surprise that the one-fourth pound red or white hots — a white hot is a Rochester original — served plain or with chili and cheese, are a specialty. But the restaurant also has a reputation for cooking up fantastic cheeseburgers and fried fish. Seasoned curly fries or fried cauliflower accompany your burger or fried haddock, and selected locations serve locally renowned Abbott's Frozen Custard for dessert. No alcohol available. Serving lunch and dinner daily. 100 Midtown Plaza, Rochester, NY 14580. (585) 232-4760. Multiple locations. Go to: www.wtle.com/21775. ***Burgers, Fish Fry, Hot Dogs. $.***

Conesus Inn ~ *Best Steak House*

Conesus Inn is the place to go "For the Prime of Your Life," as the restaurant advertises, where you get a view of scenic Conesus Lake from both the patio and the dining room. For more than 40 years, this homey roadhouse has exemplified what a family-owned steak and seafood house does best — provide consistently good meals in a friendly environment. The slow-roasted prime rib is the specialty of the house, but there are plenty of cuts to suit other tastes, including a classic Delmonico in two sizes and a huge porterhouse. Besides steaks, Conesus prepares delicious chicken Wellington, roast rack of lamb and Alaskan king crab. Beer and wine available. Closed during winter, but otherwise serving dinner Tue–Sun. Closed Mon. 5654 E. Lake Rd., Conesus, NY 14435. (585) 346-6100. Go to: www.wtle.com/17663. ***American Traditional, Seafood, Steak House. $$$.***

Highland Park Diner ~ *Best Breakfast, Best Diner*

In its nearly 60-year history, Highland Park Diner in the quaint Swillburg neighborhood of southeast Rochester has undergone a few changes in ownership and function, including one stint as an off-track betting parlor. But for the past 20 years or so, the local institution has remained true to the tradition of gleaming neon-and-chrome diners, serving comfort food in gargantuan portions. Breakfast-all-day specialties include a sweet cheese-topped Belgian waffle and the Highland skillet bowl, a medley of eggs, home fries, gravy and shredded cheese. The current owners have added Greek specialties to complement the traditional diner fare, but thankfully, they've kept the classic hand-dipped milkshakes and the renowned apple pie and coffee. No alcohol available. Serving breakfast and lunch daily, dinner Mon–Sat. 960 Clinton Ave. S., Rochester, NY 14620. (585) 461-5040. Go to: www.wtle.com/17562. ***Breakfast, Burgers, Diner. $.***

Horizons Restaurant

With live jazz every night and a spectacular hilltop view of the Rochester skyline from every table, Horizons Restaurant at the Woodcliff Hotel & Spa is the perfect place to watch the sunset while you enjoy a spectacular meal and the restaurant's charming and elegant ambiance. Straightforward, attractively plated cuisine enhances the setting, making Horizons one of the city's favorite spots for romantic evenings, as well as breakfast, lunch and Sunday brunch (11 am–2 pm). Begin your meal with the signature lobster bisque, and move on to the house-specialty salmon with Grand Marnier barbecue sauce. Other favorites include the Kansas City veal steak and the rack of lamb. Dessert selections vary according to the whim of the in-house pastry chef. Serving breakfast, lunch and dinner daily. 199 Woodcliff Dr., Fairport, NY 14450. (585) 248-4825. Go to: www.wtle.com/17564. ***Breakfast, Brunch, Contemporary, Hotel Restaurant. $$$.***

The King and I ~ *Best Thai*

Frequently appearing on Rochester's best-of lists for Thai cuisine, The King and I has remained a local favorite despite having moved several times over the years. With more than 200 entrée choices, a fifth of which are vegetarian, you'd have to be extraordinarily persnickety not to find something you like. For seafood lovers, there's orange roughy prepared a number of ways as well as shrimp and scallop combinations. Continue your culinary adventure with entrées such as *kang kheeo wan* chicken in a green curry sauce, Evil (in name only) Jungle Prince Pork with green beans and bamboo in a spicy sauce, or spicy lemongrass squid. Beer and wine available. Serving lunch and dinner daily. 1455 E. Henrietta Rd., Rochester, NY 14623. (585) 427-8090. Go to: www.wtle.com/17736. ***Thai, Vegetarian. $$.***

Mr. Dominic's at the Lake ~ *Best Italian*

Passionate fans of longtime Rochester favorite Mr. Dominic's at the Lake may wish that the generous helpings of Italian classics didn't generate quite so much buzz, as it remains one of the toughest places in town to get a table. The consistent quality of the cuisine is a testament to the fact that the kitchen has retained pretty much the same staff for 25 years, a not-so-common trait in the restaurant world. Regulars swear by any of the veal options, among them the winning veal French with a lemon wine sauce. Pasta lovers can dig into stuffed shells, baked ziti or manicotti Elizabeth, a house specialty with mozzarella and mushrooms. Dominic's delivers locally. Full bar. Serving lunch and dinner daily. 4699 Lake Ave., Rochester, NY 14612. (585) 865-4630. Go to: www.wtle.com/17676. ***Italian. $$.***

Nick Tahou Hots ~ *Best Hot Dogs*

There is no room for culinary snobbery at Nick Tahou Hots, where the signature dish is the Garbage Plate. So beloved is this three-tiered combo plate that it has spawned a host of imitators and is considered a regional specialty. The base of the dish is always the diner's choice of two sides — home fries, french fries, macaroni salad or baked beans — topped by your choice of meat — hot dog, hamburger patty, Italian sausage, chicken tenders or others. Finally, the whole motley mixture is dressed with mustard and onions, then doused with Nick's signature hot sauce. Of course, if you don't like your food layered into a towering pile, you can still get fine hot dogs, sausages or burgers on buns. No alcohol available. Serving breakfast, lunch and dinner Mon–Sat. Closed Sun. 320 W. Main St., Rochester, NY 14608. (585) 436-0184. Two locations. Go to: www.wtle.com/22157. ***Burgers, Diner, Hot Dogs. $.***

Phillips European Restaurant ~ *Best Dessert*

A restaurant with a dessert menu that is equal in length to the dinner menu is bound to be a paradise for the sweet-tooth afflicted. Before skipping to the not-so-bitter end, though, enjoy a different sort of savory temptation at Philips European Restaurant, serving classic Continental fare such as scallops Provençale, veal Marsala and steak Diane. Assuming you have managed to stave off the hankering to eat dessert as your main course, after-dinner offerings include English trifle, crème brûlée, white chocolate carrot cake, biscotti and a variety of cheesecakes. But the stars of the dessert show may be the tortes, which run the gamut from Austrian chocolate or tiramisu to Viennese meringue or lemon mousse. Full bar. Serving lunch and dinner daily. 26 Corporate Woods, Rochester, NY 14623. (585) 272-9910. Go to: www.wtle.com/17622. ***Continental, Dessert. $$$.***

Restaurant 2 Vine ~ *Best Contemporary*

Much-heralded 2 Vine has established itself as one of Rochester's very best American contemporary restaurants, earning accolades for its excellent menu as well as its transformational architecture. Once the site of an ambulance garage, the early 20th-century building received new windows, tile, decorative glass and a canopied entrance prior to the restaurant's 1999 opening. French bistro standards, such as steak frites and *moules marinière* (mussels steamed in white wine), share the menu with American-inspired favorites, such as pan-roasted duck breast and grilled pork or lamb chops. Nightly rotating entrées range from bouillabaisse to prime rib. Full bar. Serving lunch Mon–Fri, dinner Mon–Sat. Closed Sun. 24 Winthrop St., Rochester, NY 14607. (585) 454-6020. Go to: www.wtle.com/21799. ***Bistro, Contemporary. $$.***

Rooney's Restaurant ~ *Best Continental*

For years, Rooney's Restaurant, located in a circa-1890s converted saloon in the tiny neighborhood of Swillburg (formerly known for its prominent pig farms, where "swill" was customarily left out on porches to serve as pig feed — hungry yet?), has been one of Rochester's go-to spots for romantic dining and creative Continental cuisine. High ceilings, a fireplace, exposed brick walls and exceptional service set the scene for a memorable meal. Begin with appetizers from the daily changing menu such as salmon spring rolls or escargot with a blue cheese demi-glaze. For entrées, the array of wood-grilled meats is always top-notch, and you can't go wrong with specialties such as plantain-crusted shrimp or the house-made spinach walnut ravioli. Full bar. Serving dinner nightly. 90 Henrietta St., Rochester, NY 14620. (585) 442-0444. Go to: www.wtle.com/17594. ***Contemporary, Continental. $$$.***

SACRAMENTO
CALIFORNIA

10 LOCAL FAVORITES

Sacramento's somewhat-underrated restaurant culture *includes a number of much-praised contemporaries, although no eatery in town is more revered than Willie's Burgers & Chiliburgers.*

Biba ~ *Best Italian*

Renowned chef Biba Caggiano has been helping place Sacramento on the national culinary map since her authentic Italian eatery opened in 1986. When not starring on her internationally syndicated television show, this hard-working mother and grandmother — a Bologna, Italy, native — keeps herself busy by personally altering the menu with the season, signing copies of her best-selling cookbooks and even overseeing the restaurant's finances. Hand-made pastas, veal shank, grilled lamb skewers and various seafood specialties have guests wondering if they're not in a larger city, or in Italy itself. Don't miss Biba's superior dessert list featuring daily house-made gelato. Full bar. Serving lunch Mon–Fri, dinner Mon–Sat. Closed Sun. 2801 Capitol Ave. Sacramento, CA 95816. (916) 455-2422. Go to: www.wtle.com/13297. ***Italian. $$$.***

Corti Brothers ~ *Best Deli*

A 60-year staple for Sacramento's epicurean shoppers, Corti Brothers has been bringing premium specialty foods, wines and products from around the globe to its Folsom Boulevard location since 1947. The old-fashioned deli boasts a vast selection of the world's most happening meats and cheeses, realized in all the traditional sandwiches plus a dozen or so Corti originals. Portions are large, but don't worry: The storefront scale, a popular amusement for many a customer and random passerby, reads about three pounds under actual weight. Forget that little tidbit, and reward your sweet tooth with Swiss chocolate, peanut butter cookies or other imported goodies on the way out. Beer and wine available. Serving lunch and dinner daily. 5810 Folsom Blvd., Sacramento, CA 95819. (916) 736-3800. Go to: www.wtle.com/13008. ***Deli, Takeout/ Gourmet Takeout. $.***

La Provence Restaurant & Terrace ~ *Best French*
With one of the city's favorite outdoor dining venues, La Provence is Roseville's neighborhood staple for classically modern French cuisine. The restaurant, which in fall 2007 underwent a change in ownership and chefs, features a seasonal menu of traditional French bistro flavors prepared in a decidedly contemporary California style, from sophisticated sautéed diver scallops and pan-roasted duck breast to more casual croque-monsieurs (grilled ham and cheese sandwiches) and a kid-friendly brunch menu. Full bar. Serving lunch and dinner Tue–Sat. Sun brunch 10 am–2:30 pm. Closed Mon. 110 Diamond Creek Pl., Roseville, CA 95747. (916) 789-2002. Go to: www.wtle.com/13061. ***Brunch, French. $$$.***

Lemon Grass Restaurant ~ *Best Asian Fusion*
Lemon Grass's prominent chef/owner Mai Pham, who has earned much national praise for her meticulous proficiency in her native Thai and Vietnamese cuisines, brings recipes derived from her childhood to her labor-of-love Munroe Street eatery. Pham's purist tendencies separate the two cuisines rather than fuse them, and thus her menu offers the traditional curries and satays of Thailand alongside the classic salads, salad rolls and noodle dishes of Vietnam. For example, her Siamese seafood bouillabaisse proves a flavorful Thai-style fish stew that is not to be missed, while Mom's Catfish in Clay Pot arrives as a caramelized garlic catfish filet just like her Vietnamese mother used to make. Full bar. Serving lunch Mon–Fri, dinner Mon–Sat. Closed Sun. 601 Munroe St., Sacramento, CA 95825. (916) 486-4891. Go to: www.wtle.com/11164. ***Asian Fusion, Thai, Vietnamese. $$.***

Mikuni Japanese Restaurant & Sushi Bar
~ *Best Japanese/Sushi*
A longtime local favorite for Japanese cuisine, the original Mikuni Japanese Restaurant & Sushi Bar has grown since its

1987 opening in Fair Oaks to include several restaurants in the Sacramento Valley. At each of the hip locations, patrons down sake cocktails and feast on Americanized Japanese favorites. A lengthy list of traditional tempura, teriyaki and noodle dishes round out a creative sushi menu, all packed with fresh seafood that is flown in daily and accompanied by the unique house sauces that differentiate Mikuni from the competition. And for those who prefer meals on wheels: Book the traveling sushi bus, popular among the business lunch crowd and Kings season ticket holders. Full bar. Serving lunch and dinner daily. Hours vary by location. 4323 Hazel Ave., Fair Oaks, CA 95628. (916) 961-2112. Multiple locations. Go to: www.wtle.com/21456. ***Japanese/Sushi. $$.***

The Mustard Seed Restaurant ~ *Best Bistro*

For more than 20 years, chefs/owners Paul and Robyn Bergman have helped set the standard in California cuisine with their quaint little eatery in the heart of Davis. The Mustard Seed Restaurant's picturesque cabin setting creates an ideal atmosphere for this Wine Country bistro, which evolved into a full-service restaurant upon moving to the old Soga's building several years ago. Although the menu changes weekly, expect a stellar list of contemporary fare featuring the freshest fish, natural meats and locally grown organic produce. You might find the likes of pan-seared duck, crab and asparagus pasta, or grilled Hawaiian swordfish. Full bar. Serving lunch Tue–Fri, dinner Tue–Sat. Closed Sun–Mon. 222 D St., Davis, CA 95616. (530) 758-5750. Go to: www.wtle.com/ 11705. ***Bistro, Contemporary. $$$.***

Restaurant 55 Degrees

Kicking Capitol Mall up a notch with cutting-edge cooking and design since October 2005, Restaurant 55 Degrees offers a contemporary dining experience from polished steel surroundings on the ground floor of an office park. The downtown business crowd, in particular, adores the brasserie setting and the progressive fare, designed by a talented kitchen whose collective resume rivals any in the city. Robust French and Belgian cooking with a tangential fascination with the Sunshine State's agricultural bounty plays out in the vivid flavors of gourmet steak frites, Syrah reduction pork chops and Maine roasted monkfish. But perhaps the best option remains a plate of mussels paired with a draft Belgian white beer. The wine cellar, with its optimal temperature that gives the restaurant its name, offers an excellent and complementary selection, as well. Full bar. Serving lunch Mon–Fri, dinner Mon–Sat. Closed Sun. 555 Capitol Mall, Sacramento, CA 95814. (916) 553-4100. Go to: www.wtle.com/ 23019. ***Contemporary. $$$.***

Slocum House ~ *Best Brunch*

A longtime local favorite for special-occasion dining, Slocum House's history dates to the early 20th century. Today, community founder Charles Slocum's home and gardens, nestled in secluded Fair Oaks, create the perfect ambiance for a classy meal. While lunch and dinner offer a global selection of well-executed seafood, steaks and pasta dishes, the big event remains the highly popular Sunday brunch (10:30 am–1:30 pm). A complimentary glass of California sparkling wine begins the starter buffet, where fresh fruits and decadent pastries form a beautiful spread. The prix fixe menu may include anything from Dungeness crab and Brie scramble to champagne-and-orange poached king salmon. Full bar. Serving lunch Tue–Fri, dinner Tue–Sun. Sun brunch. Closed Mon. 7992 California Ave., Fair Oaks, CA 95628. (916) 961-7211. Go to: www.wtle.com/11100. ***Brunch, Contemporary. $$$.***

The Waterboy ~ *Best Contemporary*

From its elegant Midtown setting, The Waterboy gives the cuisines of southern France and northern Italy a California kick, making this local institution a favorite stop for a seasonally changing selection of impeccable meats, fish and pastas that incorporate the hottest regional epicurean trends. Chef/owner Rick Mahan offers a menu that particularly excels with sweetbreads and seafood, though creative entrées may range from pan-roasted duck breast to house-made lamb sausage. Fresh bread provided by Grateful Bread and a fail-proof gourmet dessert list bookend a near-perfect dining experience. Full bar. Serving lunch Mon–Fri, dinner nightly. 2000 Capitol Ave., Sacramento, CA 95814. (916) 498-9891. Go to: www.wtle.com/13068. ***Contemporary. $$$.***

Willie's Burgers & Chiliburgers ~ *Best Burgers*

Willie's Burgers & Chiliburgers more than holds its own among the highly competitive California burger pantheon. A neighborhood alternative to popular chains, the tidy little burger joints, located downtown and also in Carmichael, do not serve such tidy food — but that's what the paper towels mounted on the wall are for. That little convenience proves quite indispensable, especially with orders of the house-specialty chiliburger and chili fries. You'll need a fork, too, to manage the toppings on Willie's excellent hot dogs. With beignets for breakfast, what more could you ask for in a burger joint? Beer and wine available. Serving breakfast, lunch and dinner daily. 2415 16th St., Sacramento, CA 95818. (916) 444-2006. Two locations. Go to: www.wtle.com/21525. ***Breakfast, Burgers, Hot Dogs. $.***

SALT LAKE CITY
UTAH

10 LOCAL FAVORITES

The mountain oasis that is Salt Lake City *features a number of historic and classic restaurants, including circa-1919 Lamb's Grill Cafe, Emigration Canyon fixture Ruth's Diner, and the cherished Hires Big H drive-in.*

Bambara ~ *Best Contemporary*

The solemn stone Norse gods who guard this former Continental Bank building must be dying to peek inside at Bambara's lively atmosphere. With big, bright artwork, colorful plates and the exhibition kitchen filling the room with rich aromas of grilled meats, fresh seafood and house-baked breads, this busy dining room has become famous for creative food and exceptional hospitality. Salmon hash is offered at breakfast, while dinner may feature cedar plank wild salmon and locally raised Morgan Valley lamb, along with the three-course nightly specials. Full bar. Serving breakfast and dinner daily, lunch Mon–Fri. 202 S. Main St., Salt Lake City, UT 84101. (801) 363-5454. Go to: www.wtle.com/13793. ***Breakfast, Brunch, Contemporary, Hotel Restaurant. $$.***

Franck's

From its cozy setting in a renovated home on the Tuscany property, Franck's is the relatively new home of French chef Franck Peissel. Keep an eye on *Salt Lake* magazine's Best Chef of 2007, who works his magic from an open kitchen that is monitored by a "chef cam" displayed in the dining room. This friendly neighborhood place offers both American comfort food — from fried chicken to meat loaf — as well as classic French dishes such as escargot, cheese fondue and duck confit. Don't miss the butterscotch pudding with a hidden layer of chocolate. Full bar. Serving dinner Mon–Sat. Closed Sun. 6263 S. Holladay Blvd., Holladay, UT 84121. (801) 274-6264. Go to: www.wtle.com/22908. ***Bistro, Contemporary. $$.***

Hires Big H ~ *Best Burgers*

The Hires Big H original Salt Lake location remains surprisingly unchanged: Founder Don Hale, well into his 80s, still comes into work every day to greet a hungry population of students, who've been a major part of the clientele since this drive-in opened in 1959. But locals of all ages, as well as reporters from *The Wall Street Journal* and *Gourmet* magazine, love the classic offerings, available from several Hires restaurants across the city. Favorites include the famous Hires Big H hamburger, hot dogs, fries and onion rings, frosty mugs of Hires root beer (in five sizes), and root beer floats. Thick shakes are available in more than 15 flavors, including grasshopper, candy bar and marshmallow. No alcohol available. Serving lunch and dinner Mon–Sat. Closed Sun. 425 S. 700 E., Salt Lake City, UT 84102. (801) 364-4582. Go to: www.wtle.com/13995. ***Burgers, Diner. $.***

Lamb's Grill Cafe ~ *Best American Traditional*

Lamb's Grill Cafe stakes claim as the state's oldest restaurant, as Greek immigrant George P. Lamb founded the first incarnation in Logan, Utah, in 1919. Not much has changed since the restaurant moved downtown in 1939. Locals still enjoy three meals a day in surroundings familiar to previous generations. For breakfast, try the grilled trout or the traditional Scottish dish finnan haddie. Lunch favorites include soups, salads and sandwiches, while substantial dinner entrées feature the likes of beef stroganoff and red snapper. Top it all off with rice pudding or a big slice of chocolate cake. Full bar. Serving breakfast, lunch and dinner Mon–Sat. Closed Sun. 169 S. Main St., Salt Lake City, UT 84111. (801) 364-7166. Go to: www.wtle.com/13823. ***American Traditional, Breakfast. $$.***

Lugano Restaurant ~ *Best Italian*

Lugano Restaurant's chef/owner Greg Neville remains one

of the busiest proprietors in Salt Lake City. Besides teaching cooking classes, he oversees the kitchen and constantly tweaks his snug little eatery's selection of rustic northern Italian fare. Although the menu is rather simple, extravagant appetizers can include clay pot mussels or focaccia covered with grilled pears, caramelized onions, Gorgonzola and pine nuts. Linguine and clams or parsley chicken breast make fantastic dinner entrées. Beer, including on-tap microbrews, and *Wine Spectator* award-winning wine list available. Serving dinner nightly. 3364 S. 2300 E., Salt Lake City, UT 84109. (801) 412-9994. Go to: www.wtle.com/14861. ***Italian. $$.***

Market Street ~ *Best Seafood*

The locally acclaimed Market Street restaurants — including Market Street Oyster Bar, Market Street Grill and the fresh fish markets — serve a similar selection of fine seafood dishes with Gastronomy, Inc.'s signature reputation for excellent service. From clam chowder in a bread bowl and several different varieties of oysters on the half shell to halibut fish and chips and non-ocean options such as prime rib, the high quality remains constant. For brunch (not served at the University location), try the succulent steak and eggs Benedict. Full bar. Serving lunch and dinner daily. Sun brunch (call for hours). 48 W. Market St., Salt Lake City, UT 84101. (801) 322-4668. Multiple locations. Go to: www.wtle.com/15206. ***American Traditional, Brunch, Seafood. $$.***

Mazza ~ *Best Middle Eastern*

Locals fell in love with Mazza when this popular Middle Eastern restaurant was serving paper plates of carry-out hummus and falafel. Today, dining at refurbished Mazza is a little more indulgent: Beef and okra stew, kabob platters and the signature chicken and potatoes *mutabbak* (with onion slices and tamarind sauce) arrive with real flatware accompanied by a selection of Lebanese, Armenian, Turkish and Moroccan beers and wines. Although it now caters to the sit-down crowd, the restaurant still serves a great deal of quick meals and takeout. Beer and wine available. Full bar at 9th and 9th location. Serving lunch and dinner Mon–Sat. Closed Sun. 1515 S. 1500 E., Salt Lake City, UT 84105. (801) 484-9259. Two locations. Go to: www.wtle.com/24504. ***Middle Eastern. $$.***

The New Yorker ~ *Best Steak House*

Though The New Yorker (another smash hit from

Gastronomy, Inc.) is technically a private club due to local liquor laws, non-members hankering for a quality steak can pay a temporary fee to experience some of Salt Lake City's best cuts of beef. Housed in the historic New York Building, with its stained glass windows and plush booths, the Dining Room serves top-notch filets, rib eyes, game and seafood. The separate café is a popular after-work spot for drinks or casual fare, from Maryland crab cakes to lobster shepherd's pie. Full bar. Serving lunch Mon–Fri, dinner Mon–Sat. Closed Sun. 60 W. Market St., Salt Lake City, UT 84101. (801) 363-0166. Go to: www.wtle.com/15224. ***Café, Contemporary, Steak House. $$$.***

The Paris Bistro, Zinc Bar & Grill ~ *Best Bistro, Best French*

This Emerson Heights hot spot not only derives its name from now-closed historic local department store The Paris, but also houses many of its antiques and collectables, creating an engaging atmosphere that is ideal for sampling veteran chef/owner Eric DeBonis' French- and Mediterranean-inspired bistro fare. His passion for locally available and seasonal ingredients is evident on his highly praised menu. Anything, from oven-roasted beet salad to steak tartare, is excellent, especially when topped off with a dazzling dessert such as lemongrass crème brûlée or crêpes Suzette. Full bar. Serving dinner nightly. 1500 S. 1500 E., Salt Lake City, UT 84105. (801) 486-5585. Go to: www.wtle.com/13857. ***Bistro, Contemporary, French. $$.***

Ruth's Diner ~ *Best Breakfast, Best Diner*

In 1930, the feisty Ruth Evans opened Ruth's Hamburgers downtown and immediately began attracting a wealth of loyal customers (many of whom knew her from her days as a cabaret singer). Despite the restaurant's move to a converted trolley car in nearby scenic Emigration Canyon in 1949, Ruth's Diner remains a popular Salt Lake fixture for belly-warming, down-home eats. Whether chicken-fried steak and eggs for breakfast, meat loaf and Swiss cheese burgers for lunch, or spicy Jamaican chicken for dinner, the menu reflects its founder's classic yet undeniably saucy personality. Full bar. Serving breakfast, lunch and dinner daily. 2100 Emigration Canyon, Salt Lake City, UT 84108. (801) 582-5807. Go to: www.wtle.com/13864. ***Breakfast, Diner. $$.***

SAN ANTONIO TEXAS

10 LOCAL FAVORITES

***The roots of San Antonio's thriving** restaurant scene date back several generations, as evidenced by the time-honored appeal of Mexican cuisine at La Fonda on Main (circa 1932) and the chicken-fried steak from DeWese's Tip Top Cafe (circa 1938).*

The River Walk

Azúca ~ *Best Latin/South American*

At Azúca, chef L. Rene Fernandez is intent on illustrating that south-of-the-border cuisine extends far beyond Mexico. The space is brightly colored and full of blown-glass vases and light fixtures, complemented by the equally colorful cocktails and artistic fare. Flamenco, salsa and tango dancing enliven the adjoining bar. The dishes are described as Nuevo Latino and are inspired by culinary techniques that range from the Caribbean to Central and South America. Begin with a ceviche trio or some melt-in-your-mouth *amarillos*, fried plaintains served with sour cream. Notable entrées include Latin paella and the Chef's Trio: a sampling of beef tenderloin, sautéed shrimp and seared tuna. Full bar. Serving lunch and dinner daily. 713 S. Alamo, San Antonio, TX 78205. (210) 225-5550. Go to: www.wtle.com/509. ***Latin/South American. $$.***

Biga on the Banks ~ *Best Contemporary*

Located on a slightly less congested part of the River Walk, the elegant lofted dining room at Biga on the Banks features windows that stretch from floor to ceiling and scenic alfresco dining. If you prefer a more interactive dining experience, sit at Table 31 — the chef's table — and watch chef/owner (and local celebrity) Bruce Auden in the kitchen. The cuisine, which changes daily, is cutting-edge and contemporary; starters may include apple-smoked salmon nachos or chicken-fried oysters on squid ink linguini. Inspired dishes such as 11-spiced venison chops with grilled quail or the "Close-to-bouillabaisse" — shellfish, mahi mahi, tuna, grouper and lobster — round out the entrées. Full bar. Serving dinner nightly. 203 S. St. Mary's St., San Antonio, TX 78205. (210) 225-0722. Go to: www.wtle.com/9132. ***Contemporary. $$$.***

DeWese's Tip Top Cafe ~ *Best Diner*

The Tip Top Cafe, owned by the DeWese family, opened its doors in 1938 and began serving heaping plates of fried food to customers. Almost 70 years later, not much has changed: The restaurant is still owned and operated by family members, and diners drive for miles to get their fill of all things battered and fried. Mementos of the family and the diner's history are mounted on the wall, including the memorable stuffed bass. Onion rings and fried chicken are house specialties, but for a true taste of Texas, try the chicken-fried steak — crispy on the outside, tender on the inside and covered in rich gravy — which ranks among the state's best. No alcohol available. Serving lunch and dinner Tue–Sun. Closed Mon. 2814 Fredericksburg Rd., San Antonio, TX 78201. (210) 732-0191. Go to: www.wtle.com/428. ***American Traditional, Diner. $.***

La Fonda on Main ~ *Best Mexican*

La Fonda on Main, which opened in 1932 at its Main Street location, is steeped in tradition, having served clientele including world leaders FDR, Lyndon Johnson and the king of Siam himself, Yul Brynner. In 1997, local restaurateurs Cappy and Suzy Lawton purchased the eatery and made serious renovations, resulting in a fresh, uncluttered space complete with an upscale patio. Among the stellar dinner entrées is the Pescado Veracruzana: a choice of fish filet or shrimp, sautéed in Veracruz sauce made with fresh tomatoes, olives, chiles and capers. The menu also features enchiladas de mole Xiqueño: two chicken enchiladas drenched in mole sauce and covered in sautéed vegetables and queso. Full bar. Serving lunch and dinner daily. 2415 N. Main Ave., San Antonio, TX 78212. (210) 733-0621. Go to: www.wtle.com/536. ***Mexican. $$.***

La Scala ~ *Best Continental*

La Scala, a hidden gem named after the world famous opera

house in Milan, continues to be a leading upscale dining option in the San Antonio area. Its classic European dishes, attentive service, large windows and mirrors, and spacious interior with plenty of fresh flowers are perfect for a special occasion, a pre-theater meal or just an exceptional night out. For dinner, choices include filet au poivre served with a brandy red wine sauce, French-cut lamb chops, and Norwegian grilled salmon in a saffron cream sauce. Complete your meal with a selection from the famed pastry cart, and feel free to slow-dance the calories away to the romantic live music on weekends. Full bar. Serving lunch and dinner daily. 2177 N.W. Military Hwy., San Antonio, TX 78213. (210) 366-1515. Go to: www.wtle.com/54. ***Continental, Italian. $$.***

Las Canarias ~ *Best Brunch*
Located in the historic Omni La Mansión del Rio hotel along the River Walk, Las Canarias derives its name from the 1731 band of Canary Islanders, who were integral in the founding of San Antonio. Experience the elegant yet relaxed, Spanish-inspired ambiance in the two-tiered dining room or on the outdoor patio overlooking the river under the shade of palms. Signature dishes include buffalo carpaccio, crab-stuffed swordfish tempura and roasted rack of lamb. The Sunday champagne brunch (10:30 am–3 pm) is a local favorite featuring a large selection of meat carvings, Texas cheeses, omelets, Belgian waffles and even sushi. Full bar. Serving breakfast, lunch and dinner Mon–Sat. Reservations required for Sun brunch. 112 College St., San Antonio, TX 78205. (210) 518-1063. Go to: www.wtle.com/65. ***Brunch, Contemporary. $$$.***

L'Etoile ~ *Best French*
The variety of elegant rooms provides a range of differing dining experiences at L'Etoile in Alamo Heights, but all patrons will receive the same excellent service and deliciously authentic French cuisine. The restaurant's brazen credo is "the time of your life," and chef/owner Thierry Burkle rarely disappoints with his progressive French fare that emphasizes fresh fish, seafood and produce. Offerings change daily, but notable starters may include baked Brie and goat cheese wrapped in pastry, or foie gras with apple chutney. The menu has featured entrées such as sea scallops with mushroom risotto and mahi mahi served with jicama and crab relish. Full bar. Serving lunch Mon–Sat, dinner nightly. 6106 Broadway, San Antonio, TX 78209. (210) 826-4551. Go to: www.wtle.com/59. ***French, Seafood. $$$.***

Le Rêve

Ranked as not only one of the best restaurants in Texas, but among the finest in the nation, Le Rêve is "the dream" of chef/owner Andrew Weissman, a local product who returned home after sharpening his culinary skills in France and New York. This 40-seat intimate dining room on the River Walk specializes in modern French cuisine that is prepared "à la minute" and consequently served at a leisurely pace. But that leaves more time to linger over notable appetizers such as caramelized onion tart or foie gras with pear, apple and peach salad. Past main courses have featured beef tournedos and diver sea scallops with lime leaf and coconut broth. Jacket required. Reservations required. Beer and wine available. Serving dinner Tue–Sat. Closed Sun–Mon. 152 E. Pecan St., San Antonio, TX 78205. (210) 212-2221. Go to: www.wtle.com/58. ***French. $$$.***

Paesanos ~ *Best Italian*

In recent years, Paesanos has expanded from its beginnings as an Italian restaurant in the Alamo Heights neighborhood to include two other locations. The interior, characterized by beautifully decorated vaulted ceilings and elegant lighting fixtures, creates an atmosphere appropriate for casual outings and wedding receptions alike. Paesanos defines its food as classic Italian favorites with a contemporary Mediterranean twist. Regular patrons know that if you can only order one dish, it should be the Shrimp Paesano, an oversized pasta dish of shrimp drenched in a lemon garlic sauce. In addition to a variety of pizzas, other dishes include veal Marsala and poached salmon with mushrooms. Full bar. Serving lunch and dinner daily. 555 E. Basse Rd., San Antonio, TX 78209. (210) 828-5191. Multiple locations. Go to: www.wtle.com/19707. ***Bakery, Italian. $$.***

Schilo's Delicatessen ~ *Best German*

The Schilo family came to Texas in 1914 and three years later opened their namesake delicatessen that would become a San Antonio institution, serving authentic German food that hasn't changed (for good reason) in years. There's an array of German sausages and deli sandwiches, including one of the best Reubens in town. But Schilo's is best known for its split pea soup, overflowing frosty mugs of draft root beer and decadent cheesecake. On weekends, live accordion music accompanies your dining experience. Beer and wine available. Serving breakfast, lunch and dinner Mon–Sat. Closed Sun. 424 E. Commerce St., San Antonio, TX 78205. (210) 223-6692. Go to: www.wtle.com/352. ***Breakfast, Deli, German. $$.***

SAN DIEGO CALIFORNIA

10 LOCAL FAVORITES

***San Diego's beauty follows suit in its rich and eclectic restaurants**, from the tranquility of a brunch at the Crown Room at Hotel Del Coronado to the giddy hubbub of Hash House A Go Go.*

San Diego Mission

Café Sevilla ~ *Best Spanish*

A flamenco guitarist strums to a hip after-work crowd chilling in the lively tapas bar. A romantic date unfolds over Castilian-style filet medallions and a live dinner show in the elegant dining room. Girls' night out takes a rowdy turn, followed by some quick-serve paella, at the basement Latin dance club. To its three disparate dining experiences, downtown's Café Sevilla brings its outstanding menu of authentic Spanish cuisine. Have a ceviche small plate in the dining room, or enjoy an entrée portion of roasted pork tenderloin in the tapas bar: The mix-and-match menus are designed to suit a diner's mood rather than to limit his or her desired dishes to one room. The several variations of house-specialty paella, rich with fresh seafood, are available in all three areas. Full bar. Serving dinner nightly. 555 4th Ave., San Diego, CA 92101. (619) 233-5979. Go to: www.wtle.com/16101. ***Small Plates, Spanish. $$.***

Crown Room at Hotel Del Coronado ~ *Best Brunch*

There's no place like home — except for maybe Hotel del Coronado's resplendent Crown Room, once the haunt of *The Wizard of Oz* author and Coronado resident L. Frank Baum.

Though Sunday brunch (9 am–2 pm) is the only meal offered in the elegantly offbeat dining room, the elaborately expansive buffet remains undoubtedly one of the city's best ways to spend a weekend morning. Dim sum choices, tastes of Mexican cuisine and an entire station devoted to fine cheeses complete a list of American breakfast favorites such as made-to-order omelets and waffles. And no ruby red slippers are needed to take a trip to the divine chocolate fountain. Full bar. Serving Sun brunch. Closed Mon–Sat. 1500 Orange Ave., Coronado, CA 92118. (619) 522-8490. Go to: www.wtle.com/15720. ***Brunch, Hotel Restaurant. $$$.***

Donovan's Steak & Chop House ~ *Best Steak House*

A consistent winner of local media's annual best-of polls, Donovan's Steak & Chop House finds an appropriate home in La Jolla's Golden Triangle financial district. A beveled, mirror-topped bar serves stiff cocktails and complimentary mini-filet sandwiches, while the outdoor heated cigar tent remains one of the last smoking oases in California. All the steak house favorites, from filet mignon to the massive 24-ounce rib eye chop, are offered, as well as an excellent skillet-fried potato side with onions and peppercorn gravy. *Wine Spectator* award-winning wine list and full bar. Serving dinner Mon–Sat. Closed Sun. 4340 La Jolla Village Dr., La Jolla, CA 92122. (858) 450-6666. Go to: www.wtle.com/16124. ***Steak House. $$$.***

Hash House A Go Go ~ *Best Breakfast*

Everything about Hash House A Go Go is big: Big portions. Big waits. Big fun. In fact, chefs and co-owners Craig "Andy" Beardslee and Johnny Rivera's two-point mission statement centers on putting the fun back into food and the dining experience in general. The early morning lines of anxious diners wrapping around their legendary Hillcrest eatery prove the success of their mantra. Gourmet Midwestern comfort food comes in the form of pizza-sized flapjacks for breakfast, the BBBLT (with three servings of bacon) for lunch, and gargantuan cuts of crispy stuffed pork tenderloin for dinner. Just be prepared to share a meal or bring home leftovers. Full bar. Serving breakfast, lunch and dinner daily. Sat–Sun brunch 11 am–2:30 pm. 3628 5th Ave., San Diego, CA 92103. (619) 298-4646. Go to: www.wtle.com/15598. ***American Traditional, Breakfast, Brunch, Home-style. $$.***

Kemo Sabe ~ *Best Asian Fusion*

Blurring the boundaries between food and art, Kemo Sabe

brings to its posh Hillcrest quarters hoards of venturesome foodies seeking an out-of-this-world meal. Executive chef/ partner Deborah Scott blends Eastern sensibilities with Western flavors, making for one of the country's most visionary menus of American Southwestern-flaired Pacific Rim cuisine. Crediting her creative mind, Scott glazes smoked ribs with peanuts and Kahlua, mixes chiles and lemongrass in her Thai fish stew, and plates jalapeño corn bread and sautéed collard greens with 10-spice honey chicken. The full bar features a number of draft local microbrews. Serving dinner nightly. 3958 5th Ave., San Diego, CA 92103. (619) 220-6802. Go to: www.wtle.com/15543. ***Asian Fusion. $$.***

The Marine Room

As trying as Mother Nature may be, the pounding surf crashing outside The Marine Room comprises a fundamental component of this La Jolla dining landmark's history. The former inn, converted to a restaurant in 1941, has undergone multiple renovations at the mercy of the mighty Pacific, most notably after damage caused by 1982 El Niño-induced storms. But, on the same note, the dramatic waves must be credited for their breathtaking backdrop, as well as for providing a habitat for much of the restaurant's divine menu. From spinach-wrapped oysters to sesame-peppered ahi, dishes show global influence rooted in French fundamentals. The Marine Room also excels with game dishes. Check the restaurant's website for a schedule of the high tide so you can watch Mother Nature in action as you dine. Full bar. Serving dinner nightly. 2000 Spindrift Dr., La Jolla, CA 92037. (858) 459-7222. Go to: www.wtle.com/15630. ***Brunch, French, Seafood. $$$.***

Mille Fleurs ~ *Best French*

From the heart of tony Rancho Santa Fe, the extraordinary Mille Fleurs remains one of San Diego's most beloved special-occasion dining destinations. A popular outdoor patio, a swanky piano bar and the newly remodeled dining room make for an all-around elegant experience. Mille Fleurs specializes in expertly prepared, modern French cuisine incorporating fresh produce from renowned neighbor Chino family farm. Locals enjoy live music as they feast on such delicacies as squab breast, New Zealand venison loin and sautéed frog legs. Gourmet desserts range from passion fruit crème brûlée to chilled rhubarb-strawberry soup. Full bar. Serving lunch Mon–Fri, dinner nightly. 6009 Paseo Delicias Ave., Rancho Santa Fe, CA 92091. (858) 756-3085. Go to: www.wtle.com/15831. ***French. $$$.***

Old Town Mexican Café ~ *Best Mexican*

A staple in San Diego's historic Old Town for more than a quarter-century, Old Town Mexican Café consistently packs in both locals and tourists thanks to its festive, family-friendly atmosphere, lively bar, and extensive menu of well-prepared, traditional Mexican fare. Mariachis stroll between tables loaded down with substantial portions of house-specialty carnitas, Mexican-style pork ribs and old standbys such as tacos, enchiladas and fajitas. A few American morning standards supplement the otherwise-authentic border breakfast menu of huevos rancheros and Spanish omelets. Full bar. Serving breakfast, lunch and dinner daily. 2489 San Diego Ave., San Diego, CA 92110. (619) 297-4330. Go to: www.wtle.com/15952. ***Breakfast, Mexican. $$.***

Parallel 33

The menu is all over the map at the eclectic and modernly exotic Parallel 33 restaurant in Mission Hills. Inspired by the earth's 33rd parallel — which crosses San Diego, Morocco, Lebanon, India, Pakistan, China and Japan — the kitchen, now under the able hands of chef Benjamin Moore (star-chef/co-owner Amiko Gubbins has left), creatively fuses the wide spectrum of culinary influences. Dishes show no bounds in combination or in flavor with such past entrées as grilled rib eye with wasabi mashed potatoes, Moroccan lamb tajine and pan-seared, coriander-crusted scallops. Full bar. Serving dinner Mon–Sat. Closed Sun. 741 W. Washington St., San Diego, CA 92103. (619) 260-0033. Go to: www.wtle.com/15792. ***Contemporary. $$$.***

The Prado at Balboa Park ~ *Best Contemporary*

With a prime location, a hotshot chef and a something-for-everyone contemporary menu, The Prado at Balboa Park has earned its place as one of San Diego's most beloved, versatile restaurants. This crown jewel of the local Cohn Restaurant Group assumes a whopping 22,000 square feet in the ornate House of Hospitality in the heart of Balboa Park, home of the San Diego Zoo and a number of the city's top museums and theaters. From saffron lobster broth-infused paella to braised boneless beef short ribs, the playful menu melds Latin and Italian cuisines with deft flair, inspiring many local brides and event planners to choose this gem as a party or special-occasion venue. Full bar features specialty martinis and house-made sangria. Serving lunch daily, dinner Tue–Sun. 1549 El Prad, San Diego, CA 92101. (619) 557-9441. Go to: www.wtle.com/15513. ***Contemporary. $$.***

SAN FRANCISCO CALIFORNIA

10 LOCAL FAVORITES

***With its cosmopolitan sensibility and history as a cultural vanguard**, San Francisco claims a dining scene as progressive and diverse as its inhabitants, including pioneer of vegetarian cuisine Greens Restaurant and one of the country's most acclaimed Vietnamese eateries, The Slanted Door.*

"Painted Ladies" in Alamo Square

Buckeye Roadhouse ~ *Best American Traditional*

Constructed about the same time as the neighboring Golden Gate Bridge, Mill Valley's Buckeye Roadhouse has been a favorite fill-up for local doctors, families and passers-through since 1937. The ski lodge interior, complete with roaring fire, offers a cozy setting for Bay Area residents to enjoy a creative cocktail or fine wine with some belly-warming, gourmet comfort food. From Dungeness crab cakes and baby back ribs to mushroom lasagna and braised lamb shank, the something-for-everyone menu highlights the best of traditional American cuisine. The popular Sunday brunch (10:30 am–3 pm) is a gastronomic hit with the likes of smoked barbecue hash, ahi Benedict and brioche French toast. Full bar. Coffee and espresso drinks, juice, and pastries available Mon–Fri beginning 6 am. Serving lunch and dinner daily. 15 Shoreline Hwy., Mill Valley, CA 94941. (415) 331-2600. Go to: www.wtle.com/16244. ***American Traditional, Brunch, Dessert. $$.***

Delfina ~ *Best Italian*

With one foot anchored in the Old World and the other guiding the way in the New, Delfina has served as the Mission District's funky, cutting-edge neighborhood trattoria since opening to rave reviews in 1998. Chef/owner Craig Stoll, a James Beard award nominee, hones his soulful Italian cuisine in the kitchen while partner and wife Anne's convivial presence warms the intimate dining room. Mr. Stoll's seasonal menus favor the elemental cooking of Italy, incorporating local ingredients and modern sensibilities. From grilled calamari with white bean salad to roast duck with fresh figs, it's nearly impossible to go wrong. Just don't skip the decadent buttermilk panna cotta. Beer and wine available. Serving dinner nightly. 3621 18th St., San Francisco, CA 94110. (415) 552-4055. Go to: www.wtle.com/16442. ***Italian. $$.***

The Dining Room at The Ritz-Carlton

One of only a handful of restaurants given four stars by the *San Francisco Chronicle*, The Dining Room at The Ritz-Carlton, San Francisco, is as elite as its Mobil Five-Star and AAA Five Diamond ratings indicate. From the first appearance of the champagne and sparkling wine cart down to the last bite of sublime caramel pot de crème, dinner in this spectacular room is a world-class experience. Modern French cuisine with Japanese influence plays out in such upscale dishes as suckling pig and poulard with black truffle risotto. Award-winning wine list to boot. Full bar, including an extensive single malt Scotch collection. Serving dinner Tue–Sat. Closed Sun–Mon. 600 Stockton St., San Francisco, CA 94108. (415) 773-6168. Go to: www.wtle.com/16393. ***Continental, French, Hotel Restaurant. $$$.***

Fleur de Lys ~ *Best French*

Many say that Nob Hill's renowned French gourmet mainstay Fleur de Lys emerged better than ever from a 2001 fire that could have destroyed this local institution. A 10-month rehab restored one of the most romantic dining rooms in San Francisco, making it even more opulent and breathtaking than before. Chef/co-owner Hubert Keller, a French native and James Beard award winner, appropriately began to renovate his already esteemed menu of complex but enticingly innovative variations on classic French cooking. Three, four or five courses play out in such dishes as pistachio-crusted king salmon, foie gras- and truffle-stuffed roasted squab breast and marinated venison loin. Full bar. Serving dinner Mon–Sat. Closed Sun. 777 Sutter St., San Francisco, CA 94109. (415) 673-7779. Go to: www.wtle.com/16542. ***Continental, French, Vegetarian. $$$.***

Greens Restaurant ~ *Best Vegetarian*

Adopting the standards of upscale dining to its meatless philosophy, Greens Restaurant revolutionized the world of vegetarian cuisine upon opening in 1979. The refurbished warehouse at historic Fort Mason offers spectacular views of the marina and the Golden Gate Bridge, and its award-winning menu attracts vegetarians and carnivores alike. Weekday à la carte menus feature the likes of spinach and braised endive pizza, Vietnamese yellow curry, and mesquite-grilled vegetable skewers, while Saturday night's fixed price dinner may offer gourmet tartlettes and vegetable-stuffed phyllo pastries. Beer and wine available. Serving lunch Tue–Sat, dinner nightly. Sun brunch 10:30 am–2 pm. 1298 Market St., Bldg. A, Fort Mason Center, San Francisco, CA 94123. (415) 771-6222. Go to: www.wtle.com/16543. ***Brunch, Vegetarian. $$.***

Michael Mina

Michael Mina opened his namesake restaurant in the exquisite Westin St. Francis hotel in 2004. The refined space perfectly suits the chef's sophisticated textures and flavors, artfully showcased on hand-selected china. Mina is devoted to the concept of culinary trinities: Each of the three courses on the prix fixe menu features a trio of playfully linked items. A meal, then, might include a starter of beef carpaccio over three types of chilled noodles, an entrée of rack of lamb with three variously stuffed vegetables, and a dessert of berry shortcake with raspberry, blueberry and strawberry ice creams. When all is said and done, a guest at Michael Mina may sample 12 different flavors over the evening — that is, if he or she can manage to stick to his or her own meal. Extensive wine list and full bar. Serving dinner nightly. 335 Powell St., San Francisco, CA 94102. (415) 397-9222. Go to: www.wtle.com/16409. ***Contemporary, Hotel Restaurant, Vegetarian. $$$.***

The Slanted Door ~ *Best Vietnamese*

Making Vietnamese food hip since 1995, The Slanted Door packs in locals, who've made days- or weeks-in-advance reservations for a table in the sleek Ferry Building bearings. Sweeping views of the Bay and a relaxed atmosphere complement the traditional Vietnamese cooking, which makes this destination-dining spot one of the country's most acclaimed Vietnamese restaurants. Local ingredients find their way into traditional cooking methods, making for attractive combinations such as caramelized chicken clay pot with ginger and chiles, five-spiced duck legs, and spicy Japanese eggplant with coconut milk. Wines, cocktails and specially imported teas enhance the dining experience. Full bar. Serving lunch and dinner daily. 1 Ferry Building, San Francisco, CA 94111. (415) 861-8032. Go to: www.wtle.com/16550. ***Vietnamese. $$.***

Swan Oyster Depot ~ *Best Seafood*
Polk Street's tiny Swan Oyster Depot has been a San Francisco institution since 1912. With only 18 or so tottering barstools along the marble counter top, seats are like thrones for those lucky patrons who've earned — with sometimes hour-long waits — a spot to dine in seafood heaven. (Plenty choose to stand around the counter as well.) Locals say no choice is a bad choice from the hand-written menu on the wall: From indigenously rooted crab Louie to New England clam chowder, this is some of the freshest sea bounty in the area. At least four different kinds of half-shell oysters are available daily, and whole lobsters are cooked to order. Beer and wine available. Serving during breakfast, lunch and early dinner hours Mon–Sat. Closed Sun. 1517 Polk St., San Francisco, CA 94109. (415) 673-1101. Go to: www.wtle.com/16503. ***Oysters, Seafood. $$.***

Yank Sing ~ *Best Chinese*
Yank Sing — meaning "city of the ram," in reference to Canton, the capital of the Chinese Guangdong province famous for dim sum — was one of only a few area dim sum restaurants when Alice Chan opened the eatery in 1958. Now run by a third generation of the Chan family, the restaurant shines even among many, thanks to its nearly 100 varieties of Chinese small plates served daily. The two Financial District locations bustle with heavy lunchtime crowds, as banking professionals down plates of pork dumplings, curried shrimp- and cheese-stuffed won tons, and deep-fried crab claws. Full bar. Serving lunch daily. 49 Stevenson St., San Francisco, CA 94105. (415) 541-4949. Two locations. Go to: www.wtle.com/21177. ***Chinese. $.***

Zuni Café ~ *Best Brunch, Best Contemporary*
Helping keep the national culinary compass pointed toward California cuisine, Zuni Café has been keeping certain other highly lauded East Bay restaurants on their toes since opening in 1979. James Beard award-winning chef and co-owner Judy Rodgers offers her cutting-edge cooking in the quirky, multileveled eatery, once named No. 37 on *Gourmet* magazine's America's Top 50 Restaurants list. A neighborhood spot through and through, national press doesn't stop this place from flawlessly executing burger- and Caesar salad-like standards next to sublime ricotta gnocchi and a vast array of first-rate oysters. When in doubt, choose seafood. The loyal, diverse-as-San-Francisco clientele also love Rodger's Sunday brunch (11 am–2:30 pm) — perhaps because it includes some of the city's best Bloody Marys. Full bar. Serving lunch and dinner Tue–Sun. Closed Mon. 1658 Market St., San Francisco, CA 94102. (415) 552-2522. Go to: www.wtle.com/16242. ***Brunch, Contemporary, Oysters. $$$.***

SAN JOSE CALIFORNIA

10 LOCAL FAVORITES

Best known for its Silicon Valley of high-tech companies, *San Jose doesn't cede dining dominance to its more publicized Bay Area neighbors to the north, thanks to regionally and nationally renowned restaurants such as California Cafe and Manresa.*

The dome at San Jose City Hall

Amber India Restaurant ~ *Best Indian*

Don't judge Amber India Restaurant by its unassuming strip mall setting. Rather, the choice original artwork hanging on the walls makes for a better preview of some of South Bay's favorite northern Indian cuisine. The wait for a seat at the popular original Mountain View spot and the second Santana Row location is eased by a specialty cocktail such as the Pink Elephant (vodka, black-raspberry Chambord and lychee fruits). The lunch buffet and à la carte dinner menu offer excellent versions of the standard curry, tandoori and kabob dishes in addition to unique specialties that can't be found elsewhere, such as *tawa* salmon, a sautéed filet with mint, bell peppers and tomatoes. A quick-serve spin-off, Amber Café in Mountain View, serves "Indian bits and bites" such as wraps and Indian pizza. Full bar. Beer available at Amber Café. Serving lunch and dinner daily. 2290 W. El Camino Real, Mountain View, CA 94040. (650) 968-7511. Multiple locations. Go to: www.wtle.com/21952. ***Indian. $$.***

Blue Mango ~ *Best Vegetarian*

As refreshing as its homey décor, Blue Mango welcomes

omnivores, vegetarians and vegans alike to indulge in its popular Thai-inspired menu. This consistent winner of local media best-of polls charms many a Silicon Valley resident with its artfully plated stir-fries, curries and noodle dishes, which can be prepared on a spicy scale of one to 10. Those overestimating their heat tolerance can cool off with a Thai iced tea or a creative dessert to the tune of pineapple-coconut ice cream tempura, a mango samosa or a fresh fruit sorbet. Beer and wine available. Serving lunch Mon–Sat, dinner nightly. 4996 Stevens Creek Blvd., San Jose, CA 95129. (408) 248-7191. Go to: www.wtle.com/16808. ***Thai, Vegetarian. $$.***

California Cafe ~ *Best Brunch*

Though most look to restaurant all-star Chez Panisse for a California cuisine prototype, many locals prefer neighborhood gem California Cafe for everyday and, often, special-occasion dining. Several locations across the country include two favorably situated South Bay spots: the historic, vine-covered Stanford Barn (a former winery) in Palo Alto, and a quaint, cozy Old Town building in Los Gatos. Chef-driven menus feature robust Asian flair, making everything from the popular Asian chicken salad to the gourmet Kobe flat iron steak with lobster tail and tempura shrimp memorable. Award-winning wine list and full bar. Los Gatos: Serving lunch and dinner daily. Sun brunch 10:30 am–2:30 pm. Palo Alto: Serving lunch Mon–Sat, dinner nightly. Sat–Sun brunch 11 am–4 pm. 50 University Ave., Los Gatos, CA 95030. (408) 354-8118. Two locations. Go to: www.wtle.com/21934. ***Brunch, Contemporary. $$.***

Chef Chu's ~ *Best Chinese*

First opened in 1969, Lawrence Chu's 12-item takeout stand has evolved into a colossal two-story restaurant that has become one of the most well regarded on the Peninsula, as has the chef. The beautiful glassed-in exhibition kitchen allows those dining in — about 40 percent of business remains carry-out — to observe the chefs in action, as they diligently prepare the likes of Mongolian beef, *kung pao* prawns and Hunan chicken. Although the cuisine leans more toward Americanized than authentic, dishes such as Chef Chu's Famous Chicken Salad and the Peking duck (which must be ordered 24 hours in advance) leave diners saying, "P.F.-what's?" Full bar. Serving lunch and dinner daily. 1067 N. San Antonio Rd., Los Altos, CA 94022. (650) 948-2696. Go to: www.wtle.com/16796. ***Chinese. $$.***

Forbes Mill Steakhouse ~ *Best Steak House*

A Los Gatos favorite for fine dining, after-work cocktails

and all-around elegance, Forbes Mill Steakhouse sets the Peninsula's steak standard from its fancy downtown digs on Santa Cruz Avenue. An impressively extensive wine list and a highly professional waitstaff enhance the comfortable rustic-hideaway feeling. If top cuts of prime-certified Angus beef, cooked precisely to temperature, and a host of pastas, chops and seafood dishes for the beef-averse don't make its patrons feel privileged enough, there's always the selection of the exclusive Kobe beef, available in three cuts. Try the Kona coffee crème brûlée for dessert. Full bar. Serving dinner nightly. 206 N. Santa Cruz Ave., Los Gatos, CA 95030. (408) 395-6434. Go to: www.wtle.com/17035. ***Steak House. $$$.***

Habana Cuba ~ *Best Cuban*

Whether sipping mojitos on the hip outdoor patio, relaxing to live music with a glass of house-made sangria on a Friday night, or splitting a bottle of a South American wine in the double-decker dining room, locals love Rose Garden's Habana Cuba. Specialty drinks aside, the tender grilled pork of the sandwich Cubano and addictive fried green plantains are reason enough to stop in for lunch. Authentic, down-home Latin specialties such as *ropa vieja* (shredded beef stewed in a spicy tomato broth) make this sexy eatery the ideal spot for a romantic date or special night on the town. Full bar. Serving lunch Tue–Fri, dinner Tue–Sun. Closed Mon. 238 Race St., San Jose, CA 95126. (408) 998-CUBA. Go to: www.wtle.com/16814. ***Cuban. $$.***

Harry's Hofbrau ~ *Best Home-style*

In accordance with the Bay Area hofbrau tradition, in which establishments would give beer drinkers free access to the buffet, Harry's Hofbrau features a reasonably priced cafeteria-buffet hybrid, in addition to strategically placed televisions and over 100 beers. The menu's highlight is the traditional, freshly carved meat, including house-specialties roasted turkey, pork loin, baked ham and pastrami. Have them on a stacked-high sandwich, or try a daily special such as turkey stroganoff, spinach lasagna or shrimp Creole. And in the German tradition of the hofbraus' historical connection with royal courts, an in-house pastry chef bakes daily pies, cakes and cookies fit for a king. Full bar. Cash only. Serving lunch and dinner daily. 390 Saratoga Ave., San Jose, CA 95129. (408) 243-0434. Go to: www.wtle.com/16894. ***German, Home-style. $$.***

Le Papillon ~ *Best French*

Pampering Silicon Valley's top technology executives and locals seeking an extra-special meal, Le Papillon has been providing one of San Jose's most sophisticated dining experiences since 1977. At this DiRoNA restaurant, coats are taken at the door and chefs will accept requests for old favorites no longer on the menu. On the cutting edge of French cuisine, tasting and à la carte menus infuse Asian technique and ingredients, making for an excellent selection of pan-seared foie gras, braised duck breast and grilled rack of lamb. Top it all off with a poached pear tart or a traditional crème caramel. Extensive wine list and full bar. Serving lunch Thu–Fri, dinner nightly. 410 Saratoga Ave., San Jose, CA 95129. (408) 296-3730. Go to: www.wtle.com/16888. ***Continental, French. $$$.***

Manresa ~ *Best Contemporary*
Mobil Four-Star, Michelin two-star Manresa proves day after day that its half-decade history of excellence continues, having once been named No. 42 on *Gourmet* magazine's America's Top 50 Restaurants list. This crown jewel of California cuisine hosts a Los Gatos patronage, eager to sample chef/proprietor David Kinch's French-inspired, Spanish-flaired seasonal menus. Many of the fruits and vegetables, including heirloom tomatoes, are grown at nearby LoveApple Farm. One midsummer, four-course chef's tasting menu included such delicacies as beefsteak and oyster tartare, asparagus with black truffles, rustic chicken stew with sun-chokes, and green apple parfait with cold rhubarb soup. Serving dinner Tue–Sun. Closed Mon. 320 Village Ln., Los Gatos, CA 95030. (408) 354-4330. Go to: www.wtle.com/16619. ***Contemporary. $$$.***

Stacks' ~ *Best Breakfast*
Hungry locals have been stacking up like pancakes since 1992 for the all-American breakfasts and lunches of beloved Stacks'. Regulars don't mind queuing around the block, as this well-oiled machine consistently fills bellies with all the morning favorites — omelets, skillets, pancakes and waffles — plus the specialty crêpes stuffed with anything from fruit to crabmeat. Lunch's burgers, salads and sandwiches are just as familiar, and just as satisfying, making both the Menlo Park and the Burlingame locations ideal stops for the entire family. No alcohol available. Serving breakfast and lunch daily. 600 Santa Cruz Ave., Menlo Park, CA 94025. (650) 838-0066. Two locations. Go to: www.wtle.com/16698. ***Breakfast, Diner. $.***

SEATTLE WASHINGTON

10 LOCAL FAVORITES

***A gateway to the Pacific Rim,** Seattle's abundance of outstanding restaurants includes some of the nation's very best Asian and seafood eateries (Wild Ginger and Ray's Boathouse, respectively) along with nationally renowned contemporaries (Dahlia Lounge and Lark).*

13 Coins Restaurant ~ *Best Diner*

Like Vegas' swanky steak-seafood-breakfast-anytime haunts, Seattle's landmark 13 Coins Restaurant is a 24-hour diner that features crab cakes, escargots and a notable wine list alongside chicken-fried steak and eggs. With its dark, polished, leather-padded walls, high booths, and high-back chairs, the remodeled restaurant shows off more of a sophisticated metropolitan sensibility than that of a neighborhood diner. The 24-hour menu runs the gamut from Dungeness crab omelettes and New York steak and eggs to Australian rock lobster and veal scallopini. Full bar. Open 24 hours daily. 125 Boren Ave. N., Seattle, WA 98109. (206) 682-2513. Two locations. Go to: www.wtle.com/7317. ***American Traditional, Breakfast, Diner. $$.***

Cafe Juanita ~ *Best Italian*

Chef/owner Holly Smith took over Cafe Juanita — one of Seattle's most reliably superb restaurants in neighboring suburb Kirkland — in 2000, and since then has created an innovative menu celebrating both northern Italy's cuisine and the bounty of the Northwest. Serenely located on the edge of Juanita Creek, the café's cozy, softly lit dining room overlooks a garden that provides many ingredients for the menu. Start with octopus salad and a pasta course such as rabbit raviolini with sage butter. Oregon lamb with chickpea purée and braised beef cheek with fava beans are entrées that display Smith's artistry. Full bar. Serving dinner Tue–Sun. Closed Mon. 9702 N.E. 120th Pl., Kirkland, WA 98034. (425) 823-1505. Go to: www.wtle.com/8272. ***Italian. $$$.***

Campagne ~ *Best French*
Campagne's auspicious location has both aesthetic and practical advantages: It not only features a scenic view of Elliott Bay, but also lies directly above the Pike Place Market, which in large part dictates the seasonally changing menu's abundance of fresh produce. Choose between the minimalist, romantic main room, the lively, intimate bar, or the courtyard (weather permitting), and enjoy the world-class professional service and French cuisine. Glazed guinea hen on risotto and foie gras with roasted grapes and shallots exemplify the noteable starters. Large plates may include sautéed wild mushrooms with house-made gnocchi and roasted veal sweetbreads with fennel. Full bar. Serving dinner nightly. 86 Pine St., Seattle, WA 98101. (206) 728-2800. Go to: www.wtle.com/21589. ***French. $$$.***

Dahlia Lounge ~ *Best Contemporary*
Owner/chef Tom Douglas, who with wife Jackie Cross owns several other popular Seattle restaurants, keeps locals and tourists alike flocking to Dahlia Lounge with a menu that is part Northwest haute cuisine, part comfort food. Tom Hanks ate here in the hit movie *Sleepless in Seattle*, and though Dahlia has moved since the filming, it continues to win awards (much like Hanks). Here, international influences, dramatic presentations, superb seasonal ingredients and creative accompaniments define Northwest fare. Begin with the likes of curried vegetable samosas or shrimp-scallion pot stickers. Dungeness crab cakes and rotisserie roast duck are recommended entrées. And such desserts! How about made-to-order doughnuts? Full bar. Serving lunch Mon–Fri, dinner nightly. 2001 4th Ave., Seattle, WA 98121. (206) 682-4142. Go to: www.wtle.com/6248. ***Contemporary. $$.***

The Georgian ~ *Best Continental*
Housed inside the historic Fairmont Olympic Hotel, with its spectacular Palladian windows, striking chandeliers and lavish Italian Renaissance architecture, The Georgian is one of Seattle's most luxurious dining experiences. Flawless service and a seasonal Continental menu featuring

Northwestern foodstuffs render this restaurant perfect for special occasions. Start with the seafood sampler, consisting of prawns, oysters, Dungeness crab and smoked salmon. Entrées such as roasted rack of lamb and smoked wild king salmon are available à la carte or on the three- and seven-course tasting menus. Full bar. Serving breakfast and lunch daily, dinner Mon–Sat. 411 University St., Seattle, WA 98101. (206) 621-7889. Go to: www.wtle.com/7338. $$. 9428. ***Breakfast, Contemporary, Continental, Hotel Restaurant. $$.***

The Harvest Vine ~ *Best Spanish*

Through the years, The Harvest Vine has evolved from a catering company to a takeout and wine shop to the popular and critically acclaimed restaurant offering gourmet tapas that showcase the regional specialties of Spain and the Basque country. The cozy dining room doubles as a wine cellar with floor-to-ceiling wine racks, hand-hewn beams and 200-year-old Spanish doors. Expert chef/owner Joseba Jiménez de Jiménez's creative menu includes cold tapas such as white anchovy filets marinated in vinegar, and hot selections, including award-winning pimiento de Padrón (fried Galician green peppers). Meatier options are available such as rib eye of ox grilled rare, or pan-seared breast of duck with tri-color roasted carrots. Beer and more than 300 Spanish and Basque wines available. Serving dinner nightly. 2701 E. Madison St., Seattle, WA 98122. (206) 320-9771. Go to: www.wtle.com/9428. ***Small Plates, Spanish. $$.***

Lark

The exposed wooden beams across the ceiling and the diaphanous curtains at Lark on Capitol Hill conjure the warmth of a rustic cabin, but the cuisine is the antithesis of simple and old-fashioned. John Sundstrom, recipient of the James Beard Foundation's 2007 Best Chef: Northwest award, specializes in creating inspired small plates intended to be shared among dining companions. The table may begin with a trio of exotic cheeses before moving on to notable seafood small plates such as carpaccio of yellowtail or Sun Hollow raw oysters. Indulge in other offerings such as crispy duck leg or rotisserie pork belly. Try the chocolate madeleines for dessert. Full bar. Serving dinner Tue–Sun. Closed Mon. 926 12th Ave., Seattle, WA 98122. (206) 323-5275. Go to: www.wtle.com/6254. ***Contemporary. $$.***

Metropolitan Grill ~ *Best Steak House*

In Seattle, "The Met" is not a venue that houses a collection of Egyptian artifacts and European masterworks, but rather a celebration of one of America's greatest contributions to the world: the perfect steak. With massive granite columns reaching to the ceiling, an elegant, 50-foot black marble bar and oversized plush booths, The Met is the essence of old-school. The "Guess the Dow" competition at the bar should be a tip-off to the type of crowd that gathers here. They start with corn-fed Nebraska beef steaks grilled to order over live mesquite and offered in petite and Metropolitan sizes. Entrées include the New York peppercorn steak, the blackened prime rib and the lobster tail. Full bar. Serving lunch Mon–Fri, dinner nightly. 820 2nd Ave., Seattle, WA 98104. (206) 624-3287. Go to: www.wtle.com/9446. ***Steak House. $$.***

Ray's Boathouse and Cafe ~ *Best Oysters, Best Seafood*

If your out-of-town guests are afraid of heights, the Space Needle is out. If they spent the early 90s singing along to *The Bodyguard* soundtrack instead of Nirvana, that disqualifies The Crocodile Cafe or any grunge music sites of interest. One Seattle institution that will not fail to impress is Ray's Boathouse. With a 50-foot Ray's sign and over 60 years of history, this is not a landmark to be missed. The casual, upstairs café is renowned for its cocktails (cucumber-lime mojito, rosemary-grapefruit drop), affordable dishes, and outdoor dining with a magnificent view of Puget Sound and the Olympic Mountains. The downstairs, more of a fine-dining restaurant, focuses on local, sustainable seafood: Featured entrées include sablefish in sake *kasu*, Alaskan red king crab legs and grilled white prawns. Full bar. Café serving lunch and dinner daily. Restaurant serving dinner nightly. 6049 Seaview Ave. N.W., Seattle, WA 98107. (206) 789-3770. Go to: www.wtle.com/8723. ***Oysters, Seafood. $$.***

Wild Ginger ~ *Best Asian Fusion*

After years of traveling and researching the traditional cooking styles and recipes of China and Southeast Asia, owners Rick and Ann Yoder opened Wild Ginger in 1989 to immediate popularity. The spacious dining room's neutral color palette with Asian art downplays the hectic evening pace, and the service is invariably accurate and prompt in spite of the crowds. The new satay bar is sure to please meat-on-stick enthusiasts with offerings such as Bangkok boar and lemongrass chicken. For dinner, recommended entrées include the vegetarian Monk's Curry, seven-flavor beef and the house specialty: fragrant duck, seasoned with cinnamon and star anise, served with six small steamed buns in a sweet plum sauce. Full bar. Serving lunch Mon–Sat, dinner nightly. 1401 3rd Ave., Seattle, WA 98101. (206) 623-4450. Go to: www.wtle.com/6494. ***Asian Fusion. $$$.***

ST. LOUIS MISSOURI

10 LOCAL FAVORITES

***Home to the Gateway Arch, the Cardinals and Budweiser**, St. Louis boasts culinary icons, too, most notably Ted Drewes Frozen Custard and the many stellar Italian restaurants in the neighborhood known as The Hill.*

Blueberry Hill ~ *Best American Traditional*

You very well could find your thrill at this landmark neighborhood bar, grill and nightclub in The Loop. Memorabilia ranging from baseball cards to *Wayne's World* action figures — excellent! — decorates the whimsical dining room, while one window features a display with alternating themes (Elvis, Superman, "flamingo dinner party," et al.), sometimes utilizing live performers. If this overwhelming amount of oddities fails to entertain you, there is live music in adjoining rooms, a famously extensive jukebox and a number of dartboards to distract you. The menu consists of classic diner fare — terrific burgers, dogs, chili, macaroni and cheese — while other highlights include jerk chicken breast, trout Almondine and a number of breakfast items. Full bar. Serving lunch and dinner daily. 6504 Delmar Blvd., St. Louis, MO 63130. (314) 727-4444. Go to: www.wtle.com/13416. ***American Traditional, Burgers, Diner, Hot Dogs. $.***

Chez Leon ~ *Best French*

It's easy to mistake Laclede Avenue in St. Louis' Central West End for a side street in Paris, thanks to Chez Leon's red restaurant front with its tall French doors and patio. The elegant seasonal menu continues the tradition of classical and provincial French cuisine. Items are available à la carte or on a reasonably priced three-course, prix fixe menu. For starters, try smoked salmon with capers and onions or a salad with warm bacon and poached eggs. Entrées can include fare such as steak frites, braised sauerkraut with a smoked pork chop and sausage, and roasted free-range chicken with truffle sauce. Full bar. Serving dinner Tue–Sun. Closed Mon. 4580 Laclede Ave., St. Louis, MO 63108. (314) 361-1589. Go to: www.wtle.com/13562. ***French. $$$.***

Crown Candy Kitchen ~ *Best Diner*
Harry Karandzieff and best friend Pete Jugaloff merged their entrepreneurial dreams and candy-making skills in 1913 to open Crown Candy Kitchen in now-historic Old North St. Louis. A classic diner menu, featuring house-made egg or tuna salad sandwiches, Reubens, and chili dogs, complements the retro décor complete with soda fountain and pictures of WWII bombers. The kitchen still makes its own chocolate for candies and to top their legendary ice cream. The signature items, however, are the 24-ounce malts and milkshakes, with flavors ranging from the classic chocolate to marshmallow, pineapple, and seasonal delights such as pumpkin and eggnog. No alcohol available. Serving lunch and dinner daily. 1401 St. Louis Ave., St. Louis, MO 63106. (314) 621-9650. Go to: www.wtle.com/13554. ***Diner, Ice Cream/Confections. $.***

Cyrano's ~ *Best Dessert*
Cyrano's (the city's first and only European-style coffeehouse) first introduced its flavored coffees, decadent desserts and small-portioned entrées to St. Louis in 1960 and immediately became a favorite spot. But it closed its doors in 1996 only to reopen in 2003 when a group of nostalgic restaurateurs reinvented the beloved spot as a café/wine bar. Now just as popular as the original, the new Cyrano's features a coffee bar, lounge and dining room decorated with some of the original restaurant's artwork and antiques. The seasonal menu offers stellar appetizers and entrées with Continental flair, but the main event is still dessert. The acknowledged-by-name queen is the chocolate-encased Cleopatra sundae with vanilla ice cream, bananas, strawberries and dark chocolate, but the menu also includes flambés for two, éclairs, tortes, puddings and cakes. Full bar. Serving lunch and dinner daily. Late-night Fri–Sat. Sun brunch 11 am–3 pm. 603 E. Lockwood Ave., St. Louis, MO 63119. (314) 963-3232. Go to: www.wtle.com/13547. ***Brunch, Contemporary, Dessert. $$.***

King and I ~ *Best Thai*
Located on increasingly diverse South Grand Boulevard, King

and I has been torching tongues with its spicy curries, noodles and Thai specialties for years. The pad thai, simmered in a fermented fish sauce, is a delicious variation on the traditional dish. Other entrées include the Forrest Gump — not surprisingly a shrimp dish — and cross-cultural experiments such as Thai fajitas and Thai ravioli. To douse the fire and regain articulation, order an exotic cocktail such as the Fog Cutter (pineapple juice, rum and brandy) or the Siam Stinker (rum, gin and fruit juice). Full bar. Serving lunch and dinner Tue–Sun. Closed Mon. 3157 S. Grand Blvd., St. Louis, MO 63118. (314) 771-1777. Go to: www.wtle.com/13953. ***Thai. $$.***

O'Connell's Pub ~ *Best Burgers*

How often are legendary burgers served alongside a gallery of fine art and antiques? You'd be hard-pressed to find one example aside from O'Connell's Pub, an institution since opening in the city's famed Gaslight Square in 1962. Beveled glass windows, dim lighting — assisted by two chandeliers from the 1904 World's Fair in St. Louis — and dark wood paneling create classic pub ambiance. Nine-ounce juicy burgers and the hefty roast beef sandwiches (best with rare beef) can prove to be irresistible, but the fish and chips on Friday or rib tips on Saturday are delicious alternatives. The crisp French fries and fried mushrooms are award-winning as well. Full bar. Serving lunch and dinner daily. 4652 Shaw Ave., St. Louis, MO 63110. (314) 773-6600. Go to: www.wtle.com/13516. ***Burgers, Irish/British, Sports Bar/Pub Food. $.***

Sidney Street Cafe ~ *Best Contemporary*

Benton Park neighborhood mainstay Sidney Street Cafe has been attracting loyal diners for 20-plus years with its adventurous American contemporary cuisine. The modest yet elegant surroundings — a century-old storefront building with an old-fashioned mahogany bar, exposed bricks and hardwood floors — are inviting for a casual or romantic dinner. Asian influences and accents in addition to creative presentations enliven the menu's traditional steak and seafood selections. Begin with appetizers such as lobster turnovers and veal dumplings. The menu varies nightly with the exception of a few items such as the sun dried tomato-encrusted Tuscan sea bass, and steak wasabi served with tempura vegetables. Full bar. Serving dinner Tue–Sat. Closed Mon. 2000 Sidney St., St. Louis, MO 63104. (314) 771-5777. Go to: www.wtle.com/13398. ***Contemporary. $$$.***

Sweetie Pie's ~ *Best Soul Food*

Before Robbie Montgomery was the star of the show at her

revered soul food restaurant, Sweetie Pie's, she sang backup as an Ikette in the St. Louis-based Ike and Tina Turner revue. She now showcases her talent via mouthwatering soul food at the original Sweetie Pie's on Florissant in Dellwood and at a second, more spacious location on Manchester in Forest Park. Food is served cafeteria-style, and the choices change daily. Among the specialties of the house: smothered pork with gravy, baked chicken, Salisbury steak, barbecued ribs, and fried catfish accompanied by sides of sweet corn, fried okra, cooked cabbage and sweet potatoes. No alcohol available. Cash only. Serving lunch and dinner Tue–Fri and Sun. Closed Mon and Sat. 9841 W. Florissant Ave., St. Louis, MO 63136. (314) 521-9915. Two locations. Go to: www.wtle.com/13931. ***Home-style, Soul Food. $.***

Ted Drewes Frozen Custard ~ *Best Ice Cream*
A St. Louis icon as legendary as its location on old Route 66, Ted Drewes Frozen Custard has attracted legions of locals and tourists to its walk-up windows since Ted Drewes Sr. opened his first frozen custard stand in 1931. While the custard does indeed stand on its own as a perfectly delectable treat, the signature item is the "concrete:" a thick milkshake concoction with a combination of fruit, candy, nuts and cookies folded in the layers of custard. The All Shook Up Concrete (peanut butter cookie and banana) is a deliciously clever tribute to the King's favorite snack. Per tradition, come November and December (not exactly ice cream season), Ted Drewes sells freshly cut Christmas trees. No alcohol available. Generally serving during lunch, dinner and late-night hours. Closed mid Dec–mid Feb. Call for hours. 4224 S. Grand Blvd., St. Louis, MO 63111. (314) 352-7376. Two locations. Go to: www.wtle.com/21370. ***Ice Cream. $.***

Trattoria Marcella ~ *Best Italian*
One of St. Louis' most renowned Italian restaurants, Trattoria Marcella is located just south of the traditional Italian neighborhood known as The Hill. It has undergone renovations multiple times to accommodate the crowds that it attracts with its rustic cuisine. Start with the acclaimed calamari or a plate of wild mushrooms served over polenta fries with caramelized sweet Marsala wine and Gorgonzola cheese sauce. Move on to a pizza or pastas such as farfalle Alessandra — bow-tie pasta tossed with salmon in a lemon cream sauce — and chicken and spinach cannelloni. Stuffed veal scaloppini and lamb loin chops with eggplant risotto round out the entrées. Full bar. Serving dinner Tue–Sat. Closed Sun–Mon. 3600 Watson Rd., St. Louis, MO 63109. (314) 352-7706. Go to: www.wtle.com/13884. ***Italian. $$.***

TAMPA BAY
FLORIDA

10 LOCAL FAVORITES

***From fried grouper sandwiches** to Spanish paella, the seafood is, of course, stellar in Tampa Bay's top restaurants, while Bern's ranks among the country's oldest and most renowned steak houses.*

Bern's Steak House ~ *Best Steak House*

Cherrywood booths, bronze pillars and ornate gilded furnishings contribute to the Old World atmosphere at locally renowned Bern's Steak House, open since 1956. Its wine cellar is regarded as one of the largest and best in the world, with nearly 7,000 unique labels and 200 wines available by the glass. Dry-aged steaks are custom cut for each patron and may be topped with sauces specially made from the wine collection. The formidable menu includes everything from caviar and vegetarian options to steak-ordering instructions. You may want to retire to one of the 48 phone-equipped private nooks in the Harry Waugh Dessert Room to order flambés, banana chocolate cheesecake or one of the dozens of other tantalizing treats. Full bar. Serving dinner nightly. 1208 S. Howard Ave., Tampa, FL 33606. (813) 251-2421. Go to: www.wtle.com/21914. ***Steak House. $$$.***

Bob Heilman's Beachcomber Restaurant ~ *Best American Traditional*

Open since 1948, Bob Heilman's Beachcomber Restaurant has a breathtaking view of Clearwater Beach. Patrons find comfort in the old-fashioned, traditional American menu and the uniquely decorated dining rooms featuring model sailboats, a live piano bar and a central fireplace surrounded by booths. For dinner, choose from appetizers such as fried onion rings or clams casino with three peppers in garlicky butter. The Back-To-The-Farm Chicken is a local favorite (and a Heilman family recipe since 1910). Other excellent choices are the veal piccata, sautéed chicken livers with mushrooms and the Beachcomber Seafood Platter. Full bar. Serving lunch and dinner daily. 447 Mandalay Ave., Clearwater, FL 33767. (727) 442-4144. Go to: www.wtle.com/18616. ***American Traditional. $$.***

Ceviche ~ *Best Spanish*

Ceviche boasts some of the finest Spanish small plates from its two area locations: One relocated in early 2008 to Howard Avenue in Tampa and the other is in St. Petersburg's Theater District. Both offer romantic settings and nearly 50 varieties of hot and cold tapas. The excellent signature cold tapas dish, the ceviche de la casa, offers lime-marinated shrimp, scallops, squid and fish, tossed with tomatoes, scallions and peppers, seasoned with cilantro and tequila. Hot tapas have included veal and chorizo meatballs in tomato sauce or braised lamb ribs with white beans and roasted tomatoes. Live Spanish music on weekends. Full bar. Serving dinner nightly. St. Petersburg location closed Mon. 1502 S. Howard Ave., Tampa, FL 33606. (813) 250-0134. Two locations. Go to: www.wtle.com/18822. ***Small Plates, Spanish. $$.***

Chateau France Restaurant ~ *Best French*

Chateau France is the crème de la crème of French haute cuisine in St. Petersburg. Housed in an early-1900s Victorian mansion in the Historic District, the romantic dining areas are adorned with fine furnishings, lace curtains draped over bay windows, and candlelit tables. The extensive menu invites you to indulge in the beloved foods that have made France a culinary beacon for chefs worldwide. For appetizers, there are scallops au citron or house-made pâté. Try the specialty Dover sole or the signature French bouillabaisse as your entrée. For dessert? Soufflé, but of course! The 15,000-bottle wine cellar has selections to harmonize with every course. Dress is formal. Reservations required. Full bar. Serving dinner nightly. 136 4th Ave., N.E., St. Petersburg, FL 33701. (727) 894-7163. Go to: www.wtle.com/18670. ***French. $$$.***

Columbia Restaurant ~ *Best Latin/South American*

Opened in Tampa's historic Ybor City by Casimiro Hernandez Sr. in 1905, the still family-owned-and-operated Columbia Restaurant, with locations throughout Florida, is one of the most acclaimed Spanish- and Latin American-inspired restaurants in the United States. The Tampa location encompasses an entire city block. There, diners enjoy hand-painted Spanish tile, flamenco shows and the special house paella, served in one of 15 dining rooms, each with its own personality. Choose several tapas dishes to share, such as a casserole of shrimp, crab and artichoke hearts, or spicy beef turnovers with corn and black bean salsa. On the dinner menu, recommended entrées include red snapper Alicante and roast pork a la Cubana. Full bar. Serving lunch and dinner daily. 2117 E. 7th Ave., Tampa, FL 33605. (813) 248-4961. Multiple locations. Go to: www.wtle.com/18591. ***Cuban, Latin/South American, Small Plates, Spanish. $$.***

Frenchy's Original Cafe ~ *Best Seafood*

Colorfully cluttered surroundings and fabulous seafood draw crowds to the multitude of Frenchy's restaurants on or near Clearwater Beach. Frenchy's Original Cafe opened in 1981 as a hole-in-the-wall haven for waterlogged and sand-caked beachgoers. Shortly thereafter, crowds were lining up around the block for the signature fried grouper sandwiches. Though casual and whimsical in nature, Frenchy's takes fresh seafood seriously: The fish, caught by one of the company's 10 boats, has likely been out of water for only a few hours. Favorites include the Crabby Shrimp Sandwich, the Super Seafood Gumbo and the Baja fish tacos. Beer and wine available. Serving lunch and dinner daily. 41 Baymont St., Clearwater, FL 33767. (727) 446-3607. Multiple locations. Go to: www.wtle.com/18804. ***Seafood. $$.***

Lenny's Restaurant ~ *Best Breakfast*

Neighbors and tourists alike jam into quirky Lenny's Restaurant for its huge all-day breakfasts and deli-style lunches and dinners. Second-generation family owners have kept founder Lenny Farrell's spirit alive by maintaining the eccentric décor, complete with stuffed animals, baseball memorabilia, family portraits, autographed celebrity photos and numerous knickknacks. Hungry patrons appreciate the famed pastry basket that comes complimentary with most breakfasts. Well-priced breakfast items include pancakes, and omelets with pastrami, salami or corned beef hash. Lunch centers on hot dogs and deli sandwiches. No alcohol available. Serving breakfast and lunch daily. 21220 U.S. Hwy. 19 N., Clearwater, FL 33765. (727) 799-0402. Go to: www.wtle.com/18540. ***Breakfast, Deli. $.***

The Maritana Grille

The flamingo-pink Don CeSar Beach Resort has been a St. Pete Beach landmark since 1928. Original Italian marble and crystal chandeliers greet visitors making their way through the hotel lobby to the chic Maritana Grille inside. From your table, you can view the waterfront or find amusement in the wall of salt water aquariums filled with colorful native Florida fish. The restaurant, like the menu, is small and classy. Start with chilled avocado soup with jumbo lump crab or foie gras with a porcini mushroom tart, and move on to entrées such as filet mignon with truffle mashed potatoes and pan-seared scallops with lobster risotto. Full bar. Serving dinner nightly. 3400 Gulf Blvd., St. Pete Beach, FL 33706. (727) 360-1881. Go to: www.wtle.com/18931. ***Contemporary, Hotel Restaurant. $$$.***

Mise en Place ~ *Best Contemporary*
One of Tampa-St. Pete's most highly regarded restaurants, Mise en Place specializes in American contemporary fine dining with a focus on fresh local ingredients. Located across the street from the University of Tampa, the restaurant is popular for both romantic dates and power lunches. Chef/owner Marty Blitz's menu changes constantly, but when available, start with chicken liver pear port mousse pâté, a gourmet pizza or an artisanal cheese plate. Palate-pleasing entrée options may range from veal scaloppini with lobster ravioli to peppercorn-crusted tuna. If you're finding it hard to choose, try the multi-course "Get Blitzed" tasting menu of chef-selected courses paired with complementary wines. Full bar. Serving lunch Tue–Fri, dinner Tue–Sat. Closed Sun– Mon. 442 W. Kennedy Blvd., Tampa, FL 33606. (813) 254-3392. Go to: www.wtle.com/18623. ***Contemporary. $$$.***

SideBern's ~ *Best Dessert*
SideBern's labels itself the "progressive little sister to Bern's Steak House." Little sister or not, this theater district restaurant, serving contemporary American fare and decadent desserts, ranks as one of Tampa's top dining experiences. As for the menu, let's begin with the glorious end. Desserts are prepared daily and can include: a chocolate sampler (with a chocolate shake, chocolate crème brûlée and a mini liquid-center cake with mint ice cream) or fruitier confections, such as the Tahitian vanilla bean crème brûlée with berry mango salad, or the tropical fruit bombes. "No dessert until you finish your dinner" proves to be an idle threat, though, as you'll have no problem savoring every last bite of exotic (in both name and execution) dishes that may include Fulton's Yellowfin Tuna Evolution or blood orange & pink peppercorn crusted duck breast. Full bar. Serving dinner Mon–Sat. Closed Sun. 1002 S. Howard Ave., Tampa, FL 33606. (813) 258-2233. Go to: www.wtle.com/18661. ***Contemporary, Dessert. $$$.***

WASHINGTON D.C.

10 LOCAL FAVORITES

Restaurants in the nation's capital have been hosting the power elite *for a couple of centuries, and boardinghouse-turned-saloon Old Ebbitt Grill has served most of them since the days of President Ulysses S. Grant.*

Thomas Jefferson Building of the Library of Congress

Citronelle

Internationally esteemed Michel Richard was educated in some of France's most prestigious kitchens, has opened highly popular restaurants from coast to coast, and achieved the world's top culinary honors, from the James Beard Foundation's Outstanding Chef 2007 to a 2003 induction into renowned French culinary society Relais & Châteaux. But the ambitious chef considers Georgetown's Citronelle his flagship. With the tony Latham Hotel as a backdrop, Richard pairs with his fellow James Beard award-winning sommelier to produce a menu of imaginative French-Californian cuisine. One midsummer, 10-course Chef's Table menu featured the likes of chestnut and peanut soup, a lobster burger, roasted squab, and chocolate three ways. Jacket required. Full bar. Serving dinner nightly. 3000 M St. N.W., Washington, D.C. 20007. (202) 625-2150. Go to: www.wtle.com/13682. ***French. $$$.***

Five Guys ~ *Best Burgers*

Two words: Burgers. Fries. Four more: Juicy. Crisp. Hot. Salty. With a multitude of locations in the D.C. area and across the Eastern Seaboard, Lorton, Va.-based Five Guys dishes out hand-patted, never-frozen burgers topped with a range of (free) extras including hot peppers, sautéed mushrooms, A1 and barbecue sauce. The food here gets a lot of ink: Local media have named it best burger, best bargain or best fries nearly every year. That may be due to the quality, or possibly to the ubiquity. There's almost always a Five Guys near enough that there's no excuse for eating burgers from the big national chains. No alcohol available. Serving lunch and dinner daily. 4626 King St., Alexandria, VA 22302. (703) 671-1606. Go to: www.wtle.com/12849. ***American Traditional, Burgers. $.***

The Inn at Little Washington

The kind of place where sorbets mediate every course, where napkins are always folded upon returning to the table, where once-in-a-lifetime meals take place: The Inn at Little Washington has been a world-class dining experience since 1978. The luxuriously charming inn, nestled into a postcard-worthy rolling landscape 70 miles from downtown D.C., has amassed nearly every bestowable honor over the years, including being the first establishment to receive five stars from Mobil Travel Guide and five diamonds from AAA for both its hotel and restaurant. Choose a seat among the intimately clustered tables, flex that wallet, and prepare to be dazzled by the grandeur and precision of the ever-changing selection of seasonal offerings, from grilled prawns with mango mint salsa to veal cheeks with Virginia ham ravioli. Full bar. Serving dinner nightly. 309 Middle St., Washington, VA 22747. (540) 675-3800. Go to: www.wtle.com/14769. ***Contemporary, Hotel Restaurant. $$$.***

Kinkead's ~ *Best Seafood*

Rub elbows with the Capital City's movers and shakers at this four-star Foggy Bottom mainstay, where textbook attention to detail and a superb wine list combine with some of the area's freshest seafood. A seat in the elegant upstairs dining room or in the more casual downstairs raw bar requires weeks-in-advance reservations for a sample of James Beard award-winning chef Bob Kinkead's creative, much-sought-after fare. On the daily changing menu — which is even adjusted between lunch and dinner — you will always find premium oysters, the local-favorite grilled squid and polenta, and the highly popular signature pepita-crusted salmon. Full bar. Serving lunch Sun–Fri, dinner nightly. 2000 Pennsylvania Ave. N.W., Washington, D.C. 20006. (202) 296-7700. Go to: www.wtle.com/14194. ***Contemporary, Oysters, Seafood. $$$.***

L'Auberge Chez François ~ *Best French*

Evoking the spirit of the quaint, family-run bed and breakfasts that spot the French countryside, L'Auberge Chez François offers an almost otherworldly charm from its suburban cottage location. Monsieur François moved the now half-century-old eatery to Great Falls in 1976, and has since handed over the kitchen to son Jacques, whose culinary prowess and popular cookbooks have gained further recognition for the legendary dining destination. Classic Franco-Alsatian cooking is the real deal: roasted rack of lamb, sautéed Dover sole and classic Châteaubriand for two. The amuse-bouche, the superior service and a host in each dining area are just a few of the extras. Full bar. Serving dinner Tue–Sun (Sun dinner begins 1:30 pm). Closed Mon. 332 Springvale Rd. Great Falls, VA 22066. (703) 759-3800. Go to: www.wtle.com/13684. ***French. $$$.***

Old Ebbitt Grill ~ *Best Breakfast*
Dating back to 1856, Old Ebbitt Grill remains one of D.C.'s most beloved, historic restaurants. This boardinghouse-turned-saloon was a known haunt of President Grant and, given its proximity to the White House, has hosted numerous other Capitol Hill elite since converting to a full-service restaurant in 1971. Many a political deal has occurred over gin and tonics at the mahogany bar, while hearty portions of frittatas and buttermilk pancakes have helped push political policy amid the polished leather banquettes. Creative American lunch, dinner and Sunday brunch (8:30 am–4 pm) favorites offer something for everyone, while the oyster bar remains one of the area's best-known. Full bar. Serving breakfast, lunch and dinner daily. 675 15th St. N.W., Washington, D.C. 20005. (202) 347-4800. Go to: www.wtle.com/12947. ***Breakfast, Brunch, Contemporary, Oysters, Seafood. $$$.***

Ray's the Steaks ~ *Best Steak House*
No white linens top these tables, nor do celebrity caricatures decorate the walls: Ray's the Steaks provides the anti-chain experience in favor of true neighborhood flavor. Loyal patrons will gladly drive from the beef emporium that is D.C. to the unassuming Arlington, Va., strip mall where chef/owner Michael Landrum offers the same top-drawer cuts of meat for substantially smaller prices. Amid the tiny yet bustling 45-seat room, enjoy gargantuan New York strips, bacon-wrapped filets and rib eyes, served with two heaping cast-iron skillets of mashed potatoes and creamed spinach (at no extra charge). Excellent wine list and house-made pies to boot. Full bar. Serving dinner Tue–Sun. Closed Mon. 1725 Wilson Blvd., Arlington, VA 22209. (703) 841-7297. Go to: www.wtle.com/14379. ***Steak House. $$$.***

TenPenh ~ *Best Asian Fusion*
The American embassy of feng shui might rest at this Pennsylvania Avenue hot spot, where ultra-stylish décor and a gastronomic harmony of texture and flavor have been the code of conduct since July 2000. Grab a signature TenPenhpolitan or one of the 10 on-tap beers, and observe the beautiful people as they gossip over appetizers of sweet-and-spicy barbecue short ribs and steamed shrimp-and-chive dumplings. The Pan-Asian menu spans the cuisines of Vietnam, the Philippines, China, Japan and Thailand, while the in-house pastry chef applies Eastern flavors to classic Western desserts. (Think mango crème brûlée and ginger lemongrass pound cake.) Full bar. Serving lunch Mon–Fri, dinner Mon–Sat. Closed Sun. 1001 Pennsylvania Ave. N.W., Washington, D.C. 20004. (202) 393-4500. Go to: www.wtle.com/12930. ***Asian Fusion. $$.***

Vidalia ~ *Best Contemporary*
Following in the footsteps of chef/owner Jeffrey Buben, Vidalia's chef de cuisine R. J. Cooper was named James Beard Foundation's 2007 Best Chef: Mid Atlantic. This award-winning team is dedicated to American regional cuisine, and though the Dixie accent is slightly less detectable than in its early years, the menu still pays tribute to Southern flavors. Practically-all-lump crab cakes, creamy sweet shrimp and grits, and slightly crisp veal sweetbreads are the excellent result, all of which can be paired with an outstanding supporting cast of sides such as baked macaroni and cheese with goat milk cheddar. The impressive selection of wines includes multi-course friendly sampler flights, three-ounce pours and half bottles. Full bar. Serving lunch Mon–Fri, dinner nightly. 1990 M St. N.W., Washington, D.C. 20036. (202) 659-1990. Go to: www.wtle.com/12841. ***Contemporary. $$$.***

Zaytinya ~ *Best Middle Eastern*
With a menu as sexy as its crowd, sleek Penn Quarter resident Zaytinya bills itself as a "*mezze* specialist," mezze being the small plates of the Eastern Mediterranean. Loyal patrons marvel at the multitude of Greek, Turkish and Lebanese bite-sized dishes and how each seems to be bursting with a vastly different flavor than the last. Mussels in light tomato broth, house-made lamb sausage, and succulent *kibbeh* (spiced minced meat) and wheat fritters add up to a well-rounded, authentic meal without too much strain on the wallet. The extensive wine list features superior choices predominantly from oft-overlooked Greece, Turkey and Lebanon. Full bar. Serving lunch and dinner daily. Sat–Sun brunch 11:30 am–2:30 pm. 701 9th St. N.W., Washington, D.C. 20004. (202) 638-0800. Go to: www.wtle.com/14137. ***Brunch, Greek, Middle Eastern. $.***